DEGAS

THE LIFE AND WORKS OF
DEGAS

AN ILLUSTRATED EXPLORATION OF THE ARTIST, HIS LIFE AND
CONTEXT, WITH A GALLERY OF 500 OF HIS FINEST PAINTINGS
AND SCULPTURES

JON KEAR

HERMES
HOUSE

This edition is published by Hermes House an imprint of Anness Publishing Ltd, Blaby Road, Wigston Leicestershire LE18 4SE info@anness.com

www.hermeshouse.com
www.annesspublishing.com

Anness Publishing has a new picture agency outlet for images for publishing, promotions or advertising. Please visit our website www.practicalpictures.com for more information.

Publisher: Joanna Lorenz
Editorial Director: Helen Sudell
Editor: Simona Hill
Designer: Sarah Rock
Editorial Reader: Penelope Goodare
Production Controller: Mai-Ling Collyer

ETHICAL TRADING POLICY
Because of our ongoing ecological investment programme, you, as our customer, can have the pleasure and reassurance of knowing that a tree is being cultivated on your behalf to naturally replace the materials used to make the book you are holding. For further information about this scheme, go to www.annesspublishing.com/trees

PUBLISHER'S NOTE
Although the advice and information in this book are believed to be accurate and true at the time of going to press, neither the authors nor the publisher can accept any legal responsibility or liability for any errors or omissions that may have been made nor for any inaccuracies in this book.

PICTURE CREDITS
AKG: Page 151, 162t, 174c. Alamy: Page 50, 110, 117b, 122b, 125t, 128b, 129t, 152t, 158t, 161t, 163b, 187b. Bridgeman Art Library: Private Collection, Page 1, 13b, 29l, 37cr, 42b, 50l, 54t, 57t, 73tl, 74t, 79br, 82t, 83b, 85b, 95b; 3, 39l, 41l, 47tr, 52, 71tr, 73tr, 86, 90t (Photo © Christie's Images); 5l, 13t, 94b (Roger-Viollet, Paris); 14–15, 64r, 68, 69t, 69bl, 69br (The Stapleton Collection), 19b (Photo © Peter Nahum at The Leicester Galleries, London); 25b, 28bl, 31b, 47tc (Giraudon), 28br (Ken Welsh); 55tr (Archives Charmet); 62r, 67b, 75t, 87tl (Photo © Lefevre Fine Art Ltd., London); 74b, 84t (Peter Willi); 84b (Photo © Boltin Picture Library); Samuel

Courtauld Trust, The Courtauld Gallery, London, UK, 2; Musée d'Orsay, Paris, France, 7b, 8–9, 16t, 21b, 46, 57t, 66t, 78, 79, 87b, 93b; (Giraudon); 6b ,7t, 10, 12r, 22b, 23b, 25t, 26t, 31tr, 32t, 33b, 35t, 38b, 42t, 47b, 59l, 59r, 61b, 65, 72, 76, 85t, 89t, 90b; (Peter Willi) 12l, 26b; Metropolitan Museum of Art, New York 49t; Art Gallery and Museum, Kelvingrove, Glasgow, Scotland © Culture and Sport Glasgow (Museums) 5r, 79bl; © Walters Art Museum, Baltimore, USA 11; Van der Heydt Museum, Wuppertal, Germany (Giraudon) 14tl; (Giraudon) 14tr; Art Gallery of New South Wales, Sydney, Australia 15t; National Gallery, London, UK 16b, 24b, 43t; © Dahesh Museum of Art, New York, USA 17b; Louvre, Paris, France, 17t (Peter Willi); 18, 37tr, 81b (Giraudon); Musée Bonnat, Bayonne, France 19t (Giraudon); Museo e Gallerie Nazionale di Capodimonte, Naples, Italy 20t (Alinari); Roger-Viollet, Paris 20b; © Birmingham Museums and Art Gallery 21t; Brooklyn Museum of Art, New York, USA 22t, 27b, 71br; Galerie Neue Meister, Dresden, Germany 23t (© Staatliche Kunstsammlungen Dresden); Fogg Art Museum, Harvard University Art Museums, USA, 24t (Friends of the Fogg Museum Fund, the Alpheus Hyatt Fund, the William M. Prichard and Francis H. Burr Memorial Funds); 51t (Gift of Herbert N. Straus); 61tr, 97t (Bequest from the Collection of Maurice Wertheim, Class 1906); 80t (Gift of Mrs J. Montgomery Sears); Minneapolis Institute of Arts, MN, USA 27t ; Bibliotheque Nationale, Paris, France, 29r (Giraudon); 55tl (Archives Charmet); Hamburger Kunsthalle, Hamburg, Germany 30, 33t; Burrell Collection, Glasgow, Scotland © Culture and Sport Glasgow (Museums) 31tl; 48t; Municipal Museum of Art, Kitakyushu, Japan 32b; Museu Calouste Gulbenkian, Lisbon, Portugal, 34l (Giraudon); Kunsthaus, Zurich, Switzerland, 34r (Giraudon); Bibliotheque de l'Opera Garnier, Paris, France, 35b (Giraudon); 64l (Archives Charmet); Museum of Fine Arts, Boston, Massachusetts, USA, 6t, 54b (1931 Purchase Fund); 36 (Gift of Mr and Mrs John McAndrew); 37l (Gift of Robert Treat Paine, 2nd); 38t (S. A. Denio Collection); Musée de la Ville de Paris, Musee Carnavalet, Paris, France, 45t 49b (Giraudon); National Gallery, London, UK, 81t, 82b; 66b (Giraudon); Detroit Institute of Arts, USA, 39b Gift of W. Warren & Virginia Shelden in memory of Mrs. Allan Shelden; Philadelphia Museum of Art, Pennsylvania, PA, USA 40; Sterling & Francine Clark Art Institute, Williamstown, USA 41tr, 75b; © Nationalmuseum, Stockholm, Sweden 43t; Musée d'Art et d'Histoire, Saint-Denis, France, 44 (Giraudon); © Samuel Courtauld Trust, The Courtauld Gallery, London, UK, 45b; Norton Simon Collection, Pasadena, CA, USA; 48b; Musee des Beaux-Arts, Pau, France, 51b (Giraudon); Fitzwilliam Museum, University of Cambridge, UK 53, 58r, 71tl; 76bl, 77br; Musée Marmottan Monet, Paris, France, 55b (Giraudon); 94t, 95t; Petit Palais, Geneva, Switzerland, 56l; © National Gallery of Scotland, Edinburgh, Scotland, 56r, 91t; ©

Walker Art Gallery, National Museums Liverpool 58l; Musée des Beaux-Arts, Lyon, France, 60 (Giraudon); Ashmolean Museum, University of Oxford, UK, 61tl; Musée de la Chartreuse, Douai, France, 62l (Giraudon); Galleria d'Arte Moderna, Florence, Italy, 63t; National Gallery of Art, Washington DC, USA, 63b; The Art Institute of Chicago, IL, USA, 67t, 97b; National Portrait Gallery, Smithsonian Institution, USA, Art Resource, 70 (Giraudon); Musée Rodin, Paris, France, 73b (Peter Willi); Philadelphia Museum of Art, Pennsylvania, PA, USA, 77t; Hermitage, St. Petersburg, Russia, 80b (Giraudon); Musée des Beaux-Arts, Reims, France, 83t; Musée des Beaux-Arts, Rouen, France, 87tr (Giraudon); Bibliotheque Litteraire Jacques Doucet, Paris, France, 88 (Archives Charmet); Archives Larousse, Paris, France, 89b (Giraudon); Museu de Arte, Sao Paulo, Brazil, 91br (Giraudon); Bibliotheque Historique de la Ville de Paris, Paris, France, 92, 93t (Archives Charmet); 97t, 100, 102t, 102b, 103t, 103b, 104t, 104b, 105t, 105b, 106t, 106b, 107t, 107b, 108t, 108b, 109t, 109c, 109b, 110t, 111t, 111b, 112t, 112b, 113t, 113b, 114, 115t, 115b, 116t, 116c, 116b, 117t, 118t, 118b, 119t, 119b, 120t , 120b, 121c, 121t, 121b, 122t, 123t , 123b, 124b, 125b, 126t, 126b, 127t, 128t, 129c, 129b, 130r, 131tr, 131c, 131b, 132t, 132b, 133t, 133b, 134t, 134b, 135t, 136t, 136b, 137t, 137b, 138t, 138b, 139t, 139c, 139b, 140t, 140c, 140b, 141t, 141b, 142t, 142b, 143b, 144t, 144b, 145tl, 145tr, 145b, 146t, 147t, 147b, 148t, 149t, 149b, 150t, 150b, 152b , 153t, 153b, 154t, 154b, 155tl, 155tr, 155br, 156t, 156b, 157t, 157b, 158t, 159t, 159c, 159b, 160t, 160b, 161b,162c, 163t, 163c, 164t, 164b, 165t, 165b, 166t, 166c, 166b, 167t, 167b, 168t, 168b, 169t, 169t, 170t, 170c, 170b, 171t, 171b, 172t, 172c, 172b, 173t, 173c, 173b, 174t, 174b, 175t, 175b, 176t, 176b, 177t, 177c, 177b, 178t, 178b, 179t, 179c, 179b, 180t, 180b, 181t, 181b, 182t, 182b, 183t, 183b, 184t, 184b, 185t, 185c, 185b, 186t, 186c, 186b, 187t, 188, 190t, 190b, 191t, 191c, 191b, 192t, 192b, 193t, 193b, 194t, 194c, 194b, 195t, 195b, 196, 197t, 197c, 197b, 198t, 198c, 198b, 199t, 199b, 200t, 200b, 201t, 201c, 201b, 202t, 202b, 203t, 203c, 203b, 203r, 204b, 205t, 205c, 205t, 206t, 206b, 207t, 207b, 208t, 208b, 209t, 209b, 210t, 210b, 211t, 211b , 212t, 212b, 213t, 213c, 213b, 214t, 214b, 215t, 215c, 215b, 216t, 216b, 217t, 217c, 217b, 218t, 218b, 219t, 219b, 220t, 220b, 221t, 221b, 222t, 222b, 223t, 223b, 224t, 225t, 225b, 226t, 226b, 227t, 227b, 228t, 228b, 229t, 229b, 230, 231t, 231b, 232t, 232c, 232b, 233t, 233b, 234t, 234b, 235t, 235b, 236t, 236b, 237t, 237c, 237b, 238, 240t, 240b, 241t, 241b, 242t, 242b, 243t, 243b, 244t, 244b, 245t, 245b, 246t, 246b, 247t, 247b, 248t, 248b, 249t, 249b, 250, 250b. Corbis: Page 98–9. Superstock: Page 101, 130l, 146b,162b,189, 239 The Art Archive: Page 251.

CONTENTS

Introduction 6

DEGAS: HIS LIFE AND TIMES 8
THE ENIGMATIC ARTIST 10
BETWEEN TRADITION AND MODERNITY 52

THE GALLERY 98
PAINTINGS AND PASTELS 100
DRAWINGS, PRINTS AND OIL SKETCHES 188
SCULPTURES 238

Index 252

INTRODUCTION

Regarded even in his own lifetime as a modern master, since his death in 1917 Degas has been recognized as one of the greatest artists of all time. His work remains extraordinarily vital and is still loved and admired for its originality, wit and penetrating visual analysis.

Degas lived in turbulent times marked by radical political and social change. In his lifetime France was transformed into a modern industrial nation and the city of Paris where Degas was born and lived saw dramatic changes. The Paris that emerged in the course of the Second Empire and the early decades of the Third Republic (1870–1940) was to furnish him with the subject matter he became famous for: ballerinas, horse-races, cafés and café-concerts, and the work, life and entertainments of the city. Born into a wealthy and aspiring banking family, Degas is the documenter of the lifestyle and values of the haute bourgeoisie, though his eye roams further afield, taking in the more marginal aspects of Parisian life, including the impoverished lives of the city's working classes.

A DEVELOPING CAREER

Degas' career can broadly be divided into three phases: between 1855–65 he sought to become a history painter in the grand tradition; the period 1865–85

Above: Degas developed an artistic style in which he depicted real life as if a moment captured on camera.

marks his emergence as a Realist with close ties to the Impressionist group; the final period from 1885 onwards reflects his increasing preoccupation with aesthetic form. It is at this time that the human body and its movement became his dominant themes. In this period we see an intensification of his attempts to reconcile his admiration of the old masters with the originality and experimentation of his own work. Though one of the most innovative modern painters, Degas was an artist who kept in mind the art of the classical masters, which he admired and emulated in his own works.

A LIFE DEVOTED TO ART

Degas was completely absorbed by his work. He did not marry and little is known of his life beyond the discreet reminiscences of his circle of friends, whose salons he frequented or who had the rare privilege of being visitors to his

Left: Ballet dancers preoccupy Degas' later artistic career, and he built up a knowledgeable repertoire of the movements, as well as depicting last-minute costume adjustments, as here.

studios on the slopes of Montmartre. The picture revealed to us by these friends is of an intensely private man, dismissive of his fame, who could be gregarious, generous and witty, but also abrasive, unapproachable and reclusive.

The last years of Degas' life were not happy ones. Increasingly isolated, largely by his own design, he spoke often of his loneliness. The abiding image we have of Degas is as an artist tirelessly devoted to his craft, endlessly reworking the subject matter that dominated his art. His life was organized around a daily routine of working in his studio, obsessively making studies, tracing and retracing his drawings of the bathers and ballerinas that populated his later art. Never content with what he had achieved, he remained focused on making progress in his art. When declining health and eyesight put an end to this, he was robbed of the one thing that had given his life purpose and meaning. Degas outlived his powers as an artist, as well as many of the contemporary artists that helped define the era. When he died he left behind a unique and exceptional body of work.

Right: Café culture was a new phenomenon in 19th-century Paris, and the subject of many of Degas' paintings.

Below: Degas' bathers link his later work to that of the old masters.

DEGAS: HIS LIFE AND TIMES

Degas' art was intimately related to his own life and times. Closely associated with the rise of Realism and the Impressionist movement, Degas was a constant innovator in art. Born in Paris at a time of great change, he would make the sights and spectacles of Parisian life the abiding subject of his work. Degas painted the world around him: the ballet dancers he saw at the Opéra Garnier, the Paris theatre and opera house, the ambience and entertainments at the cafés and café-concerts he frequented in the evenings, and the world of horse-racing, which enjoyed its heyday in this period. Few painters have produced such a penetrating image of their times.

Left: The Dancing Class, *by Degas, c.1873–76. This painting showing ballerinas rehearsing reveals Degas' preoccupation with the theme of movement, disciplined training and the backstage life of the ballerinas that dominated his art throughout his career.*

THE ENIGMATIC ARTIST

Degas received a conventional artistic education, studying at the
Academy's École des Beaux-Arts, before spending some years in Italy
learning from the Renaissance masters at first hand. These experiences left
Degas with a profound and enduring respect for tradition, matched only
by his originality and experimentation. During the early 1860s Degas
aspired to be a history painter, but struggled to find themes and realize his
most ambitious pictures. The paintings he produced from this time are
often enigmatic and unresolved. By the end of the 1860s, however, Degas
had re-invented himself as a painter of the contemporary Parisian milieu;
the world of the new modernized city now became his subject matter.

Above: Before the Races, *by Degas, c.1882. Degas' interest in horse-racing coincided
with the golden age of this sport in France.*
Left: Self Portrait, *by Degas, 1855. This self-portrait, showing Degas holding a chalk
holder, makes a forceful statement about his ambitions to be an artist.*

FAMILY AND EDUCATION

Degas' attitudes and the direction his art took were shaped by his family, whose tastes and values influenced his own. His upbringing and the experiences of his childhood and youth left an impression on Degas that remained with him for the rest of his life. They also left an indelible influence on his art.

Hilaire-Germain-Edgar Degas was born on 6 July 1834 at 8 rue Saint-Georges in Paris. The family home was located on the Right Bank, near the cathedral of Notre-Dame-de-Lorette. The 9th Arrondissement, in which his home was situated, was a favoured location of the haute bourgeoisie, to whose ranks Degas belonged. Its streets were a mixture of elegant 18th-century townhouses and the neo-Grec and neo-Roman style favoured by financiers and real estate brokers, earning the quarter the nickname Nouvelle Athènes. Close by, signs were evident of the political volatility that characterized the age. In the year of Degas' birth, the French monarch Louis-Philippe restored order in the nearby working-class Beauborg district. By the time Degas was 14, a second French revolution had swept the monarch from power.

DEGAS' FAMILY

Auguste, Degas' father, was half French and half Italian and spent most of his youth in Naples, the seat of the family banking enterprise. In his early 20s he came to France to take charge of a newly established Paris branch. On 12 July 1832, he married Célestine Musson, a 19-year-old American Creole of French descent from Louisiana. Edgar was the first of five children, comprising

Left: Portrait of Lorenzo Pagans. *Music was a very important part of the Degas household. This picture shows the Spanish tenor Lorenzo Pagans (1838–83) performing at the family home while Degas' father, Auguste (1807–74), listens attentively in the background.*

Below: Portrait of René-Hilaire Degas, *(1770–1858), the artist's grandfather, by Degas, 1857. René-Hilaire was a successful and innovative entrepreneur who was to exert a very important influence on the family's fortunes and on Degas' early career.*

Above: A black and white photograph of Edgar Degas (1834–1917). As a young man Degas prided himself on being a fashionable dandy and man around town.

Above: Self portrait, by Degas, c.1857. This assertive self-portrait, perhaps influenced by the portraits of Agnolo Bronzino (1503–72), is one of a series in which Degas stares questioningly back at his own mirror image.

three brothers and two sisters. Their mother died prematurely when he was only 13, leaving a family dominated by patriarchs. Degas' grandfathers were also to be an important influence on the family's economic circumstances and on the class outlook of the young Edgar. Each played a role in shaping the course Edgar's life and art took. During his youth he would spend time with both at the family seats in Naples and New Orleans. The family fortune was to give him the financial independence crucial to the development of his art.

His grandfathers René-Hilaire Degas, after whom Degas was named, and Germain Musson were self-made men who acquired huge fortunes, the former in banking, the latter in exporting cotton and other goods. René had fled France during the years of the first French Revolution, after the execution of his fiancée for treason; his experience of Jacobin terror left a lasting impression on the family's outlook. After short military interludes in the Napoleonic army, René

ended up in Naples, Italy's largest city and at the time under French occupation, where he quickly established a successful banking operation that benefited from royal patronage. A shrewd businessman, René advanced the careers of his three sons in the business, while also socially raising the family's status through the marriage of his daughters to Italian aristocrats and senators.

Germain Musson led a similarly picaresque life. Born in Saint Dominique, he became an adventurer and exporter

of sugar, coffee, cotton, cocoa and indigo cultivated on African slave plantations. He settled in New Orleans in 1810 and took advantage of the boom years in the opening up of trade along the Mississippi River. After the death of his wife he brought his five daughters to Paris to be educated, before eventually resettling in Louisiana.

ASPIRING IDEALS

Degas benefited from the aspirations of the haute bourgeoisie. Like many in their class, they emphasized education, social refinement and cultivated knowledge of the arts. Edgar was sent to the Lycée Louis-le-Grand where he graduated in 1853 with a baccalauréat in literature. The family fostered his attraction to painting, contemporary classical music and opera.

STARTING OUT

Degas' artistic education followed a conventional academic route. Though he ultimately turned away from academic principles, the training instilled in him an enduring love of tradition. His work combined a desire for originality with a deep appreciation of the techniques and themes of classical art.

Degas began his artistic instruction at drawing classes at the Lycée Louis-le-Grand, alongside Léon Bonnat (1833–1922), a future director of the École des Beaux-Arts and academic painter, Henri Rouart (1833–1912), a part-time painter and industrialist, Paul Valpinçon (1834–94), a childhood friend, and the author and playwright Ludovic Halévy (1834–1908), establishing close friendships with the latter three. Degas' grades were not exceptional, but he applied himself to copying Renaissance masters after engravings and drawing from casts of ancient statuary. He benefited from the teaching of Léon Cogniet (1794–1880); Degas' notebooks reveal he planned his own version of Cogniet's renowned *Tintoretto Painting His Dead Daughter* (1845).

EARLY INFLUENCES

Degas' interest in art was fostered by his father, who on Sundays would take him to the Louvre, where he lingered in the galleries of the Italian masters of the

Below: Hémicycle of the École des Beaux-Arts, *by Delaroche, c.1834–36. Delaroche's grand 27m (29½yd) long mural adorned the École des Beaux-Arts. Its depiction of 75 great artists of the past in conversation alongside various female muses made a powerful statement about the academic artistic tradition.*

Above: Nude Study, *by Degas, c.1858–60. This early academic study shows Degas acquiring the skills in depicting the figure that the École training sought to foster. The nude was to remain an important subject for Degas and one that allowed him a dialogue with the works of the old masters.*

Cinquecento; on one visit he recalled seeing Eugène Delacroix. He also had access to major art collections among the family's friends, including the collections of 17th- and 18th-century masters of Dr Louis La Caze and François Marcille, and that of Édouard Valpinçon, which included Jean Auguste Dominque Ingres' *Valpinçon Bather* (1808) as well as some of his drawings. Ingres (1780–1867) was to be the presiding influence on Degas' artistic

Above: The Greek Room of the École Nationale Supérieure des Beaux-Arts provided classical artefacts that were copied by students at the École as part of their training to be history painters.

career. His father's small collection of pastels by Jean-Baptiste Perronneau (1715–83) and Quentin de la Tour (1704–88) also left a lasting impression.

In 1853 Degas registered to study law at the prestigious Faculté de Droit, but his irregular attendance indicated his ambitions lay elsewhere. Earlier in the year, when registering at the print collection at the Bibliothèque Nationale, he had stated his profession as artist and signed himself a pupil of Félix-Joseph Barrias (1822–1907), his then instructor. His father later replaced Barrias with Louis Lamothe (1822–69)

Above: The Anatomy Class at the École des Beaux-Arts *by François Salle (1839–99), 1888. This painting, rendered in a style of academic naturalism, shows a professor posing the model in a life class at the École des Beaux-Arts. The depiction of the nude in the life class was the focus of artistic training.*

and Degas spent much of his time at Lamothe's studio, copying at the Louvre and State print collections, while preparing for the entrance examinations for the École des Beaux-Arts.

THE ÉCOLE DES BEAUX-ARTS

The French Academy's school was an essential component of the training of ambitious 19th-century artists. Delaroche's imposing *Hémicycle des Beaux-Arts* (1836), adorned the interior,

emphasizing the importance of tradition. Successful students enjoyed lucrative state commissions and official awards, yet they faced a wearying curriculum copying from engravings and classical statuary. Only drawing was taught and instruction focused on bodily anatomy and movement. The École was structured around a series of competitions; winners of the most prestigious, The Prix de Rome, were rewarded with four-year studentships in Rome to study the Renaissance masters.

Degas' day was divided into morning classes at the École and afternoons copying at the Louvre and visits to the Musée Luxembourg, which housed the State collection of contemporary art. He supplemented École instruction with attendance at Lamothe's studio, where he learned to paint and studied the life

ÉCOLE TRAINING

Over the four years of enrolment at the École, students progressed from copying engravings and plaster casts concerned with antique statuary to the life class, where the figure was posed in the Classical style. Through this process, students learned to conceive of the figure in terms of its structure and honed their skills in line drawing, which was considered to be the primary principle of good composition. The aim was to teach students to articulate the body in harmonious compositions and to instil through long practice habits of the eye and composition that would then become natural. Learning the mastery of the body taught students the skills needed to be a painter of multi-figure historical subjects.

model. Degas' notebooks show him absorbing the style and lessons of the canon, most especially classical statuary, the Italian primitives, high Renaissance painters and French 18th-century Neoclassicists. Despite his endeavour he performed indifferently and became disenchanted with the teaching he received at the École, and left in the summer of 1856. He then worked with Nicolas Soutzo (1834–1907), a painter and engraver, who encouraged an interest in studying after nature. Yet Degas remained preoccupied with the figure, producing portraits and works that betray the influence of Ingres, Jacopo da Pontormo (1495–1557) and Agnolo Bronzino.

FRENCH ART IN THE 1850s

The art world of Degas' youth was very different from the one in which he would make his career. In the 1850s French art was dominated by the rivalry between the schools of Neoclassicism and Romanticism. It was this rivalry that conditioned Degas' ideas about art.

French art in the first half of the 19th century was governed by the Academy, formed in 1648. Members, alongside government officials, sat on the jury of the Salon, the annual official exhibition of contemporary art, and exerted a dominant influence over the training of artists. Academic art emphasized the artists' relationship to the grand tradition, and sought artistic continuity with the art of the Italian Renaissance and antiquity. The Academy fostered the idea of a hierarchy of genres with historical and narrative subjects at its apex and non-figurative subjects like landscape and

Below: Execution of Lady Jane Grey, by Delaroche, 1833. Delaroche's academic style and historical subjects made him one of the most successful artists of his time. During the first half of the century his work was seen as offering an alternative to the rivalry between the Classical and Romantic schools.

Right: The Source, by Ingres, 1856. Ingres' sensual nudes asserted their relationship to the classical tradition, depicting subjects that were regarded as timeless and universal.

still-life at the bottom. The art world revolved around an official system of rewards and state patronage. Artists competed for lucrative public commissions for morally elevated subjects to decorate civic buildings, churches and monuments. Leading artists of the first half of the 19th century invariably emerged from the Academy's ranks. Ingres, widely recognized as the greatest draughtsman and painter of his generation and heir to the French classical tradition of Nicolas Poussin (1594–1665), was among these. For Ingres, the artist was a public educator, transmitting timeless and universal artistic values, and the mission of art was to perpetuate and extend the example of the old masters.

THE RISE OF ROMANTICISM

By the 1820s these classical values began to be challenged as a new movement emerged in France associated with the work of Théodore Géricault (1791–1824) and Eugène Delacroix (1798–1863), though, ironically, its roots lay in the innovations of Davidian-trained painters like Baron Antoine-Jean Gros (1771–1835). The Romanticism of these artists focused on a more subjective, individualized and original approach to painting based on artistic will and temperament. Delacroix believed the classical tradition needed to be renewed in relation to the turbulent spirit of the times. France had experienced violent revolution in 1789, the Napoleonic wars with Europe (1803–15), the Restoration

of the Bourbon monarchy (1814–30) and a second revolution in 1848. To his most fervent admirer, the poet Charles Baudelaire (1821–67), Delacroix's violent subject matter, treated in bold, animated and unorthodox compositions that used heightened colour and vibrant brushwork, expressed the volatility and underlying disquiet of the period.

NEW DEVELOPMENTS

At the beginning of the century French art was dominated by Neoclassicism and Romanticism, but by the 1830s other tendencies emerged that would eventually eclipse them. Paul Delaroche (1797–1856) pioneered the popular genre historique, anecdotal and melodramatic portrayals of historical subjects that exploited the French fascination with the English Civil War and the popularity of the novels of Sir Walter

THE RIVALRY OF INGRES AND DELACROIX

By the 1840s the conflict between Ingres and Delacroix had become a dominant feature of the French art world, with their respective merits debated by younger artists. Ingres sought to emulate artists like Raphael (1483) and Poussin, who were regarded as exemplars of the classical tradition and refined taste. Delacroix, on the other hand, looked to the vibrant and animated paintings of Titian (c.1490–1576), Rubens (1577–1640), Rembrandt (1601–69) and Michelangelo (1475–1564), whose works were seen as a unique expression of their individual temperaments. Ingres and Delacroix had contempt for each other. When Delacroix was elected to the Academy's ranks at the end of his life, Ingres voted against his nomination.

Scott. Despite his desire for accuracy, in dramatizing his subjects, Delaroche took artistic licence in depicting the historical events he represented to make them relevant to a contemporary audience. The theatrical lighting of the *Execution of Lady Jane Grey* (1833), the blindfolded Jane's pale appearance and her groping towards the block, all heighten the emotive quality, but have little basis in fact.

Realism was also emerging as a tendency, arising out of the demands within Romanticism for contemporary subjects and the renewal of artistic conventions in relation to nature. Many

of the most important realists, like Gustave Courbet (1819–77) and Jean-François Millet (1814–75), had begun their careers painting in a Romantic style, but in the late 1840s moved toward a conception of art that rejected idealism and imagination and sought subjects drawn from nature.

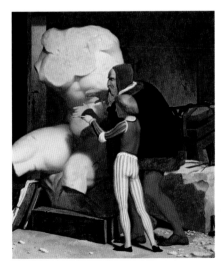

Right: Michelangelo (1475–1564) Showing a Student the Belvedere Torso, *by Jean–Léon Gérôme, (1824–1904), 1849. Michelangelo was revered as an artist that combined exemplary knowledge of tradition with originality and personal expression. His work was admired by romantics and classicists alike.*

THE IMPORTANCE OF INGRES

Of all the artists who influenced Degas, the French Neoclassicist Jean Auguste Dominque Ingres remained the most significant. In the first half of the 19th century Ingres redefined the classical tradition and was recognized as the most brilliant draughtsman of his time.

Degas' admiration of Ingres' work was first awakened by his visits to the Valpinçons, where he could study Ingres' seminal *Valpinçon Bather*. This was deepened during the four years he studied with Louis Lamothe, who had been a pupil of Ingres, and also of Ingres' star pupil, Jean-Hippolyte Flandrin. Under Lamothe's guidance Degas learned the key principles of Ingres' art, above all that "Drawing is the probity of art." His own later artistic maxims, such as: "Drawing is not the same as form, it is a way of seeing form", bear the imprint of Ingres' trenchant views.

ADMIRATION AND INFUENCE

The influence of Ingres, filtered through Lamothe, accounts for Degas' decision to spend a summer copying works by Flandrin and ancient and Renaissance art in Lyon, the spiritual centre of Ingres' followers. It also determined the appreciation in his early career for Raphael and other Italian Renaissance artists such as Mantegna (1431–1506), Perugino (1446–1524), Bronzino (1503–72) and Pontormo (1494–1557), as well as his admiration of Flaxman's illustrations for *The Illiad* and *The Odyssey*. Ingres' influence may also explain Degas' choice of obscure classical subjects, of the kind Ingres favoured. Although Degas' taste would broaden by the beginning of the 1860s to encompass Ingres' enemy Delacroix, Ingres continued to exert a huge influence on him; Degas' portraits, self-portraits and bathers are inconceivable without Ingres' example and often make overt references to their source. Degas' most accomplished early self-portraits mirror those of Ingres and his ambitious *The Bellelli Family* (c.1858–67) closely recalls Ingres' *Portrait of the Gatteaux Family* (1850). Years later he spoke of Ingres' drawings as "those marvels of the human spirit".

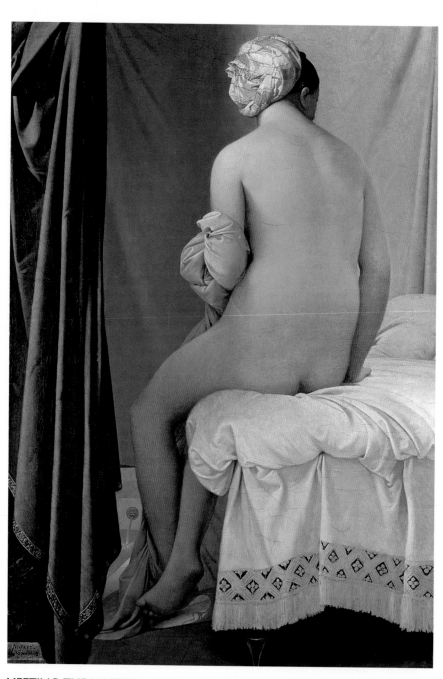

MEETING THE MASTER

In 1855 Degas made a copy after Ingres' *Valpinçon Bather*. His veneration for Ingres is clear from an anecdote from that time saying that on hearing Edouard Valpinçon had refused Ingres' request to lend the picture for his retrospective at the 1855 Universal

Above: The Bather, *known as* Baigneuse Valpincon, *by Ingres, 1808. Ingres' great masterpiece demonstrates the stylization and sensuality of his female bathers, which place a strong accent on the fluid line of the contours of the body. It is a work with which Degas was fascinated.*

Left: Study for The Turkish Bath, *by Ingres, c.1859. Degas imitated the work of Ingres and later explored the expressive possibilities of this pose in his bathers' pictures of the 1880s.*

was a pupil of Ingres, and any mention of this always pleases him, for he looks upon Ingres as the first star in the firmament of French art."

When in later life Degas was wealthy enough to buy art, he established a collection of Ingres, including 20 paintings and 90 drawings. Letters to Paul Durand-Ruel show him pleading with the dealer to sell him pictures by Ingres. Paul Valéry recalled Degas telling him how when he visited Ingres in 1855, "while they were talking, (he) cast an eye around the pictures on the walls". Fifty years later, he owned many of them.

Exhibition, Degas exploded with a rage that so shook Edouard, he decided to lend it after all and beg Ingres' pardon. Degas accompanied the picture to Ingres' apartment in the neighbouring rue de Lille, where he met the great artist. On a later visit Degas revealed he was an aspiring painter. "Draw lines, young man", Ingres advised him, "lots of lines, never from nature, always from memory and the engravings of the masters." Degas' early drawings, mainly after Raphael and the antique, show he took Ingres' advice to heart and at the 1855 Ingres retrospective he assiduously made drawings after many of Ingres' mythologies, paying particular attention to details. In copying after Ingres Degas was absorbing his artistic style. Reviewing Degas' *Portrait of Edmond Duranty* (1879) at the Impressionist show in 1880, Charles Ephrussi wrote that Degas was "not only a draughtsman of more than estimable ability, but a pupil of the great Florentines…and above all of a great Frenchman, M. Ingres". In 1890 the writer George Moore wrote: "Degas

Right: Saint Symphorian after Ingres, *by Degas, c.1855. After Ingres'* Martyrdom of Saint Symphoriam, *1834, this study shows the influence that Ingres' linear style had throughout Degas' life.*

TRAVELS IN ITALY

Though by the end of the 18th century the centre of the art world had shifted to France, the achievement of Italian Renaissance artists and the classical heritage of Rome still exerted a powerful influence over French art. Degas' travels in Italy certainly shaped the development of his art.

It was traditional for prize-winning students at the École des Beaux-Arts to finish their education by studying the Italian old masters at the French Academy in Rome. Though Degas did not enter the École's most prestigious competition, his commitment to the classical tradition was sufficient for him to follow this custom and study in Italy. On 15 July 1856, he set sail. Arriving in Naples, where he stayed at his grand-father's grand palazzo, Degas settled into a routine of studying from the Museo Nazionale Romano collection, which contained murals from the ruins of Pompeii, Herculaneum and Stabiae, as well as an excellent collection of Italian masters, including Titian's *Portrait of Pope Paul III* (1543) and works by Veronese (1528–88). During his stay Degas read

Below: Portrait of Gustave Moreau (1826–98), by Degas. During his stay in Italy Degas became friends with Symbolist painter Moreau, who would be one of the leading painters of the fin-de-siècle.

works by Dante (1265–1321) and journeyed along the coast of Sorrento where, inspired by an Italian landscape by Claude Lorrain (1600–82) at the Nazionale, he made sketches of the local scenery. Degas also made a number of sketches and portraits of his family. Of these, it was his father's troubled sister, Laura Bellelli, whom Degas was most drawn to.

VOYAGE TO ROME

At the beginning of October Degas departed for the Roman port of Civitavecchia, staying at the Villa Medici. There he became friends with many Academy students and established an informal group called Caldarrosti (Roast Chestnuts), named after the Roman street vendors. The Caldarrosti met regularly at the Caffé Greco to talk about art, music and literature. Goethe (1749–1832), Byron (1788–1824), Shelley (1792–1822), Leopardi (1798–1837), Stendhal (1783–1842) and the composer Berlioz (1803–69) featured heavily in their discussions, as did the respective merits of Delacroix and Ingres. Like his comrades Degas busied himself with copying after the art and antiquities in Rome. Degas studied paintings in the

Left: Portrait of Alessandro Farnese (1468–1549) Pope Paul III, by Titian c.1488–1576. Degas was impressed by Venetian Renaissance artists such as Titian. The rich, highly saturated colour schemes left a lasting impression on him.

Vatican including *Saint Jerome* (1480) by Leonardo da Vinci (1452–1519) and *Perseus* (c.1800) by Antonio Canova (1757–1822), as well as the magnificent Papal collection of Greek and Roman statuary. He also made copies after Domenichino's (1581–1641) fresco in the chapel of Sant'Andrea in Mantua, and the mosaics, then attributed to Giotto (1267–1337), in St Peter's, Rome, as well as engravings in the Villa Medici, Rome. Degas also made many sketches of the Roman Forum and the villa Borghese Gardens. At this time he also began work on religious and mythological subjects intended for exhibition at the Salon. Degas made many studies for an aborted *Saint John the Baptist and the Angel* and contemplated many paintings based on Dante's work among other themes; however, during their development he was wracked with doubt and uncertainty, and these came to nothing.

On 1 August 1857 Degas returned to Naples, and set about copying the Pompeian murals, but by mid-October he was back in Rome where he became close friends with the charismatic Gustave Moreau (1826–98). Ingres was still strongly on Degas' mind, as the portrait of his grandfather René-Hilaire, shows, but working with Moreau he began to appreciate the achievements of Delacroix, Rembrandt and the Venetians. After brief stays in Arezzo, Assisi and Perugia, on 4 August 1858 Degas arrived in Florence, where he lodged with his aunt, Laura, at the Bellelli's apartment. Degas would later immortalize her in his most accomplished painting to date, *The Bellelli Family*.

In Florence Degas was soon hard at work again, studying the Florentine masters and reading Pascal's *Pensées* (1660). He also worked on a *David and Goliath* and a version of the *Blind Oedipus*, as well as other historical and mythological themes. In a long letter to Moreau he writes, "There is an emptiness that even art cannot fill", which conveys Degas' melancholy at this time. His mood may have been partly due to his grandfather's death in August that year, as well as Laura's absence attending to René-Hilaire's estate. On her return he worked energetically on preparatory sketches

Below: The Bellelli Family, *by Degas, 1858–67. This family portrait was Degas' most consummate work at that period, revealing his talent for capturing the individual character and psychology of his portrait sitters.*

for her portrait. By the following spring, with Moreau about to leave for France and one eye on the Salon, Degas was keen to return to Paris. He wrote to his father urging him to find a suitable studio to complete the portrait.

Left: A Roman Beggar Woman, *by Degas, 1857. Degas liked to capture local scenes of the ordinary people he encountered during his stay in Rome.*

THE BELLELLI FAMILY

Regarded as Degas' earliest masterpiece, *The Bellelli Family* is a complex group portrait. Many preparatory studies were produced, as he searched for a form that would deepen the psychological themes. Laura's refined countenance bears the influence of Ingres and Bronzino. The pyramidal composition of Laura with her daughters, Giulia and the more informally posed Giovanna, separates the group from the seated Gennaro. Laura is dressed in mourning for her father. Her austere appearance, juxtaposed with her husband whose preoccupation with business, signalled by his position at his desk, indicates the profound distance between them.

A CHANGING ART WORLD

The 1860s represented a decisive moment in French art, when changes in artistic taste and the structure of the art world began to pave the way for the emergence of modern painting. Variants of naturalism and realism emerged that challenged the dominance of the classical and romantic traditions.

By the end of the 1860s many of the great French artists who had dominated the first half of the century had passed away. The influential Paul Delaroche died in 1856 and Eugène Delacroix seven years later. Ingres' death at the age of 86 on 17 January 1867 was widely considered a watershed moment, signalling the passing of the old order. The French art world was changing.

A PERIOD OF REFORM

Already by the late 1850s discontent with the status quo was evident. The Academy's policy of exhibiting only works that conformed to their own traditionalist ideals at the annual Salon led to public demonstrations by excluded artists. In 1863 Napoleon III, in a liberalizing gesture, intervened in these disputes to allow a Salon des Refusés. Though many artists did not wish to exhibit under a banner of the refused, Edouard Manet (1832–83), James McNeill Whistler (1834–1903),

Henri Fantin-Latour (1836–1904), Félix Bracquemond (1833–1914), Alphonse Legros (1837–1914), Camille Pissarro (1830–1903), Johann Jongkind (1819–91) and Armand Guillaumin

Above: An Apple Orchard, *by Daubigny (1817–78), c.1875–77. In the 1860s the naturalist painter Daubigny became a key figure in the ascendance of landscape painting in France, much admired by the Impressionists for the informality of his style and discreet motifs.*

(1841–1927) all contributed. As Degas had not submitted to the Salon that year he was not represented, nor do we know what he thought of the exhibition. Whistler's *White Girl* (1861) and Manet's *Le Déjeuner sur l'herbe* (*Luncheon on the Grass*) (1863) were highlights of the show; Whistler's painting received much praise in comparison with the severe criticism of Manet. Despite this, Le *Déjeuner*

Left: During the 1860s, with the exhibition of Le Déjeuner sur l'herbe, *1863 and* Olympia, *1863–65, Manet became a key figure for a younger generation of modern painters who admired his updating of traditional subjects and his novel techniques.*

sur l'herbe was to have the more lasting impression on the younger generation of artists.

Though the Salon des Refusés was intended as an isolated event and generally drew bad reviews, it undermined the authority of the Academy and encouraged artists to think of alternative exhibiting venues. In the same year the École was reformed in response to widespread accusations that French art was becoming formulaic and slavishly indebted to the past. New younger professors were appointed and more liberal teaching practices put in place. These were signs of a more pluralist approach by the state toward art. As the state budget was diverted into its program of economic modernization, so funding for the arts was reduced, resulting in a decline of commissions for large-scale history paintings, on which many academic painters depended. The Second Empire (1852–70) fostered a more eclectic approach in its patronage, rewarding the public's favourites, not merely the Academy's, and allowed a

Below: Homage to Delacroix, *by Fantin-Latour (1836–1904), self-portrait with Cordier, Duranty, Legros, Whistler, Champfleury, Manet, Bracquemond, Baudelaire, and de Balleroy, 1864. Delacroix's bold colour, compositional innovation and emphasis on a personalized approach to painting made him an influential painter for later artists.*

Above: The Stone Breakers, *by Courbet (1819–77), 1849. Courbet's forceful portrayal of dehumanized and backbreaking labour established him as an uncompromising painter.*

new free market economy of the arts to flourish that would eventually usurp the old system of official awards. Galleries run by private dealers now became an increasingly familiar sight in the fashionable quarters of Paris and artists like Degas and the Impressionists were to make their careers independently of the official system.

CHANGING TASTES

Accompanying these changes in the structure of the art world were changes in the buying public. In the boom years of the Second Empire people who could not previously have done so were buying art, and their tastes were more varied. Realism was now flourishing and becoming the dominant tendency in

French art, with artists like Courbet and Millet gaining increasing critical attention and respect among younger artists. Alongside this a late romantic tendency, represented by painters such as Fantin-Latour, Legros and Whistler, sought to harness the legacy of Delacroix to these new trends in contemporary art.

More informal subjects representing diverse scenes of contemporary life and nature were becoming popular in both art and literature. By the 1860s a new taste for landscape had also emerged, associated with the Barbizon painters, whose principal members were Charles-François Daubigny (1817–78), Théodore Rousseau (1812–67), Constant Troyon (1810–65), Narcisse-Virgilio Diaz de la Peña (1807–76) and Jean-Baptiste-Camille Corot (1796–1875). The Barbizon painters were committed to sketching *en plein air* (in the open air), in order to obtain a fresh and strong impression of their motifs and to make pictures that responded to the actual appearances of nature, rather than the idealized abstractions of traditional French landscapes. Their work exercised a profound influence on the course of landscape painting in France.

SEARCHING FOR A STYLE

During the late 1850s Degas focused on large history paintings for exhibition at the Salon. However, he struggled to realize his ambitious plans for pictures that would establish his reputation. These early narrative pictures show us a direction in his art that Degas was to swiftly move away from.

Many of his preparatory drawings and studies of the nude in the 1850s reveal how guided by the example of Ingres Degas remained despite broadening his taste in Italy. However, the new-found admiration for Delacroix fostered by Gustave Moreau was beginning to make itself felt in his style, which took on a new eclecticism. Degas' studies for pictures on the themes of *Hero and Leander* (1855) and *King Candaules' Wife* (1856) reflect the style of Ingres and his followers, but *David and Goliath* (1858–59), with its freely worked brushwork and unorthodox perspective, looked to the example of Delacroix.

Degas also worked on religious themes. A series of Ingresque studies of Saint John the Baptist executed between 1856–58 suggest he was planning a work on this theme for the Salon. As Degas moved toward artistic maturity he carried with him the contradictions between these two great artistic rivals. Degas' father seems to have been sufficiently worried by his son's enthusiasm for Delacroix to ask Lamothe to steer him back to Ingres and wrote encouraging his son to avoid jeopardizing his career by becoming an "ideologue".

In the early 1860s Degas was still abandoning works and searching for a theme to make an impact at the Salon. In 1860–61 he worked on *Semiramis Building Babylon*, which depicts the Queen of Assyria standing on the banks of the River Euphrates, watching the construction of Babylon, one of the Seven Wonders of the World, a resonant theme for an ambitious young painter trying to make a reputation for himself. The painting was influenced by his visit to Arrezzo en route to Florence in 1855, where he saw the frescoes of Piero della Francesca (1415–92). Degas also took inspiration for the chariot and Semiramis' hairstyle from Assyrian reliefs recently acquired

by the Louvre. The painting shows Degas mirroring the recent processional motifs of Moreau and his knowledge of mezzotints of the visionary cityscapes of the English painter John Martin (1789–1854).

In the same period he began work on the *Young Spartans* (1860–61), a picture he described in his notebooks as

Above: Young Spartans Exercising, *by Degas, c.1860–61 and (top)* Study for the Young Spartans Exercising, *by Degas, c.1860. These two studies show Degas developing a composition he was ultimately to regard as unfinished and unresolved. Differences are to be found in the background and the attitude of the figures.*

"girls and boys wrestling in the Plane-tree grove, watched by the elderly Lycurgus and the Mothers". For his first major painting of the nude Degas made meticulous preparatory studies of the figures, working intensively on it between 1860–61 and then again around mid-decade, before possibly returning to it once more in the late 1870s. As with *Semiramis Building Babylon*, Degas chose a frieze-like arrangement for the figures

with the two groups of youths polarized, girls to the left, boys to the right, with the mothers and elder located centrally in the distance. Degas continually reworked and refined the key poses in a series of extraordinary drawings, some of which recall studies he had made at Ingres' retrospective of 1855. The final composition owes much to Ingres' Prix de Rome-winning *Achilles Receiving the*

Above: Semiramis Building Babylon, *by Degas, 1861. During the 1850s and early 1860s Degas remained preoccupied with developing ambitious history paintings for exhibition at the Salon, such as this one of the legendary Assyrian queen for whom the Hanging Gardens of Babylon were built.*

Ambassadors of Agamemnon (1801), as well as Moreau's *Athenians Delivered to the Minotaur* (1855).

The painting represents the athletic confrontation of the sexes. The gestures and poses articulate the varied responses of the figures to the contest. The boys gesticulate and prepare themselves. The girls seem caught between eagerness and reserve: one girl holds another back; another lunges toward her opponents, while still another tries to restrain her. The subject of the work seems to anticipate an abiding theme of Degas' art, the conflict between the sexes, though it may also represent a Spartan courting ritual.

BATTLE OF THE SEXES

The theme of *Young Spartans* has provoked much interpretation. Is it about conflict between the sexes, courtship, or both? It is tempting to see the picture as reflecting Degas' anxiety about women. However, Degas had read about Spartan courtship in Plutarch's (AD46–120) *Lives* and knew that Spartan girls cropped their hair before marriage, shown here by two of the females. Jean-Louis Forain (1852–1931) later recalled Degas saying the figures behind should be pregnant and the hill was where Spartans threw deformed babies. If correct, the picture is likely to represent the rituals and consequences of Spartan marriage.

Left: Saint Anthony Resuscitating a Woman Killed by her Husband, *by Degas, c.1858. This picture is one of a number of violent scenes set in the historical past that Degas was attracted to in his youth and points to his continuing engagement with Renaissance sources.*

A PERIOD OF TRANSITION

In the mid-1860s Degas still saw himself as a history painter in the traditional sense. Yet by the end of the decade his style and subject matter had changed radically. The late 1860s and early 1870s were to be a period of redefinition as the artistic preoccupations of Degas' mature style gradually surfaced.

During the 1860s Degas continued to divide his work between portraits, which show his increasing mastery of the genre, and ambitious history paintings, which posed problems of realization for him. Though Degas continued to work on his ambitious

Young Spartans with a view to making his Salon debut with it, he struggled to resolve the picture. It was listed many years later in the catalogue of the Fifth Impressionist Exhibition (1881) as *Young Spartan Girls Provoking some Boys*, but the picture was not shown and was never exhibited publicly in his lifetime. It remained, however, in his possession, a work he valued as an important moment in the transition toward his mature oeuvre.

SALON DEBUT

The first work Degas showed at the Salon was *Medieval War Scene* (1865), his only other major history painting featuring the nude and his most dramatic and violent picture to date.

Left: Portrait of a Young Woman, *by Degas, 1867. Despite his ambitions as a history painter, Degas' most accomplished work was arguably his interior, and invariably psychologically complex, portraits.*

Above: Medieval War Scene, *by Degas, 1865. The exact subject of this picture remains obscure and is most likely invented.*

The painting portrays a scene of rape and pillage, though the precise subject remains an enigma. In posthumous sales of Degas' pictures it came to be known as the *Sufferings of the Town of Orléans*, though no one knows why or even whether it was Degas who re-titled it. No recorded event in the city's history matches it.

The composition suggests Degas' interest in northern European painting and tapestries. He had copied a Bernard van Orley (1487–91) tapestry of a hunting scene. Preparatory drawings reveal his difficulty in resolving the variations in style he tried out in the initial conception. Degas continued to make amendments as he went along. At some point close to its completion he enlarged the picture, adding a third strip

of paper on the far right, to bring greater compositional breadth and introduce a rider shown abducting a woman at the right-hand margin.

The resulting composition closely parallels the frieze-like format of the *Young Spartans*, with a similar compositional division of male and female groupings at opposite sides of the picture, female victims mostly on the left, their vicious violators on the right. Naked dead bodies are slumped in the foreground, an archer sadistically fires arrows on defenceless women as the violators depart, while the town burns in the background. The central void powerfully suggests the futility and disorder of war and was a compositional device Delaroche had employed in his celebrated *Assassination of the Duc de Guise at Blois* (1834).

If Degas hoped *Medieval War Scene* would make his reputation as an innovative new history painter, he was sorely disappointed. Critical reaction was sparse and poor. Despite its brutal and sensational subject matter, it was one of a number of such pictures at the

Right: Mademoiselle Fiocre in the Ballet 'La Source', by Degas, 1866–68. *In this early ballet scene Degas anticipates the preoccupation with a subject that was to become one of the abiding themes of his art. Here Degas fuses his interest with the past with a contemporary scene taken from the theatre.*

Above: Portrait of Hortense Valpinçon as a Child, by Degas, 1869. *A frequent visitor to the Valpinçon family's estate, Degas here shows his talent for genre portraiture, creating enduring images whose intimacy and informality show his absorption of Dutch 17th-century painting.*

Salon on related themes of persecuted women and male aggressors. The portrayal of female nudes subjected to aggressive male violence had a long history in Western painting, as

exemplified by Titian's *Jealous Husband* (1511), shown stabbing his wife, and Poussin's *Rape of the Sabines* (1637–38), both of which Degas carefully copied. In the same year his friend James Tissot (1836–1902) exhibited his Renaissance costume piece, *Abduction* (1865), which has a similar composition. Degas' prior knowledge of it may have played some part in his late additions to the picture. Moreau had earlier exhibited a similar theme in his *Venetian Girls Carried off by Cypriot Pirates* (1851).

FIRST BALLET SCENE

Degas' other major costume drama of the period, *Mademoiselle Fiocre in the Ballet 'La Source'*, exhibited at the Salon of 1868, blurs the boundaries between history painting and more naturalist subject matter. The painting depicts the dancer Eugénie Fiocre (1845–1908) in the first act of Arthur Saint-Léon's (1821–70) ballet, an orientalist fantasy first performed in 1866. Critics were unsure whether to see it as a historical piece or a contemporary subject and, as Zola disparagingly noted, it falls between the two. As such it looks back to Degas' academic practice, while also anticipating the great theme of Degas' painting in the 1870s, the ballet.

PARIS MODERNIZED

When we think of the early Degas it is primarily as a painter of Paris. This was the new Paris that was substantially rebuilt during the Second Empire and the first decade of the Third Republic. It was from this modern milieu that Degas was to draw the themes and subjects of his art during the 1870s and 1880s.

With the Second Republic (1848–52) administration faltering, Napoléon III (1808–73), a nephew of Napoléon Bonaparte (1769–1821), seized power in a coup d'état in 1850, proclaiming himself emperor shortly afterwards. In 1852 the new Emperor commissioned Baron Georges Haussmann (1809–81) to draw up ambitious plans for the urban renewal of Paris. This massive project of modernization had several motives, including sanitization, slum clearance and an urgent need to revive and modernize an ailing economy. The urban structure of Paris was still much as it had been in the medieval period, a dense village-like set up with narrow meandering streets and closely packed buildings, whose unhygienic conditions made the inhabitants vulnerable to outbreaks of disease. Haussmann's

Below: The new Paris was characterized by wide boulevards, arcades, fashionable new zones of commerce and high-storied apartments offering spectacular views on to the street.

sanitization of the city included the creation of a modern subterranean sewerage system that became one of the marvels of Paris, the development of public parks and the planting of trees along many boulevards to soak up pollution from factories. These factories in turn were lured to the wastelands on the outskirts of the city by the promise of cheap rents.

The grand new boulevards of Paris were conceived to facilitate the transportation of goods in and out of the city and encourage economic modernization. The creation of new centralized zones of commerce led the way to new forms of economic activity: the building of arcades of shops selling a diverse array of goods; the development of the Bon Marché, a chain of large department stores selling objects imported from around the world; the burgeoning 'floating world' of cafés and café-concerts, theatres and other forms of commercialized entertainment. The construction of apartment buildings several storeys high,

upon which the family fortune of Impressionist Gustave Caillebotte (1848–94), among others, was made, was another new feature of Paris, elevating the view its residents had of their city.

AN IMPERIAL CITY
Napoléon III also saw the rebuilding of Paris as a way to shore up his regime and stamp the image of the Empire on to the face of the city. The new grand boulevards with their breathtaking vistas were intended to bring a new breadth, openness and majesty to the city, with the opulent Opéra Garnier as its symbolic centre. Modelled on the architecture and design of ancient Rome, the city projected an image of the Second Empire as heir to the Roman legacy.

Below: Napoléon III (1808–73) instigated the modernization of Paris from an overgrown medieval village to a grand modern city based on the model of ancient Rome.

Left: A Balcony, Boulevard Haussmann, *by Caillebotte, (1848–94), 1880, depicts the new and grand buildings that were springing up during the rebuilding of Paris.*

Below: Caricature of Baron Georges Eugene Haussmann (1809–91) as a beaver, from La Ménagerie Impériale The Imperial Zoo, *c.1870–71, by Paul Hadol, a series of prints that depicted characters who effectively controlled the new France from the 1850s to the 1870s.*

Rebuilding the city had other political motives. France had lived through a turbulent period of revolutions and insurrections and the spectre of violent revolt haunted Paris. Though the Second Empire was to be later known as a period of laissez-faire liberalization, it was initially a police state. As well as creating an atmosphere of grandeur, the wide roads would facilitate military mobilization and deter the building of barricades, and they were monitored with strategic military sentinels. Haussmann's "modernization" swept away large swathes of the older working-class areas, and much of the bohemian quarter and its quartiers dangereuses, renowned as the bedrock of radical ideas, political resistance and criminal activity.

Haussmann's new Paris was a long time in the making and it wasn't until the late 1870s that the city really began to take on its characteristic form. For many years large areas of Paris were reduced to a building site. The city that eventually resulted introduced a fully entrepreneurial capitalist system of enterprise into the city and consequently utterly changed the social and cultural experience of Parisians. This new modern capital now reflected the lifestyle of its middle classes. Modernization raised people's awareness of the immense historical changes taking place. The new city gave concrete form to the social and economic transformations of Paris fully remade in the image of commerce and capitalism. It was this Paris that Degas witnessed coming into being, as he developed from youth to maturity, and its modernity, its patterns of work and leisure and its mixture of classes were to become the subjects that preoccupied his painting. The changes implemented had a profound influence on the everyday lives of Parisians.

THE OPÉRA GARNIER

The Palais Garnier or Théâtre d'Opéra de Paris was the principal theatre for opera and ballet in Paris. It was also the home of the Académie Nationale de Musique. The Opéra Garnier was located in the 9th Arrondissement, in the most fashionable quarter of the new Paris, and built in an imposingly grand Neobaroque manner by the architect Georges Garnier. The building's ostentatious and hybrid style, combining elements of the Classical and Rococo, came to be associated with Second Empire taste. The interior was a sumptuous, glittering palace of gold with elaborate allegories on the ceilings and large mirrors lining the walls. Napoléon III had authorized Haussmann to clear 12,000 square metres (14,350 square yards) to build Europe's grandest opera house in 1858. Construction began in 1862, but was not completed until 1875.

PAINTING MODERN LIFE

During the late 1850s the notion that art should be of its time, rather than representing scenes and stories from antiquity gained increasing support, encouraged by writers and critics. The relationship between the two was to give birth to new artistic movements that would change the course of art.

By mid-century it was clear the classical tradition of French art was in decline. In its place came the Romantics, who introduced contemporary subject matter and new compositional techniques. This movement in turn encouraged the emergence of realism, with its embracing of quotidian subjects. In the 1860s this trend drew support from the critical essays of writers like Zola, Louis Edmond Duranty and Charles Baudelaire (1821–67), each of whom, in their separate ways, was

committed to an art that reflected the life around them. Zola made his name in the 1860s with a series of graphically detailed novels of the underbelly of Parisian life that scandalized the public. He also made a name for himself as an important critic arguing in favour of art as personal expression and encouraging artists to explore themes drawn from the world of Second Empire France.

In 1867 Zola wrote an important defence of Manet's *Olympia* (1863) (see page 33), that was influential in

articulating his significance for the younger generation of Impressionist artists. The novels of writers such as the Goncourt brothers, Duranty, as well as Zola, were to furnish artists with ideas, themes and subjects that dealt with the modernity of French contemporary life. The desire of these writers to find new literary styles and forms to depict modern life paralleled the artistic aspirations of modern painters.

BAUDELAIRE AND MODERNITY

The most influential of these writers was Charles Baudelaire, a close friend of Manet and a fervent champion of the work of the romantic artist Eugene Delacroix. Baudelaire's poems provide an enduring image of the Paris of the Second Empire, a vision of the modern city as a place of promise and desire but also alienation, coldness and degradation. It is a vision that often finds an echo in Degas' own depictions of Paris. Baudelaire's most important critical essay on art *The Painter of Modern Life*, was written in 1859 but not published until the end of 1863, when it appeared in two instalments in *Le Figaro*, in November and December of that year. It became a constant touchstone for modern artists. Written during the period that saw the beginnings of Haussmann's modernization of Paris, the essay argued for the painting of contemporary urban subjects and the renewal of art through the example of popular art forms. The essay describes

Left: Girls on the Balcony, *by Constantin Guys (1802–92), 1855–60. Guys was a war correspondent and illustrator who portrayed the fashions of the French Second Empire style as his theme in his drawings, prints and watercolours. Guys' subjects and his fluid style proved influential on younger Impressionist artists.*

Below: Portrait of Emile Zola (1840–1902), by Degas, 1868. Zola was an influential art critic.

Left: Portrait of Edmond Duranty, by Degas, 1879. Degas' friend Duranty was an art critic and novelist, who supported the Impressionists.

CHARLES BAUDELAIRE

Baudelaire was a much admired but controversial figure in his own lifetime. Born and raised in Paris, his poetry gives form to the turbulent age he lived through. He rejected a career in law to lead a bohemian life, always living well beyond his means. In the 1840s he established himself as a leading critic and advocate of romanticism, though only made a meagre living through his writings. During the mid-1850s Baudelaire was known as a dandy in artistic circles and during this time became a constant companion of Manet, who drew inspiration from his poems and translations of Edgar Allan Poe (1809–49). His collections of poetry *The Flowers of Evil* (1857) and *Paris Spleen* (1869) place him among the greatest poets of his or any age.

the working practices of Monsieur G. or Constantin Guys (1802–92), a popular illustrator of the fashions, manners and street life of Paris and friend of Baudelaire, providing a summary of the types, themes and subjects of his work. Guys' wit, curiosity and attentive observation, are qualities that Degas too would cultivate in his art.

Baudelaire's essay is, however, more than a description of Guys' art, with its attempt to define the new modernity of contemporary Paris. As such it describes the poet's own themes. While Baudelaire's essay suggests certain sites, types and subjects for artists to explore, his essay sketches out a project of personal investigation. In one of the key passages Baudelaire asks the artist to find amid the kaleidoscope of modern life the discreet and poetic correspondences that constitute the essential nature of modernity, to capture "that indefinable something we may be allowed to call modernity… the transient, the fleeting and the

contingent". Baudelaire's association of modernity with these qualities not only encouraged artists to explore new, transient subjects but also defined a style of engagement with these themes, encouraging the rapid, sketch-like style of modern artists in the 1860s and 70s.

Left: A photograph of Charles Baudelaire (1821–67) with engravings, c.1863, by Carjat (1828–1906).

COURBET AND MANET

Among the artists that were to influence the younger generation of painters associated with Impressionism, Courbet and Manet stand out as particularly important, though for diametrically opposed reasons. Courbet focused on the countryside, while Manet explored themes associated with the new Paris.

GUSTAVE COURBET

Born in Ornans in 1819, into a prosperous farming family with strong anti-monarchical feelings, Gustave Courbet was a radical in art and a revolutionary in politics. Arguably he was the most controversial artist of his time. In his technique and subject matter he exercised a powerful influence over early Impressionism. His larger-than-life persona sharply divided public and critics alike. In *The Painter's Studio: A Real Allegory* (1855), Courbet proclaimed himself the "visionary" painter of the future. Committed to painting the life of his native region of Ornans in the Franche-Comté, his imagery substituted a critical and politicized vision of the countryside in place of the idealized, sentimentalized images of his contemporaries.

Courbet's unorthodox technique, using thick impastoed paint often applied with a palette knife, made him

a key figure for modern landscape painters, especially Renoir, Pissarro and Paul Cézanne (1839–1906). He chose "democratic", contemporary subjects, eschewed myth and sought to embody "materialist values" in his style of painting. His status as an embattled

Above: The Painter's Studio: A Real Allegory, *by Courbet (1819–77), 1855. Courbet's studio represents a microcosm of society with himself painting a landscape at the centre. On the right are his supporters, including the critic Baudelaire shown reading at the margin.*

rebel against the artistic and political status quo helped establish the climate in which Impressionism could emerge. In the 1860s Courbet established a keen rivalry with Manet; Courbet was seen as the pre-eminent painter of the countryside and peasantry, while Manet was the painter of Paris.

EDOUARD MANET

The son of a magistrate, well-educated, witty and urbane, Edouard Manet could not seem further removed from the coarse, arrogant, peasant-like Courbet. Manet was the quintessence of the fashionable haute bourgeois Parisian and someone with whom Degas felt a close affinity. Degas made many

Left: Monsieur and Madame Edouard Manet, *by Degas, 1868–69. Manet is shown in reflective mood listening to his wife playing the piano.*

Right: Nana, by Manet (1832–83), 1877. Manet was much taken by the "precociously immoral" Nana who first featured in Zola's L'Assomoir and later became the protagonist of the novel Nana, published in 1880. The painting was sent for exhibition at the 1877 Salon but was rejected by the exhibition committee.

portrait studies of his friend that capture Manet in informal poses. By the time Manet died in 1883 he was recognized as one of France's most important contemporary artists, but during the 1860s his work caused great controversy.

In 1863 Manet painted two pictures that were to cause a scandal and elevate his status for the younger generation of artists associated with Impressionism: Le *Déjeuner sur l'herbe*, then known as Le *Bain (The Bath)* (see page 22), and *Olympia*. Like many paintings of this period these made clear references to traditional sources. In each case Manet, under the influence of the poet Charles Baudelaire, reworked these sources, placing them in a contemporary French setting. The frontal figure grouping of *Déjeuner sur*

Right: Nana, by Manet (1832–83), 1877. Manet was much taken by the "precociously immoral" Nana who first featured in Zola's L'Assomoir and later became the protagonist of the novel Nana, published in 1880. The painting was sent for exhibition at the 1877 Salon but was rejected by the exhibition committee.

l'herbe refers to Raimondi's engraving after Raphael's *Judgement of Paris* (1529), but also to Titian's *Concert Champêtre* (1508). In reworking Raphael's river gods into Parisian picnickers, *Déjeuner sur l'herbe* combined the female nude with male students in contemporary dress. *Olympia* is based on Titian's *Venus of Urbino* (1538). It was the rough reception of this work at the 1865 Salon that made him a cause célèbre

Below: Olympia, by Manet, 1863, Parisian prostitution was a key theme of many of Manet's paintings in the 1860s and 70s. Manet's treatments of the theme were bold and confrontational.

and consolidated his status for younger artists. The strange combination of the signs of high and low prostitution and the translation of Titian's iconic *Venus of Urbino*, itself a representation of a contemporary courtesan, into the contemporary milieu of Paris, left critics bewildered and scandalized. *Olympia* became a picture around which critical debates about modern painting were articulated. Fantin-Latour's *A Studio in the Batignolles* (1870), shows Manet surrounded by critics, including Duranty and Zola, and many of the artists who would become leading figures in Impressionism, such as Renoir, Monet and Bazille. For them, as for Degas, Manet was the leading modern painter of his generation.

AN ARTISTIC AFFINITY

The work of Manet was particularly important for Degas and by the end of his life Degas owned seven of his paintings. Manet was a close friend and valued colleague and Degas' own work is inconceivable without him. Many of the conventions that would later typify Degas' painting including the broad, summary modelling, arbitrary 'slice of life' compositions, abrupt cropping of figures, the combination of tradition and modernity are due to the influence of Manet. Likewise, Degas' imagery of Paris charted much the same sites, spectacles and subjects that Manet had pioneered.

MANET'S PARIS

Manet's painting, like the painter himself, moved freely across the social spectrum of Paris, taking in its fashionable high life as well as its low life. *The Old Musician* reflects the world of the dispossessed drifters of modern Paris, the ragpickers, street entertainers and beggars who were immortalized in Charles Baudelaire's poetry as symbols of the marginal and bohemian life of the city. Baudelaire himself posed for the seated figure on the right-hand margin wearing a top hat. Like *Olympia* and *Déjeuner sur l'herbe*, the painting is an updating of a picture by one of the old masters, in this instance *Los Barrachos (The Drinkers)* (1628), by the 17th-century Spanish court painter Diego Velázquez (1599–1660).

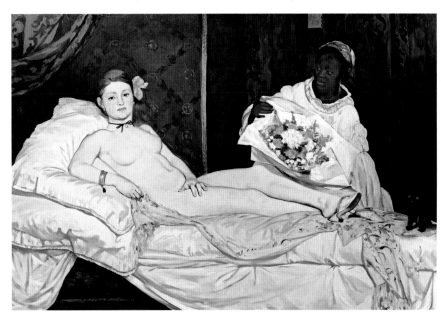

MAN ABOUT TOWN

The mid-1860s was a crucial period for Degas, marking the point of transition toward the mature phase of his art. It was now that he began to assert his independence, in life as well as art. During this period he painted his first important self-portraits.

Above Self Portrait as a Young Man, *c.1857, and left:* Self Portrait, *1862: Many of the earlier portraits are tentative and self-interrogating, though later his self-portraits become more outward-looking, assertive and express his growing confidence as an artist.*

Degas' early self portraits show him dressed as a self-confident young dandy, and an affluent and elegant man about town. He seems to be exploring his identity, projecting the melancholy artistic persona that became his enduring public image. During this time Degas rented a studio at 13 le rue de Laval, near Manet's apartment on the rue de Saint-Pétersbourg; Renoir, Frédéric Bazille (1841–70) and Fantin-Latour also lived close by. Degas was a regular visitor to the Café Guerbois, where Manet and his friends met weekly. These included many future Impressionists, the photographer

Nadar and leading critics and writers like Philippe Burty (1830–90), Théodore Duret (1838–1907) and Emile Zola. Degas quickly became part of Manet's coterie and an important figure within the group. A letter from Manet to Fantin-Latour while visiting Boulogne-sur-mer urges him to tell Degas to write to him and mentions approvingly his recent pictures of racing scenes.

EVENINGS AT THE CAFÉ GUERBOIS
Monet recalling evenings at the Café Guerbois wrote: "Nothing could have been more interesting than these talks,

with their perpetual clashes of opinion…. You always left…with stronger will, a sharpened purpose, and a clearer head." The poet Armand Silvestre remembered Degas as "humorous, extremely bantering" and already beginning to attract admirers within the group, though not everyone approved of him. "As for your friend Degas," wrote Berthe Morisot (1841–95) to her sister, "I definitely do not think he has an attractive character. He is witty, that's all." At the Guerbois Degas forged a close friendship with Duranty, a natural ally with his astringent temperament, theoretical turn of mind and interest in art with psychological complexity. Duranty was to find in Degas a painter who shared his desire for an art that represented the attitudes, feelings and sensibility of the time. Degas also attended the Wednesday night soirées of the fashionable Salon painter Alfred

Right: Self Portrait with Evariste de Valernes *(1816–96), c.1865. The 1860s saw the emergence of a new kind of psychological complexity in Degas' portraiture exemplified by double portraits of figures with contrasting attitudes.*

Stevens (1818–75) and the salon of Nina de Callias, another regular meeting place for the Batignolles group.

A LOVE OF MUSIC

Degas often attended the Opera and concerts. As a child his love of music was encouraged by his father. He was said to possess a pleasant singing voice and was a competent pianist. Though Second Empire Paris produced few great composers, the appearance of Charles Gounod (1818–93), Camille Saint-Saëns (1835–1921) and above all Hector Berlioz (1803–69) revived the French musical tradition under the influence of the great Germanic tradition of Romanticism. Opera, normally Italianate, was performed at the Palais Garnier, the Théâtre-Lyrique, Théâtre des Italiens, Opéra Comique and Bouffes-Parisiens, where Offenbach's operettas drew huge crowds. Concerts were performed on Sunday afternoons at the Cirque Impériale, where the conductor Jules Pasdeloup (1819–87) introduced German composers like Robert Schumann (1810–56) and Richard Wagner (1813–83) to a Parisian audience. Interest in the relationship between music and the visual arts was a feature of the circles in which Degas moved. Many of the Batignolles artists became ardent Wagnerians. Piano accompaniments of Germanic and contemporary French composers were a feature of the soirées the painters attended, and their circle included many talented musicians, like the pianist Edmond Maître (1840–98).

Right: The stage set for Les Troyens *by Hector Berlioz (1806–69), by Chaperon, Philippe Marie (1823–1907), 1863. In the 1860s Degas became an habitué of the theatre and opera in particular which was experiencing renewal from composers such as Wagner and Berlioz, the leading modern French composer of his age.*

OBSERVING MODERN LIFE

In the late 1860s Degas began to refocus his artistic priorities and take his work in a new direction, building on his talent for realism and psychologically searching portraits of contemporary life. It was during this period that a new artistic self-consciousness became evident in his painting.

Degas' efforts to realize ambitious historical themes came at a time when history painting was itself struggling to survive. The demise of this painting style was a constant refrain of Salon critics, who recognized that the commercial market would not support such subjects and artistic momentum was with realism and more informal, modern subject matter. Though these years are poorly documented, Degas must have realized that this course was unlikely to meet with success and that his artistic talents were best expressed in his psychologically acute portraiture. Degas had learned much from his study of Ingres' portraits. The latter's 1833 portrait of the newspaper magnate Louis-François Bertin was described by Charles Blanc as not merely an exceptional likeness, but a portrait of the age of the bourgeoisie. Blanc's comments reflected a new seriousness given to portraiture, as a genre that could reflect on the social history of the times.

A NEW STYLE OF PROFILE

From early on Degas had been interested in the double portrait as a way of bringing depth and intensity to the social analysis of his portraiture. He produced a couple of portraits of his sister Thérèse and her husband Edmondo Morbilli after their wedding in 1863, which reveal the influence of Ingres with the husband posed casually, but in a proprietorial position. Degas made several studies of the figures, attending to details of physiognomy and dress before deciding on the composition. The result captures the calm dignity and elegance of haute bourgeois life, and hints at a distant relationship between the couple and the

Left: Visit to a Museum, *by Degas, c.1879–80. This painting shows Degas exploring ways of conveying contemporary manners and affectations through the pose and body language of the figures.*

PAINTINGS IN PAINTINGS

Degas' portraits of this time often featured paintings. From his studies in the Louvre and his conversations with Duranty, Degas would have been aware of many examples of such compositions in Dutch 17th-century painting. These "paintings within paintings" had a dual purpose. They provide contextual details that convey information about the class, occupation and status of his sitters, and also illustrate Degas' pre-occupation with the nature of art itself, something that would emerge as a dominant theme of his art.

Above: Edmondo and Thérèse Morbilli, *by Degas, c.1867, illustrates Degas' interest in double portraiture as a vehicle for psychologically complex painting.*

Top right: Louis-Francois Bertin (1766– 1841), *by Ingres, 1832. This portrait was regarded as a paradigm of portraiture that reflected the age.*

Above: Portrait of James Tissot, *by Degas, 1867–68. Degas uses pictures within pictures to introduce new pictorial effects and themes into his portraits.*

social conventions of marriage at the time. The way Degas posed the figures suggests contrasts of personality and an imbalance between them, conveying in an understated way subtle tensions in the relationship: Thérèse's pliancy and melancholy contrast with her husband's robust self-assurance.

Consistent with Degas' ambition to make portraiture serve a more ambitious purpose, he began to explore theories of physiognomy, gesture and expression to deepen the intensity and modernity of his work. His notebooks show him refining Johann Kaspar Lavater's physiognomic theories from earlier in the century, revising them in a way that could give expression to, in his words, "modern feelings". "Do portraits of people in their familiar, typical postures, above all give their face the same range of expressions as one gives their body?", he instructed himself. Yet it is often the physical pose and the contextual detail that Degas emphasizes, while the expression of the face is unreadable or concealed from view. Like Manet, Degas wanted to convey "inner states" but though some figures stare directly out of the picture, he achieved his aim mostly through the unself-conscious and informal poses, often at oblique angles, and the telling gestures of his figures, interpreted in combination with the contextual detail that depicted their social setting.

A CONSUMMATE PORTRAITIST

Degas' skills as a portraitist are evident in *Portrait of James Tissot* (1867–68), his friend, who shared Degas' interest in modern life subjects. Tissot is posed informally in the context of the studio, allowing Degas to include paintings in the background that assert the artistic heritage from which both his and Tissot's contemporary paintings derive. Portraits like this won Degas praise as one of the great portraitists of his age.

A DAY AT THE RACES

Though predominantly known as a painter of ballerinas and bathers, Degas' work contains another enduring theme, the depiction of horse-racing, in the 1860s one of the most popular sports in France. Degas matured during the golden age of horse-racing and his painting is a consummate record of it.

Degas' interest in equestrian scenes is present from the start of his career. He made numerous sketches after the Parthenon friezes featuring riders, Anthony van Dyck's (1599–1641) equestrian pictures and those of other old masters. In Italy he made drawings after equestrian paintings by Paolo Uccello (1397–1475) and Benozzo Gozzoli (1421–97), and many of his early history paintings feature horses. It seems likely that Degas was familiar with and admired Géricault's equestrian pictures, which compress extraordinary energy and nervous tension into such motifs. Later, Degas became interested in Muybridge's photographic studies of horses in motion, which altered his understanding of their movement.

THE THEME OF HORSE-RACING

Though Degas made a series of hunting paintings, it was horse-racing that became his favoured equestrian motif. A subject matter that continued to interest him throughout his life, it was one of the first great modern themes to emerge in his painting and show Degas making the transition from academic art to modern life painting. From the late 1860s to the 1900s Degas explored comprehensively the motif of horses and horse-racing in paintings, pastels, prints and sculpture. It was less the race itself than the nervous agitation and expectation of the tense moments

before the race starts that caught his attention. Degas portrays horses in front of the tribunes or processing to the starting line. The theme of the 'false start' was another that captured his imagination. In a series of pictures Degas depicts the lurching, aggressive motions of the horses as their riders attempt to regain control over them. Such motifs offered Degas opportunities to show his mastery of the force and energetic movement of the horses and portray the drama of the event. The subject allowed him to make modern paintings with subtle parallels with the battle paintings of old masters. The frieze-like

Left: The Parade, *or* Race Horses in Front of the Stands, *by Degas, c.1866–68. Just as in his portraits, Degas' horse-racing pictures establish contrasts between different parts of the composition, the poise of the horses in the foreground counterpointed by the nervous rearing movement of the horse in the background.*

Above: Before the Races, *by Degas, 1868–72. Degas' horse-racing scenes often focus on the ambience before the race begins in compositions that are asymmetrical and highly innovative.*

arrangement of racehorses across the foreground alludes to his longstanding interest in ancient relief sculpture, though the bold asymmetry and disjointedness of many pictures displays a new informality of composition and realism. These reveal Degas' subtle introduction of the conventions of Japanese prints into his art.

A GOLDEN AGE IN FRANCE

Degas' lifetime coincided with a flourishing of enthusiasm for horse-racing in France. The Second Empire witnessed a golden age of horse-racing, with Longchamps, on the fringes of Paris, as the capital's premier site. Emperor Napoléon III was an avid fan, so the sport received encouragement and generous official patronage.

SPECTATING AT THE RACES

During the 1870s Degas almost obsessively returned to a drawing of a woman with field glasses looking at the viewer. For Degas it was unusual to explore the idea of using such a motif within a racing composition. He never completed his intended picture. His pictures often put the viewer in the position of a secluded onlooker at some event. His abandonment of the motif of the woman with glasses may have been due to its inversion of this relationship and the complication of the normal construction of spectators in his pictures. For once it was the viewer who was the object of the gaze rather than the person who views without being seen.

Right: Jockeys at the Racecourse, *by Degas.*

Horse-racing had been imported from Britain and English influence remained pervasive, reflecting the anglophilia of the French aristocracy and haute bourgeoisie. For the wealthy and well-connected the attraction of the races was not just for the sport but for social display. It was in October 1861, while visiting his friend Paul Valpinçon at the family estate in Ménil-Hubert in the Normandy countryside, not far from the horse-breeding establishment Haras-le-Pin, that Degas was introduced to the world of horse-breeding and the track. Being seen at the races and observing the crowd were among the foremost pleasures of such events, not least for Degas, who was attracted to their pomp and social ritual. Degas captures these features of horse-racing in pictures that examine the social customs and manners of the crowd, sometimes with them in the foreground.

Right: Jockeys on Horseback before Distant Hills, *by Degas, 1884. The realism of Degas' horse-racing pictures conceal their careful compositional design.*

MY GENRE PICTURE

In 1869 Degas began an ambitious genre picture that preoccupied him for much of the year. It seems likely he intended to exhibit it at the Salon that year, but the work was not shown until much later. The fact that Degas never parted with the picture suggests it was important to him.

Degas referred to his genre picture by the neutral title *Interior* or simply as "my genre picture" and often showed it to his visitors, but gave little away about its meaning or what it represents. It belongs to a sequence of Degas' pictures exploring male–female relationships. In the late 1860s and early 1870s much of Degas' imagery focused on men and women paired together in contrasting roles. These include double portraits featuring husbands and wives, male figures watching ballet dancers performing and ballet-masters instructing the corps de ballet. The picture also marks Degas' turn toward genre painting, scenes of everyday life, so popular in France during the 1860s. Artists like Auguste

Toulmouche (1829–90), Stevens and Tissot had popularized paintings depicting the glamorous lifestyle, fashions and customs of the haute bourgeoisie. The rise of this kind of subject matter had coincided with a new taste for English genre painting, where such pictures had a longer tradition, and the reassessment of Dutch 17th-century painting. *Interior* clearly belongs to this trend, but is something of a problem picture. Conventionally, genre pictures provided intelligible narratives with figures arranged in clear, coherent groupings. Details provided a realistic social context and reinforced the themes. All compositional elements contributed to the picture's general idea. Gestures,

expressions and the distribution of figures in meaningful relationships were regarded as integral to a successful composition. *Interior*'s subject matter is, however, difficult to discern. The composition is off-centre with an open sewing box on the top of an occasional table occupying the middle ground. The relationship between the figures, who are distant from each other both spatially and psychologically, remains ambiguous.

Below: The Interior, by Degas, c.1868. The narrative ambiguities of genre pictures were a part of the convention of genre painting, but in this picture Degas stretched these conventions to the limits of intelligibility.

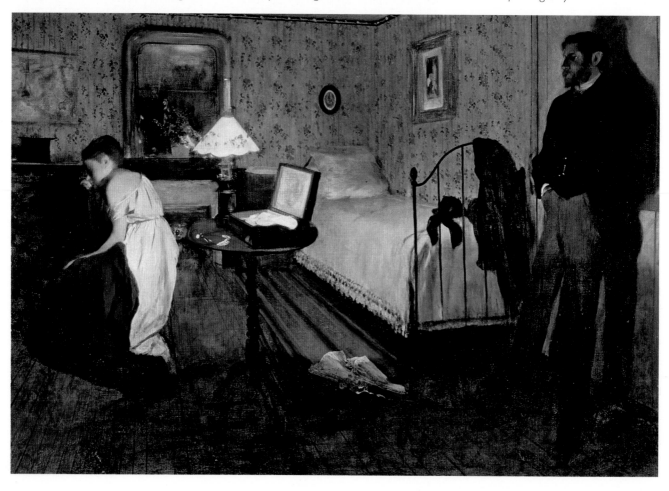

Above: Portrait of a Man Standing with his Hands in his Pockets (Study for l'Interieur), by Degas, 1868–69. *Degas meticulously planned his genre picture with sketches exploring the psychologically expressive possibilities of the figures' poses.*

LITERARY SOURCES

Several literary sources have been suggested for *Interior*, ranging from a novel by Degas' friend Duranty to Zola's *Madeleine Férat* (1868) and *Thérèse Raquin* (1867). The art historian Theodore Reff suggests the scene may depict the wedding night of Thérèse and Laurent in *Thérèse Raquin*, after their collusion in the murder of her first husband, an action that will come to divide and haunt

them. This passage matches many of the salient features of the picture and captures the disquieting atmosphere of alienation between the figures.

Laurent carefully shut the door behind him, then stood leaning against it for a moment looking into the room, ill at ease and embarrassed…Thérèse was sitting on a low chair to the right of the fireplace, her chin cupped in her hand, staring at the flames. She did not look round as Laurent came in. Her lacy petticoat and bodice showed up dead white in the light of the blazing fire. The bodice was slipping down and part of her shoulder emerged pink, half hidden by a tress of black hair.

Above: The Visit, by Alfred Stevens (1823–1906), 1870. *Salon genre scenes often represented the splendour and opulence of the life of the bourgeoisie, enticing viewers with subtle anecdotalism and understated narratives.*

Yet Degas included many details that do not appear in Zola's book: the single bed, the open sewing box and the discarded corset. Such details encourage viewers to reflect on how we interpret the picture, posing a series of questions rather than providing unequivocal meaning.

Degas initially intended to paint a more dramatic scene. A preparatory oil sketch shows a half-dressed figure suggesting a subject representing sexual conflict between lovers, possibly even a rape scene. *Interior* is more subdued and complex than this, though the suggestion of sexual disharmony remains. This was a very topical subject in the 1860s, which saw a flurry of literary representations portraying adultery and the breakdown of family life. Many painters also responded to these controversial subjects. *Interior*'s ambiguities, nevertheless, set it apart from the crowd and it remains one of Degas' most thought-provoking and opaque pictures. The painting's theme and meaning is something Degas seems to have purposely left open for discussion. He later wrote: "A painting calls for a certain mystery, some vagueness, some fantasy".

ORIGINS OF IMPRESSIONISM

Degas worked closely with the Impressionists and was considered by many contemporary critics as one of the leading Impressionist artists, though important differences existed between his work and that of many of those associated with the movement.

Impressionism as an artistic style grew from debates about realism, landscape painting and modern life subjects that emerged in the 1830s and 1840s. The term 'impression' had been used in philosophical investigations into the nature of perception in respect of whether knowledge is determined by sensory impressions of the material world, or whether our ideas condition the sensory impressions we have of the world. The term also had an artistic use, referring to a freshly worked oil sketch. From the early 19th century Romantic artists began to place new value on the sketch as the purest expression of the genesis of the idea of a picture, and a connoisseur market of collectors for such sketches arose in response.

While the term was not entirely new, its application to public exhibition pictures was. In the 1870s the term 'Impressionist' began to be used widely to describe a new modern tendency in painting represented by the work of Manet, Monet, Morisot, Pissarro, Renoir, Alfred Sisley (1839–99), Cézanne, Guillaumin, Caillebotte and Degas. It was

first used by a hostile critic, Louis Leroy, reviewing a group exhibition in 1874 which included Monet's *Impression, Sunrise*, but was quickly embraced by the artists. These 'Impressionists' exhibited together in a series of eight exhibitions from 1874–86. Impressionism was seen as part of a new demand within French art for contemporary subject matter and a breaking away from French tradition.

Above: Family Reunion, *by Bazille (1841–70), 1867. Frédéric Bazille was a key painter in the early years of Impressionism but was killed in action during the Franco-Prussian war, aged 29.*

Below: Spring, *by Pissarro, (1830–1903), 1872. Pissarro chose traditional agrarian motifs set in the countryside of Pontoise and Auvers.*

Right: La Grenouillère, *by Renoir (1841–1919), 1869. Renoir worked closely beside Monet at Grenouillère. Despite similarities in style and treatment each artist retained a distinctively personal quality to their work.*

PAINTING IMPRESSIONS

The artists generally rejected the idea that a painting should primarily respond to the work of other artists and instead spoke of their work as a direct response to nature, painting their sensations or impressions of their motifs. Nevertheless, their work was indebted to the example of other artists. The bold colour and animated compositions of Delacroix, Manet's summary brushwork, slice-of-life compositions and modern Parisian subjects and the 'impressionistic' landscapes of Courbet, Eugène Boudin (1824–98), Jongkind, and the Barbizon painters all exerted a powerful influence. The Barbizon, such as Daubigny and Théodore Rousseau (1812–67), so called because they painted *en plein air* near the Barbizon village, had exploited new commercially produced pigments in tubes and portable easels so as to paint directly from nature. Their paintings expressed a strong feeling for light, mood and atmosphere and reflected the artist's temperament and personal response to nature. Impressionist landscapists largely followed their example. Daubigny's bold brushwork and choice of banal motifs made him particularly popular among younger painters. Pissarro and Cézanne in the 1870s chose motifs similar to those of Corot and Daubigny. Their works, in Zola's words, represented "discreet corners of nature seen through artistic temperament". Monet, Renoir, Sisley and Morisot also painted en plein air, developing their artistic technique to capture fleeting perceptions of the world, though they chose ultra-modern motifs set in the city and suburbs. What

set Impressionism apart in the 1870s was the combination of innovative artistic technique with the choice of subjects not hitherto seen as suitable. In exploring the world of the new Paris they broke new artistic ground.

DEGAS AND THE IMPRESSIONISTS

Degas' relationship with his Impressionist colleagues was a complex one. He contributed to all but one of the Impressionist exhibitions, when personal and artistic differences within the group boiled over and led to his withdrawal. His relationship with the other exhibitors was often strained and it is clear he felt more affinity with the work of Manet than many of his Impressionist colleagues. Like Manet, Degas placed more value on the role of artistic tradition. His choice of motifs were similar to Manet's, remaining focused on the figure at a time when landscape had become the dominant subject for most Impressionists.

Right: Bathers at La Grenouillère, *by Monet (1840–1926), 1869. Monet's picture anticipates the broken brushwork and strongly saturated palette that would become typical of Impressionism in the mid-1870s.*

THE FRANCO-PRUSSIAN WAR

In 1870 the hedonistic years of the Second Empire were to come to an abrupt halt, as France blundered into a disastrous conflict with Prussia. The Franco-Prussian War was to leave an indelible impression on Degas, who served in the National Guard during the terrible Siege of Paris.

On 18 July 1870 Napoléon III fatefully declared war with Prussia. Relations between France and Prussia had been tense for many years over the expansion of the Germanic Empire and erupted during a diplomatic dispute about the vacant Spanish throne. The war marked the downfall of the Second Empire and had devastating consequences for France. Confident of a swift victory the French army, ill prepared for war, was soon humbled, suffering crippling defeats in Eastern France resulting in capitulation within months. At the start of September Napoléon III surrendered at the battle of Sedan, was taken prisoner and later sent into exile in London. On 4 September a mob stormed the Palais Bourbon and voted by acclamation for a new republic and a government of self-defence that would continue the war.

The war broke up the Batignolles group of Manet and his followers. On 10 August 1870, Bazille enlisted in the Zouaves regiment and was killed in

Below: An engraving showing The Last Hour of the Commune, 27 May 1871. The crushing of The Commune left a lasting legacy of divisiveness in French political and cultural life.

action four months later. Renoir accepted military service in the cavalry and left for Tarbes, while Cézanne fled south. As the situation worsened and the Prussian army began to advance on Paris almost unopposed, Monet, Pissarro and Sisley fled France for refuge in London, where Daubigny and François Bonvin (1817–87) also sought shelter. In London the Impressionists met Paul Durand-Ruel (1831–1922), who had also fled there and established a gallery on New Bond Street. He would soon become instrumental in their success.

THE SIEGE OF PARIS

In September, as Prussian troops prepared to place Paris under siege, Manet and Degas volunteered for the National Guard. Manet served in the artillery while Degas joined the infantry. While on rifle practice in Vincennes Degas discovered a fault in his right eye and transferred to the artillery, later becoming a gunner in the outer circle of fortifications. Degas was assigned to Bastion 12 on the east side of the city, just north of the Bois de Vincennes, where he served under fellow painter Henri Rouart, renewing a close friendship that would subsequently

endure. Degas supported the new republican government and remained in Paris when many were leaving. Only occasionally able to paint, Degas spent his spare moments sketching his artillery colleagues and distinguished French officers from photographs. He was much affected by the death of one of his friends, the sculptor Joseph Cuvelier, and suffered considerable privation as the siege continued deep into the winter. In

THE COMMUNE

The Paris Commune was a body of government that ruled Paris for just two months in 1871. It came into being when the working classes usurped govenment power for the first time. The Commune was forged out of an alliance of workers and political radicals who passed socialist legislation and democratic reform. The working classes resented the armistice established by the National Government of Defence with the victorious Prussian forces in the wake of France's humiliating defeat in the Franco-Prussian War. The Germans included in their peace terms a triumphal entry into Paris. The creation of a National Guard prior to the formation of the Commune resulted in hundreds of thousands of Parisians being armed and organized into a citizens' militia. The bloody repression of the Commune by National Defence troops met with fierce resistance; ferocious battles were waged street by street. An estimated 30,000 Parisians were killed, with 50,000 later executed or imprisoned; some 7,000 captives were sent into exile. These violent events reverberated politically long after the actual events.

Right: An engraving showing the entry of the German troops into Paris, 2 March 1871. The humiliation of the French military at the hands of the Prussians, symbolized by the Prussian victory parading through Paris, was a blow to French pride and ushered in a period of austerity.

January, the painter Henri Regnault, whom Degas befriended while studying together with Lamothe, was also killed. On 28 January the French high command surrendered the city and elections to appoint a new legal government were held. On 1 March, the occupying army entered the deserted streets of the city that was decked with black flags.

In mid-March the exhausted Degas took respite at the Valpinçons' estate at Ménil-Hubert in the Normandy countryside, where he sketched, rested and recuperated and began working on some portraits of the Valpinçon children, horse-racing scenes and studies of horses. These included the delightful *Hortense Valpinçon* (1871) and *Carriage at the Races* (1871–72), which shows Paul Valpinçon, his wife and their baby Henri.

THE AFTERMATH

Meanwhile in Paris the election of a monarchist National Assembly, combined with bitterness about the "dishonourable peace", led the capital to stage its own elections. The Paris Commune, a radical republican municipal council, was victorious. Courbet was elected as a representative of the people, and as president of the General Assembly of Artists. The resistance of the Commune led to fierce fighting and huge casualties. The bloody repression of the Commune was to leave deep scars in France's history. The war was over but the shock of the defeat and the legacy of the Commune's repression reverberated long after. The economic, political and cultural climate in the immediate wake of the war changed France dramatically.

Right: Woman at a Window, by Degas, c.1871–72. Degas' paintings during and immediately after the Franco-Prussian conflict are often sombre intimations of the hardship of the period.

TURNING TO THE BALLET

No subject held such a spell over Degas' visual imagination as the ballerina, a theme he represented on no fewer than 600 occasions in a variety of drawings, paintings, pastels and prints. The subject was to provide Degas with the motif of many of his most brilliant and original pictures.

Degas' first images of the ballet appeared in the 1870s, emerging out of his interest in *la vie élégante*, the tastes and pastimes of the Parisian haute bourgeoisie. The same bourgeois clientele that enjoyed the pleasures of the racetracks of Longchamps or Deauville were among those who occupied the choicest opera boxes at the luxurious Palais Garnier, where ballet was presented as an accompaniment to opera. The theme of the ballet continued to preoccupy him for the next 40 years. Degas frequently attended performances at the opera and in the course of his lifetime he acquired a connoisseur's knowledge of the terms and details of the movements that made up the art of the dance. As the most traditionally minded of the artists associated with Impressionism, Degas viewed the dance as a subject that allowed him to combine his interest in modernity with references to the antique. Asked by Louise Havemeyer, who owned one of his series of *Two Dancers*, why Degas painted the ballet so frequently, he replied, "Because…it is all that is left to us of the combined movements of the Greeks".

AN EXPANSIVE VISION

While these nostalgic sentiments indicate the deep-seated meanings the theme had for him, Degas seems to have first taken up the subject after the death of his father, when the family bank collapsed leaving considerable debts. For the first time Degas needed to sell pictures and his first ballerinas were targeted at the connoisseur market. The commercial and artistic success of his ballet scenes fast established his reputation as a specialist in this genre and these became the focus of the works he exhibited. Reviewing his ballet paintings at the Third Impressionist Exhibition in April 1877, Roger Ballu wrote: "His studies of dancers assert a

rare and original talent." By the mid-1870s his exploration of this theme had expanded dramatically to explore the full spectrum of the life of the dancer in ways that reveal the depth of his engagement with this subject.

Many of his early images of the ballet show his interest in presenting the ballerina on stage from different vantage points offered by the theatre auditorium. Often the picture's point of view, as in *Two Dancers on a Stage* (c.1874) and

Above: The Star, or Dancer on the Stage, by Degas, c.1876. Degas depicts a prima ballerina taking her applause on stage, while also hinting at the life of the backstage.

The Star (1876), suggests one of the exclusive boxes, implying not only a particular location, but the class status of the onlooker who occupies that position. Others, such as *The Opera Orchestra* (c.1870), place the viewer in the stalls.

A FALLEN FORM

In the 1870s ballet was regarded as a 'fallen' art comprising a trace of the glory of antiquity. "As we recall the dancing women in the frescoes of Pompeii…or loiter among the Atalantes in the Louvre, a deep sense comes over us of the loss…of something of wholesome refinement and infinite grace. In place of all that beautiful world of motion we merely have the ballet", wrote one commentator. Such views, also held by Degas, provide a context for the odd mixture of genuine admiration for the art of the ballet, with the wit, satire and irony in Degas' images.

In these pictures Degas also shows his fascination with the artificial ambience and distorting effects of the theatre lighting, a novel feature of these ballet pictures and a trait that recurs in his later depictions of singers at café-concerts.

Often these early ballet subjects represent the twilight world at the end of the ballet performance. We witness prima ballerinas taking 'curtain calls' and receiving tributes of bouquets. In these scenes Degas sometimes makes reference to the shadowy, half-defined presence of the wealthy abonnés, season-ticket holders who had access to the Opéra's private quarters, the foyer de la danse and the coulisses (the wings and the practice rooms). The abonnés are shown waiting in the wings to greet the ballet dancers as they retire from the stage. The depiction of the amorous intrigues of the life of the ballerina was a common theme in contemporary artistic and literary representations of the ballet. However, as Degas began to amplify and deepen his theme, he explored aspects that his contemporaries had never attempted. In his later ballet pictures the exploration of the art of the ballet becomes aligned to his art as a painter.

Above: Two Dancers on a Stage, *by Degas, c.1874. Contrasting poses add compositional expressiveness in Degas' pictures.*

Above: Dancer Standing with Hands Crossed Behind her Back, *by Degas, c.1874.*

Right: The Opera Orchestra, *by Degas, c.1870. Degas often chose novel vantage points that make the viewer conscious of the implied position in the theatre from which the scene is depicted.*

THE SCENE BACKSTAGE

During the late 1870s and early 1880s Degas began to extend his imagery of the ballet to encompass the life of the rehearsal rooms. His exploration of the scene backstage and his fascination with the ballerina's métier became enduring themes for Degas.

In 1877, a critic wrote, "For those who are partial to the mysteries of the theatre, who would happily sneak behind the sets to enjoy a spectacle forbidden to outsiders, I recommend the works of Monsieur Degas. No one has so closely scrutinized the interior above whose door is written, 'the public is not permitted here'."

Degas' preoccupation with life behind the scenes set his imagery apart from that of his contemporaries. These images of the rehearsal room sometimes feature renowned dance instructors, such as Eugène Coralli and Jules Perrot, though mostly the presence of their authority is merely implied with Degas focusing instead on the repetitive movements the dancer's body must learn to master. The knowledge Degas acquired of the life backstage and the details of their training and rehearsals transformed artistic representations of the ballet and altered the public's perception of the life of the ballerinas.

THE DANCER'S CRAFT

Though the ballet was a glamorous spectacle, for the performers it was a world of labour and craft. It is this private world of preparation for performance, the dancer's tireless exertions in bringing her art to perfection, and the fatigue and struggle this involves, that gradually captured Degas' attention. Not that these backroom images are devoid of wit and humour. As with his images of the dancers in performance, these pictures show Degas alive to the comic potential of the subject and he often suggests something of the gaucherie of the dancers. In some pictures an inanimate object creates a prosaic visual counterpart to the dancer's elaborate posture and this penchant for visual puns was a much noted feature of his painting. The critic for *La Petite République* wrote "No one, including Gavarni and Grévin, has portrayed with such humour the world of the backstage." The "vulgar physiognomies" and "lack of beauty" of the dancers were features critics frequently remarked on. Yet Degas' portrayals also reveal his deep appreciation of the dancers' art. Degas

Above left: The Rehearsal, *by Degas, c.1877. Degas's draws an analogy between the poses of the arabesque lines of the dancers and the spiral stairwell.*

Left: Waiting, *by Degas, c.1882. The strain that the training places on the body, as in this image of a ballerina rubbing her ankle, is often depicted by Degas.*

THE WORLD BACKSTAGE

In portraying the world of rehearsal, Degas represented an exclusive space, which, like the dance foyer and the wings, was off-limits to the public. Only the wealthy subscription holders were allowed privileged access. Degas, at first, had to plead with influential friends to get him a pass into this private world. Despite the realism of many of his portrayals of the rehearsal rooms, his initial depictions were works of the imagination, aided by recollections of friends. In 1882 he wrote to his friend Albert Hecht, "Have you the power to get the Opéra to give me a pass for the day of the dance examination, which, so I have been told, is to be on Thursday? I have done so many of these dance examinations without having seen them that I am a little ashamed of it."

shows the strenuous drudgery of the rehearsal room, described by one critic as "the secret miseries of these high priestesses of the harmonious art of the dance". "Look at the expressions on these faces", wrote Joris-Karl Huysmans, "the boredom of painful mechanical effort…the familiar weariness. All these things are noted with analytical insight."

SUBTLE STEREOTYPES

The coarse physiognomies of Degas' dancers reinforced the stereotype of the ballerinas' origins from the lower classes, but his imagery generally avoided the more sensationalized clichés of the dancer's life. The term "rat" to describe a young dancer began in the 19th century as a consequence of their reputation as opportunists who gnawed away at the fortunes of their amorous admirers. Jean Béraud's *In the Wings of the Opera* (1889) presents the world of the ballet as a place of sex, power and social opportunism. It is when paired with such contemporary paintings we see the distinctiveness of much of Degas' imagery.

In many of his images of backstage rehearsals we also see the dancers' mothers who accompanied their daughters to rehearsals and performances. In contemporary literature, such as Ludovic Halévy's *La Famille Cardinal* (1883), which Degas

illustrated with monotypes, they were represented as gold-diggers, brazenly seizing opportunities to match their daughters with eligible season ticket holders. Degas' depiction of mothers in his own pictures is more prosaic, showing them adjusting their daughters' costumes, offering encouragement or simply whiling away the time. These images also subtly introduce a traditional theme of the passing from youth to maturity, implying the passage from erstwhile performer to maternal companion that marks the trajectory of the dancer's life.

A CREOLE SOJOURN

In the 1870s Degas made an extended visit to New Orleans to visit family. There he began an important picture that would mark an artistic breakthrough in his painting, a significant new direction in his art and establish his reputation as a modern life painter.

Degas was fond of wryly calling himself a son of Louisiana. His mother, Célestine Musson Degas, was born into a prominent Creole family in New Orleans. In 1869 his younger brother René married his American first cousin Estelle and set himself up in the family cotton business in Louisiana with his brother Achille. During the summer of 1872 René returned to Paris on business and in October Degas accompanied him back to America. The visit to his American relatives had several timely motives. Estelle, who before her marriage had contracted ophthalmia and gone blind, was expecting a child in December. Degas, scarred from the horrors of the Franco-Prussian War and the Commune, was keen to spend time away from Paris and discover America in the still partly French city.

Degas' five-month sojourn in New Orleans came at an uneasy and decisive moment in the city's history. The Civil War had ended the privileged social status of the old Creole families and the political and economic situation was

Above: An engraving of The New Orleans Levee, c.1870. The later 19th century saw a massive commercial and industrial expansion that transformed New Orleans.

volatile, as the idealism of reconstruction gave way to division and corruption. However, living in his grandfather's palatial family mansion, Degas remained largely oblivious to the city's turmoil. Though greatly enthused by its rapid modernization, ethnic and cultural diversity and 'exoticism', he struggled to find subjects to paint and felt homesick for Paris; he described the absence of opera a cause of "terrible suffering". Quickly tiring of the portraits he painted of his relatives, Degas arrived at an impasse in his art, but he was to leave New Orleans with new artistic impetus.

THE COTTON MARKET

In February 1873 Degas wrote to Tissot that he had embarked on an ambitious multi-figure composition, *The Cotton Market, New Orleans* (1873), an ironical choice of subject given his complaints

Above: Edgar Degas lived at the family's mansion in New Orleans, Louisiana, from 1872 to 1873.

about the family's endless discussions of the cotton trade. "In it there are about fifteen individuals more or less occupied with a table covered with the precious material (cotton), and two men, one half-leaning and the other half-sitting on it; the buyer and broker are discussing a pattern." A series of portraits set in his grandfather's commercial offices, it shows the bespectacled Michel Musson, Degas' uncle, seated in the foreground looking at some cotton, and Degas' brothers René, reading the *Times-Picayune*, and Achille, in the far left background. On the right the cashier John Livaudais attends to the accounts, while behind René, James Prestidge (Musson's partner) talks to a client. The picture is notable for its acute social observation, casual but expressive poses of the figures, and contrived 'informality', demonstrating Degas' desire to capture a slice of life in an immediate, naturalistic and almost photographic fashion. Yet its informal composition is carefully choreographed and bears comparison with the ballet pictures he was working on. Shown at the Second Impressionist Exhibition in 1876, the critic Phillipe Burty praised it and compared it to the "distinguished early Flemish painters".

Impressed by Tissot's success in England, Degas conceived the picture with the British art market in mind. When in London he had met the dealer Thomas Agnew and was keen to work with him on attracting English collectors. Degas hoped that this modern, industrialized subject would find a buyer in the industrial heartland of Manchester, writing: "If a spinner ever wished to find his painter, he really ought to hit on me." On completing the picture after his return to Paris, it was eventually sold to his Parisian dealer Durand-Ruel. The sojourn in New Orleans had started unpromisingly, but ended with an artistic breakthrough.

Below: The Cotton Market, New Orleans, *by Degas, 1873. This was his most ambitious modern life subject to date.*

Above: Cotton Merchants in New Orleans, *by Degas, 1873. The sketch shows merchants inspecting a cotton bay.*

BETWEEN TRADITION AND MODERNITY

By the end of the 1860s Degas had progressed from an aspiring academic history painter to an artist of his own epoch. Though he was to work closely with the Impressionists during the next two decades, he maintained his independence and asserted the realist character of his art, rejecting Impressionism's emphasis on surface appearances. During the 1870s and early 1880s his painting sought to give form to modern subjects, but by the mid-1880s his art became more focused on movement, colour and form.

Above: Dancers in Violet Dresses, Arms Raised, *by Degas, c.1900.*
This pastel is an excellent example of the lush colours and more decorative conception of Degas' later ballerinas, which often pair figures in identical poses.
Left: Woman Drying Herself, *by Degas, c.1895–1900. The theme of women at their toilette was to become a key theme of Degas' later works.*

THE FIRST EXHIBITION

The First Impressionist Exhibition of 1874 was a key moment in the history of modern art, bringing together a group of artists who had broken with tradition and identified with a new movement. It was at this exhibition that Degas began his often-fraught association with the Impressionist movement.

During the 1860s, discontent with the authoritarianism of the Salon jury became widespread, prompting calls for new, alternative exhibiting opportunities. A letter from Frédéric Bazille to his parents in May 1867 reveals that plans for an independent show were already being discussed as early as 1866, but problems of funding proved insurmountable. With the cultural climate in the immediate post-Franco-Prussian War period hardening and Durand-Ruel, the Impressionists' dealer and primary source of economic support, experiencing financial difficulties, finding an alternative outlet for their work became urgent.

Degas was among the 16 founding members of the Société Anonyme des Artistes (Anonymous Society of Artists), the artists' co-operative that staged the exhibition. Renoir, Monet, Pissarro, Sisley, Guillaumin, Morisot, Edouard Béliard (1832–1912) and the sculptor Auguste Ottin (1811–90) were among its 16 members. The group also included three of Degas' close friends: Ludovic-Napoléon Lepic (1839–90),

Above: A Modern Olympia, *by Paul Cezanne, 1873–74. Cézanne's variation on Manet's* Olympia, *drew harsh criticism from the critics who saw it as representing the worst excesses of the new painting.*

Below: At the Races in the Countryside, *by Degas, 1869. The exhibition of this scene led one critic to comment: "No one can express with a surer hand the feeling of modern elegance".*

Above: A caricature of the First Impressionist Exhibition in Paris, "A Revolution in Painting! And a terrorizing beginning", by Cham (Amedee Charles Henri de Noe), 1874.

a student of Alexandre Cabanel (1823–89) and Charles Gleyre (1806–74), the landscapist Jean-Baptiste-Léopold Levert (1828–89) and Henri Rouart.

PLANNING THE SHOW

Degas was very active in the exhibition's organization, pressing Tissot to exhibit and seeking out other exhibitors. Yet, as Monet told Pissarro, recruitment proved difficult, with many artists worried about the risk of compromising themselves by showing with a group of little-known artists. Manet, Corot, Fantin-Latour, Henri Michel-Levy (1845–1914) and Duret all felt the Salon remained the proper arena for artists to exhibit their work and where artistic battles of the day should be fought. Eventually 30 artists were recruited and on 17 January 1874 an announcement of the formation and charter of the Société Anonyme appeared in the Chronique des Arts. By April, aided by a successful and well-publicized auction of work by Degas and his friends at the Hôtel Drouot, several newspapers contained notices of the group and its forthcoming show. The exhibition was held at Nadar's old studio on the fashionable boulevard des Capucines, in the commercial centre of the newly rebuilt Paris, and opened two weeks before the Salon on 15 April

Right: Impression, Sunrise, by Claude Monet, 1872, a work singled out by critics as representing the new tendency in modern painting.

Right: A photograph showing the vacant former studio of the photographer Nadar at 35 boulevard des Capucines where the First Impressionist Exhibition was held.

1874, remaining open for a month. Works exhibited were very diverse and included Monet's *Impression, Sunrise* (1873), Renoir's *La Loge* (1874) and Cézanne's *Modern Olympia* (1872–74). Degas was one of the exhibitors with the most work, showing ten recent works displaying the full scope of his art. These included four ballet rehearsal scenes, three race-course scenes, two pictures of laundresses, and a study of a bather.

CRITICAL REACTIONS

Many critics acknowledged the originality and innovation of the artists, but others were harsh in their judgements, with Monet and Cézanne receiving severe criticism. Degas' pictures were, by contrast, among the best-received. Though Castagnary, lamenting his choice of subjects, found his paintings "strange and sometimes even bizarre", he recognized Degas' exceptional artistic skill. Chesneau singled out *At the Races in the Countryside,* 1869, praising its "exquisite colour, draughtsmanship, exactness of pose, and accuracy of execution". Burty set Degas apart from the other exhibitors and wrote: "No one can express with a surer hand

the feeling of modern elegance. This is an artist whose capacity for observation, artistic subtlety, and taste reveal themselves in even his smallest works." While the main motive for the exhibition had been to attract buyers, Degas exhibited only pictures already in private collections. Unlike most exhibitors, he had already begun to establish strong patronage and an audience for his work. For Degas the Impressionist exhibitions were an alternative Salon that provided a revolutionary opportunity for artists to take control over what they showed and how their work was exhibited to the public.

THE NEW PAINTING

By the end of 1874 members of the artists' co-operative that had staged the boulevard des Capucines show began planning a second show, this time in Durand-Ruel's temporarily available gallery in the fashionable rue le Peletier. This show was to attract much harsher criticism than the first.

Though 13 former exhibitors, Cézanne and Bracquemond among them, withdrew from the second show, the core members remained and additional recruits, mainly brought in by Degas, brought the number of exhibitors to 20, showing a total of 252 works. These continued to range diversely from landscape scenes to depictions of the new Paris. Gustave Caillebotte, a wealthy young artist and collector, was among the new exhibitors Degas brought in. His generous patronage was to be important in sustaining Impressionism through the lean years of the 1870s, which witnessed a severe economic recession. Degas was feeling the effects of this. The perilous state of the family's finances was becoming clear, and Degas spent several weeks in Naples during the spring discussing the situation with family advisers. As a consequence Degas was keen to refresh his contacts in London, where, unlike Paris, the art market remained buoyant, and economic incentives may account for his decision to exhibit 24 pictures, including *The Cotton Market, New Orleans* and *Absinthe*, as well as a number of pictures of dancers. Degas' submissions stood apart from the landscapes of his Impressionist colleagues, adding a note of realism to the exhibition.

INTRANSIGENTS

While the First Exhibition received mixed, though generally balanced reviews, the Second attracted far harsher criticism. Some critics sympathetic to the initial exhibition now turned on the artists, questioning the continuation of the shows. The tense political and economic climate inflected the tone of the criticism, with many critics condemning what they regarded as the artists' lack of basic skills and exclusive commitment to appearances alone. Several critics described the works as intransigent, echoing the political group known as 'los Intransigentos', the anarchist wing of the Spanish Federal party, whose claims for Cantonal independence were to lead Spain into civil war. Though the rebels were eventually routed and intransigentism destroyed, France, still reeling from the events of the Commune and aware many communards had taken refuge in Spain, was watching the situation carefully, fearful of revolution spilling over the border. The association of radical painting with anarchist politics continued to colour the perception of the movement. Analogies were drawn between the artists' overturning of academic principles of composition and "democratic" style of painting, as Mallarmé described it, and forms of social and political subversion. This influenced the choice of the term "Impressionist" for the Third Exhibition, two years later. It was hoped that adopting a term that had specific artistic meanings would discourage political readings of the work.

IMPRESSIONISM EXPLAINED

At about the time of the Second Exhibition Duranty published a 38-page pamphlet entitled *The New Painting: Concerning the Group of Artists Exhibiting at the Durand-Ruel Gallery.*

Below: High and unorthodox viewpoints were a marked feature of Degas' pictures as in this portrait of the art critic Diego Martelli (1839–96).

Left: Le Pont de L'Europe, by Gustave Caillebotte, 1876. Caillebotte chose a new industrial bridge as a motif.

This important text, written by a close friend of Degas, provided the first attempt to explain the ideas and work of the artists exhibiting together. Duranty argued the artists had a complex relationship with tradition, simultaneously admiring and wishing to break free of it, and isolated four main innovations of their work: their colour use, composition, drawing and subject matter. Studiously avoiding the term Impressionism, Duranty saw the defining feature of the artists as resting with their recording of diverse aspects of modern life. Though not mentioned by name, the frequent references to the great draughtsman within the group, whom Duranty singled out as a man of "the rarest talent and rarest intellect", made clear that he saw Degas as the most important and talented of the artists.

Above: Portrait of Eugene Manet, *by Degas, 1874. This is an unusual portrait of Manet in the countryside.*

Below: The Gare St. Lazare, *by Claude Monet, 1877. Monet depicted ultra modern motifs (the railway) in the 1870s.*

DEGAS' PARIS

Degas was above all a Parisian, and in painting metropolitan subjects he charted the world in which he moved. He knew the city intimately and portrayed many different aspects of it. Degas' imagery of Paris ranged widely across its types, spectacles and patterns of leisure and labour.

The city's sights and spectacles formed one of the great themes of early Impressionism. Though Monet would later become known as an itinerant landscapist, in the late 1860s and early 1870s he painted the city and the suburbs. The Impressionists' quick notational brushwork arose as a way of capturing fleeting scenes of modern Parisian life, its pleasures and lifestyles. Though the choice of urban subjects united Impressionist painters, there were crucial differences between them. Artists like Monet, Guillaumin and Pissarro viewed their subjects primarily

as landscapes, producing topographical representations of the city's new spaces and architecture. They often chose high, distant viewpoints that accentuated the spectacular appearance of the new boulevards, fashionable quarters and parks. Degas, Manet and Renoir offered a broader and more penetrating vision of

Below: In this unorthodox composition Degas shows a laundress absorbed in her work. The compression of the room evokes the austere conditions in which laundresses, among the most poorly paid manual jobs in Paris, worked.

Paris, a detailed portrayal of the types, customs and patterns of work and leisure of Parisians, whether poor or wealthy.

CONTEMPORARY LIFE

Their pictures answered more closely Baudelaire's call to painters to capture the spirit of the modernity of Paris. Though much of Degas' imagery was of the social world of the haute bourgeoisie, his depictions of shop assistants, laundresses, popular singers and prostitutes gave representation to the lower classes in the dispassionate and objectifying manner characteristic of realist novelists of the time.

Above: From the series Celebrated Beauties by Kitagawa Utamaro, c.1797. Degas drew heavily on the asymmetry and arbitrary compositional cropping common in Japanese prints.

Above: Café Concert at the Ambassadeurs, *by Degas, 1885. Degas was fascinated by the new world of commercial popular entertainments that emerged in Paris in the 1870s.*

A DISQUIETING VISION

Though Degas revelled in the social and cultural modernity of the new Paris, his paintings are sensitive to its more disquieting aspects. *Absinthe* (1876) captures a sombre mood absent from most contemporary representations of modern life and is closer in spirit to the novels of writers like Zola and the Goncourt brothers who confronted the public with "ugly stories of the contemporary world". *Absinthe* is one of Degas' most poignant pictures. The image of demoralized working-class habitués of the Paris café-brasseries drinking themselves into a stupor would be a familiar one to readers of Zola. Degas' frowzily dressed woman and the man seated next to her seem to be

Above: In a Café, *or* Absinthe, *by Degas, c.1876. Degas' imagery encompasses the wretched, alienated conditions of the life of the working classes.*

oblivious to each other. The woman stares deep into herself, nursing a glass of absinthe. The lighting suggests it is still morning. The contrived space places the viewer as though seated at the fore-ground table watching the two figures. Degas creates a strong impression of realism. Despite this, the figures represented were the actress Ellen Andrée and Degas' friend the bohemian artist Marcellin Desboutin (1823–1902).

Degas' images of Paris remain astonishingly fresh. As a painter of contemporary life, he sought subjects that he regarded as giving form to the modernity of his time. In doing so he had few prior examples to draw on. We can, however, recognize how Degas adopted many compositional conventions of

popular prints, which had a more immediate relation to the customs and manners of their times than the high art of the French tradition. Degas was a prolific print collector, particularly of the cartoonists and caricaturists Honoré Daumier (1808–79) and Gavarni (1804–66), and admired the woodcut prints of Japanese artists of the Edo period. These provided techniques that Degas used in his 'slice-of-life' compositions, which create the impression of an observed scene captured spontaneously.

JAPANESE PRINTS

Japanese woodcuts were popular in the mid-19th century among artists and collectors, who valued their novel compositions and depiction of the *ukiyo-e*, or 'floating world'. Dating from the 17th to the mid-19th century, the prints depicted fleeting beauty and ephemeral pleasures, including the theatre and erotic entertainments. Among Degas' art collection were albums of Japanese prints, with artists such as Utamaro (1753–1806), Hokusai (1760–1849) and Hiroshige (1797–1858).

CAFÉS AND CAFÉ-CONCERTS

By the mid-1870s many of the Impressionists had become landscapists depicting the pleasures of the French countryside, but Renoir, Degas and Manet continued to pursue more urban subjects. These often concentrated on the new forms of leisure and entertainment in Paris.

Second Empire Paris saw an explosion of leisure and commercial entertainment, which became an ever more visible presence in Parisian life and drew large numbers of tourists. There were 300 theatres in Paris by 1867, providing a range of high and low entertainments including opera, comic opera, vaudeville and music halls. Parisian nightlife included an array of restaurants, popular balls, circuses, cafés and café-concerts. The massive expansion of this world was a crucial feature of the modernity of Paris and its reputation as a city of spectacle and illusion. It was this that modern artists like Degas were drawn to in representing the new Paris.

CAFÉ LIFE
The café became the meeting place for Parisians, where they could socialize and observe the city life around them. Cafés became places where artists, writers and intellectuals met to discuss their theories. Among those who attended these weekly evening meetings of Manet and his circle at the Café Guerbois were Monet, Zola, Duranty, Zacharie Astruc and Degas. After the Commune, these relocated to the Café de la Nouvelle-Athènes, pictured in Degas' *Women on a Café Terrace* (1877), on the Place Pigalle, which additionally attracted Renoir and occasionally Pissarro. The writer George Moore, who also began to attend these meetings, recalled Degas as a conversationalist whose tongue could be "sharp, ironical, cynical".

A TASTE FOR POPULAR CULTURE
Degas' notebooks from this period indicate a busy social life of regular dinners with the Rouarts and the

Halévys, attendance at the literary salon of Madame Charles Hayem and frequent visits to the Opéra-Comique and the Palais Garnier. Degas, like many of the artists and writers in his circle, also had a taste for the lowbrow and frequently visited the Café des Ambassadeurs and its nearby rival, the Alcazar d'Eté, among the most fashionable of these establishments. These café-concerts put on an array of acts in outdoor pavilions extensively lit by gaslight, whose strange, distorting illumination fascinated Degas and often

features in his pictures. Though they originated in the 1840s, the Second Empire saw the burgeoning of such popular establishments, which drew attendance from people from all classes. Manet, Degas and Renoir all savoured the ambience of these places that produced a new kind of celebrity, the popular singer. Degas ignored the men but often portrayed the leading female singers who performed there, such as Emélie Bécat and Thérèsa (Emma Valadon), whose talent Degas particularly admired. Their songs

Right: Café Concert at Les Ambassadeurs, by Degas, 1876–77. Degas was an habitué of the Café des Ambassadeurs facing on to the Place de la Concorde.

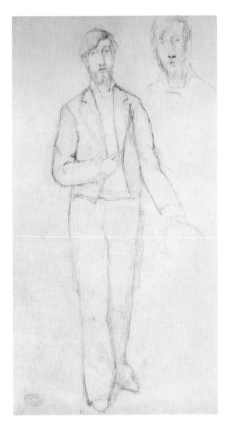

Above: Portrait of George Moore (1852–1933), *by Degas. Moore was an Irish writer and trained artist who frequented the circle of Manet and Degas.*

seemed to speak to the people, giving voice to their desires and frustrations. Degas' pictures give a vivid impression of their performances, which were by turns sentimental, coarse, aggressive and full of sexual innuendo, a mixture of the delicate and the gross, as Degas enthusiastically described it to a friend. Degas is attentive to the singers' mannerisms and gestures. Bécat was known for her jumps, twists, frantic arm-waving and coarser imploring gestures, which often injected political or sexual meaning into her songs. The government monitored these rowdy and unruly performances, which sometimes took on a political tone, and often censored the lyrics of the songs.

Degas clearly regarded such popular entertainments as spectacles that reflected the social history of his times, and also admired their energy, force and originality. In his art he often combined references to high traditions with others belonging to the low art of caricature, cartoons and popular prints.

Below: Women on a Café Terrace, *by Degas, 1877. The image probably depicts a scene of prostitutes soliciting clients.*

Above: La Chanteuse au Gant (Singer with Glove), *by Degas, c.1878. Degas was fascinated by the performances of Thérèsa.*

UNDERLYING TENSIONS

Despite Degas' long association with Impressionism he never accepted the term to describe his work and was often outspokenly critical of their artistic aims. These conflicts led to disagreements about the name of the show and arguments about Degas' invitations to his followers to participate in them.

In the late 1870s and 1880s Degas continued to exhibit with the Impressionists, though serious tensions were beginning to emerge about the organization and aims of the exhibitions. These were exacerbated by the inclusion of a growing number of Degas' followers. His Parisian scenes, portraits and most especially the ballerina pictures gained him a critical following. In an influential article the critic and naturalist novelist Joris-Karl Huysmans called Degas "one of the greatest artists we have today in France" and likened his work to that of Baudelaire, Flaubert and the Goncourts. Huysmans described Degas' work as "a remarkable, intrepid kind of painting". Degas had also begun to acquire a following among fellow painters.

Below: The Blacksmiths, by Jean-François Raffaëlli, 1884. To much consternation the realist painter Raffaëlli, whose work focused on large-scale depictions of peasants and workers, was invited by Degas to exhibit at the 1880 and 1881 Impressionist exhibitions.

DISSENT AND DISCORD

Though the Impressionist shows had largely been successful, at the fourth show, held on the Avenue de l'Opéra in 1879, Degas insisted the neutral term "Independents" be substituted for

Below: The Wings of the Opera (in the Foyer), by Jean Louis Forain, c.1887. Forain, another follower of Degas, participated in three of the four shows between 1879 and 1884. His imagery closely shadowed Degas'.

"Impressionist". Renoir, Sisley and Cézanne had all withdrawn. Despite the success of the exhibition, which attracted 16,000 visitors, Monet also withdrew after it. At the fifth show a grouping of Degas' friends and followers made their presence strongly felt within the group, leaving the Impressionist landscapists in a minority. These included Henri Rouart, Forain, Federico Zandomeneghi, Mary Cassatt (1844–1926) and Charles-Victor Tillot (1825–95). Jean-François Raffaëlli (1850–1924), his brother Jean-Marius

(1845–1916), Paul Gauguin (1848–93) and Jean-Baptiste-Léopold Levert had joined Degas' group; of those who were in the first show, only Pissarro, Morisot and Degas himself remained.

The Fifth Exhibition was marked by quarrels between Degas, Caillebotte and Pissarro over its organization. Degas objected to the poster Caillebotte had made, which left off the names of several of Degas' group. Caillebotte took strongly against the inclusion of Jean-François Raffaëlli, who tactlessly grabbed a large section of the best wall space and showed 35 works. The realist painter and printmaker Raffaëlli, was the most ambitious painter of Degas' coterie and many of the pictures of peasants, workers and ragpickers set in suburban wasteland settings were on a large scale, which rankled many of the other exhibitors. Raffaëlli's work shared with that of Degas reference points in the work of naturalist and realist writers, and he referred to his own brand of socially observant realism as caractérisme.

Degas himself seemed ambivalent about what to show. He included only 12 pictures, a mixture of ballet subjects with several drawings and etchings. Other planned inclusions, *Young Spartans* and *Little Dancer of Fourteen*, failed to materialize. After Duranty's death, shortly before the show opened, Degas again showed his portrait of the

critic. The critical attention Degas was now receiving probably worsened relations with other core exhibitors. The distinguished critic Albert Woolf asked, "Why does a man like Degas linger in this collection of non-entities?" In a long, irritable letter written to Pissarro, Caillebotte complained of Degas' "persecution mania" and his attacks on "everyone in whom he sees some talent". Acknowledging his "immense talent", Caillebotte objected to Degas packing the exhibition with his artists, "Degas has brought disarray among us…. If Degas wants to join us, let him do so, but without all those he drags along with him." Fiercely loyal and ever the peacemaker, Pissarro reminded him that Caillebotte had been among Degas' recruits to the Impressionist exhibitions. Unappeased, Caillebotte withdrew from the sixth show. The exhibition was widely seen as a Realist Salon. The catalogue listed eight entries by Degas but a number of works were added in the first week, including the long-anticipated *Young Dancer of 14*

Left: The Loge, by Cassatt, 1882. Cassatt, who was to become close friends with Degas, exhibited at four of the last five Impressionist exhibitions following Degas in pulling out of the Seventh Exhibition.

Above: Portrait of Diego Martelli, by Federigo Zandomeneghi, 1879. Shown at the 1879 exhibition, this portrait complemented Degas' earlier portrait of the art critic. Zandomeneghi, a close friend of Degas, showed at four of the Impressionist exhibitions.

Years, which materialized six days after the opening and dominated critics' coverage of the show.

DEGAS WITHDRAWS

The Seventh Exhibition in 1882 proved a predictably fraught affair, and Degas yielded to the demands that he and his protégés withdraw. At the beginning of his review of the exhibition, Huysmans lamented their absence and announced the return of Caillebotte, Renoir, Monet and Sisley. Pissarro, Morisot, Guillaumin, Gauguin and Victor Vignon (1847–1909) made up the other exhibitors. Although Degas and many of his followers would return for the Eighth Exhibition in 1886, the tensions within the group were now pulling the artists in opposite directions. Degas' will had prevailed and he had turned the Impressionist exhibition into a showcase for himself and his artistic followers, but this was not without cost. The tensions and arguments in the planning of this show signalled these group exhibitions were drawing to a close.

LA CIGALE

In the 1870s Ludovic Halévy, Degas' close friend and contemporary, was to write a topical satire about the Impressionists. This farce parodies many of the ideas of the group of artists who were fast coming to the public's attention and suggests Degas' collusion.

La Cigale (The Grasshopper), a comedy written in 1877 by Henri Meilhac and Ludovic Halévy, satirized modern artists, drawing closely on the events of the early Impressionist exhibitions. A close friend of Degas since their youth, Halévy's portrait, executed in 1879,

Below: A poster advertising 'La Vie Parisienne', an operetta by Jacques Offenbach (1819–90), by Jules Cheret, 1886.

shows him as a fellow habitué of the Paris Opéra, conversing backstage with the dilettante Albert Boulanger-Cavé. Halévy became a successful author and librettist for Jacques Offenbach, one of the most celebrated composers of the Second Empire period, and together they had an unprecedented success in 1856 with the musical parody *Orpheus in the Underworld (Orphée aux Enfers)*, written in collaboration with Hector Crémieux. In the 1860s Halévy had

begun a 20-year collaboration with Meilhac and together they produced a series of operettas, farces and comedies, satirizing the vices and follies of their time and specializing in light sketches of Parisian life. These included *Beautiful Helen (La Belle Hélène)* (1864), *Bluebeard (Barbe Bleue)* (1866), *The Grand Duchess of Gérolstein (La Grande-Duchesse de Gérolstein)* (1867), and *The Long Dinner (Le Réveillon)* (1872) which became one of the sources of Johann Strauss's operetta *The Bat (Die Fledermaus)* (1874). Today he is best known as the librettist who, in collaboration with Meilhac, adapted Prosper Mérimée's novella *Carmen* (1845) for Bizet's famous opera.

Below: Portrait of Ludovic Halévy (1834–1908), from 'La Famille Cardinal' by Ludovic Halévy, by Degas, c.1880s.

A SATIRE OF IMPRESSIONISM

The Grasshopper, a rapid-fire boulevard comedy in three acts, opened at the Théâtre des Variétés on 6 October 1877, with an adaptation following at the Gaiety Theatre in London on 13 October. Though Degas is not credited in the authorship, *The Grasshopper* appears to incorporate many of his ideas about his colleagues, and details of their lives. Degas also seems to have taken an interest in the staging and design. In a letter to Halévy written shortly before the dress rehearsal, Degas made reference to the third act and wrote:

You know that I am at your disposal for the studio of Dupuis [the actor who played the part of the painter Marignan]. It's no use my finding fault with your play; doing the thing pleases me a lot and I will do it.

The play includes jokes about 'retinalism', echoing Degas' well-known barbs about Monet's commitment to an art of optical appearances. The third act is set in the studio of an artist of the "Intentionist" tendency, Marignan. His name seems to have been composed from the names of

Above: Friends at the Theatre, Ludovic Halévy (1834–1908) and Albert Cave (1832–1910), *by Degas, 1878–79.*

a number of the painters whose works are caricatured (including Manet, Monet, Renoir, Pissarro, Cézanne and Sisley), while "Intentionist" was probably chosen for its phonetic similarity to Impressionist, though the comedy extended broadly across the concerns of modern artists. Marignan waxes lyrical about the physiognomic differences between a modern portrait with a Parisian nose and an ancient Greek nose in a classical painting. Many of the play's funniest moments point at Degas. At one point Marignan sets up a washtub and poses his model, Catherine, as a laundress scrubbing linen in a foaming lather of soapsuds. In another

scene he displays some ethereal, Whistlerian seascapes, not unlike those Degas painted in 1869. Describing a semi-abstract tableau comprising equal bands of blue sea and red sky, Marignan explains that it depicts a majestic sunset glowing over a deep blue sea, but when turned upside down it doubles as a representation of a radiant blue sky and burning red desert sands. It is said that when Degas attended the opening night, he could be heard roaring with laughter.

LUDOVIC HALÉVY

The French author and playwright Ludovic Halévy was a childhood friend of Degas. Though of Jewish ancestry Ludovic was brought up a Catholic, after his father's conversion to Catholicism before his birth. Halévy shared Degas' love of music and the opera and quickly made a name for himself as a writer of popular comedies and sketches of Parisian life and a librettist of operas and operettas. He also wrote the novels *Monsieur et Madame Cardinal* (1873) and *Les Petites Cardinal* (1880), describing the life of the lower middle classes. In his popular novel *L'Abbé Constantin* (1882), adapted for the stage in 1882, all characters are shown to be good and kind by nature, a clear rebut to the exploration of the darker aspects of human nature in Zola's novels.

THE PAINTER OF WOMEN

The great theme of Degas' art was the portrayal of women. Few painters devoted so much of their oeuvre to images of the female sex. However, Degas' feelings toward women were complex and ambivalent and this expresses itself in subtle ways in his imagery.

In Assisi the youthful Degas wrote of his desire to find "a good little wife", however, he remained a bachelor and his attitude toward marriage may have been conditioned by his upbringing. Degas was brought up in a predominantly male household. He also saw several people unhappily married: his own mother, his brother Auguste, and his aunt Laura and Gennaro Bellelli. Degas' attitudes may also have been determined by current ideas about the conflict between artistic vocation and family life. A common theme in the "studio novel" was the belief that family life could only compromise an artist's creativity. Many artists shared these beliefs. Delacroix told one of his young followers who was about to marry, "An artist must have no passion except for his work and must sacrifice everything to it." Degas echoed this view when he said: "There is love and there is art and we only have one heart." Many did not marry or, like Renoir, Pissarro, Cézanne and Manet, married late in life, though each, unlike Degas, had mistresses.

Did Degas' belief that marriage and sexual liaisons might compromise and weaken his art affect his portrayal of women? Several of his most ambitious early pictures, such as *Young Spartans*, *Medieval War Scene* and *Interior*, have been interpreted as expressing anxieties about the relations between the sexes. In his own time, Degas' portrayals of women were often regarded as cruel and his many pictures of prostitution as expressing misogynistic feelings and deep-seated anxieties about sexual desire. However, many of these themes were common subjects at the Salon.

DEGAS' AMBIVALENCE

Sometimes Degas' chauvinism was explicit. He referred to the women in his pictures as animals and is alleged to have

Above: Madame Jeantaud in the Mirror, *by Degas, c.1875. Degas uses the mirror to present two alternate views of the wife of a close friend.*

Below: Portrait of Henri Rouart's Daughter in her Father's Study, *by Degas, c.1886. The vacant chair symbolizes Rouart's presence.*

treated his models like mere objects. The views Degas expressed were not uncommon, but were part of a wider set of patriarchal attitudes that conditioned the discourses about gender and sexuality in the 19th century. However, Degas could show great tenderness to his female friends and in general took the art of the women painters in his circle very seriously. There are also anecdotes of his affection for his models and enjoyment of female company. Degas' representations of women express a wider variety of attitudes than his recorded comments might suggest. Most 19th-century artists would give men individual characters more readily than women, who were

Right: The Millinery Shop, *by Degas,
1879–86. Though Degas' formal portraits
of women are exclusively of the haute
bourgeoisie, lower-class women feature in
many of his works.*

often portrayed as types. This was only
partly true of Degas. His ballerinas and
later bathers focus mainly on the figure's
role in some activity, concentrating on
the physiognomy and sensual movement
of the body, but there is also an
engagement with the exertions and
suffering of the ballerina in perfecting her
art. Moreover, in his portraits of women,
which span all classes, he draws us
intimately into their world. These are
among the most sensitive, insightful and
sympathetic pictures of women of the
period. In them women are not simply
portrayed as types, but as individuals
who are often shown deep in thought
and with intellectual attributes not always
present in the works of Degas' peers.
In this way Degas' art exceeds the
limitations he sometimes expressed in
his attitudes about women.

ART OR MARRIAGE

The idea of incompatibility between
an artistic vocation and family life is
shown in the Goncourt brothers'
novel *Manette Salomon*, which
Degas admired and was to illustrate.
Before the artist Coriolis becomes
"enslaved" to the model Manette, it
is remarked: "Celibacy was the only
state that left artists with their
liberty, their strength, their minds and
their consciousness. He had a feeling
that it was because of wives that so
many artists slipped into weaknesses,
into complacent modishness, into
concessions to profit-making and
commerce, into denials of aspirations
…he thought it wise…to seek only
sensual satisfaction from a woman,
in a liaison without attachment".

Right: Woman doing her Hair, *by Degas,
c.1895. A major part of Degas' imagery
is women nude at their toilette. These
images rarely suggest any individual
characteristics of the women depicted.*

MONOTYPES

From the 1870s onward, Degas began to experiment with etching, lithography and monotypes. Of these it was the latter he found most amenable to his way of working. Over the course of the next few decades he was to explore its artistic possibilities to the full.

Degas' interest in monotype printing began in 1874. Attracted to the fluid, spontaneous qualities of the medium, which allowed him greater improvisation than drawing, etching or lithography, Degas produced more than 250 subjects and 400 individual monotype impressions. Degas used the 'dark-field' method, which involved covering the surface of the metal plate with ink then wiping, scratching, brushing and smudging the plate with his fingers to remove enough ink to create a representational image, which was then printed on to

paper. He usually made two impressions of each image, a stronger and a weaker, keeping the first, with its dramatic pattern of light and shade, intact and working over the lighter second in pastel and charcoal. The results create raw, bold and fresh images that incorporate chance effects. The subjects Degas represented in monotype are broad in scope and encompass the full range of his imagery, but perhaps the most intriguing and notorious are the brothel monotypes, almost all of which were produced in the late 1870s and early 1880s.

THE BROTHEL MONOTYPES

Little more than 40 monotypes of brothel subjects survive, as many were destroyed after Degas' death. We can only speculate on what these images might have looked like. The intimacy, realism and acute social observation of the surviving pictures suggest that Degas based them on his visits to the *maisons closes*, the legal brothels of Paris. The imagery varies widely, reflecting diverse aspects of the life of the brothel. Women are shown lounging around in ungraceful, candid and immodest poses, waiting for clients, amusing themselves, or simply bored. Those which show the prostitutes performing their ablutions before having sex with their clients bear similarities to Degas' images of bathers produced around the same time. Occasionally he shows something of the companionship between the women and the prosaic qualities of their lives. Often we see the 'madame' of the brothel orchestrating events in much the way the master of the corps de ballet organizes the ballerinas. Where male figures are introduced they rarely occupy the positions of authority and control typical of Degas' imagery, but often seem the object of amusement among the uninhibited prostitutes. Wary clients recoil on the edge of the picture from the brazen approaches of the prostitutes, as though having second thoughts.

A COMICAL VISION

Although some of these pictures are sexually explicit, uncouth and even demeaning, the tone is as often as not witty and comical, albeit frequently at the expense of the prostitutes. In both style and theme Degas was indebted to the caricatures and popular prints of artists

Left: In the Salon of a Brothel, *by Degas, 1879. Degas' portrayal of prostitutes emphasizes their gaucherie and vulgarity.*

Left: The Client, *by Degas, c.1877. Degas' clients rarely look comfortable in the brothel setting and the ambience is not one of sensual pleasure.*

such as Guys and Daumier. The art dealer Ambroise Vollard later used some of these monotypes to illustrate an edition of Maupassant's comical story of prostitution *The Tellier Establishment* (1881). The prints de-glamorize the image of prostitution, offering a stark contrast with the idealized portrayals of courtesans and fantasy harems found at the Salon. Degas shows the sordid and banal world of actual prostitution. Yet, if Degas avoided idealization he also avoided personalizing and individualizing the women. The simian profiles of the prostitutes and their animal-like postures and movements reflect stereotypical views of the time, associating lower-class prostitutes with atavistic behaviour.

While explicit images of prostitution were generally made for private consumption, Degas did show some of the monotypes at the Fifth and Sixth Impressionist Exhibitions, where they were praised for their telling and expressive poses, carefully observed movement and truthful conception.

Above: Admiration, *by Degas, 1879–80. A man voyeuristically admiring a prostitute posed in a tub.*

Left: The Madame's Birthday, *by Degas, 1877. Occasionally, Degas' imagery explores the communal life of the brothel.*

AN ENDURING FRIENDSHIP

The close friendship between Degas and Mary Cassatt was one of the most important in Degas' life, and each had a profound influence on the other's work. Cassatt long admired and felt a deep affinity with Degas' work, while Degas recognized in Cassatt an artist of formidable originality and talent.

Mary Cassatt was born in 1844 in Pennsylvania, USA, into a well-connected, wealthy mercantile family, and spent some of her childhood in Paris. Independent-minded, ambitious and keen to make a serious career as an artist, after graduating from the Pennsylvania Academy of the Fine Arts she returned to Paris in 1866 to further her studies, copying old masters in the Louvre and other museums.

MUTUAL ADMIRATION

Degas and Cassatt met in 1877 though they were already aware of each other's work. Recalling seeing paintings by Degas at Durand-Ruel's gallery in Paris in 1873, Cassatt wrote: "I used to go and flatten my nose against that window and absorb all I could of his art. It changed my life. I saw art then as I wanted to see it." She persuaded her friend Louise Elder, the second wife of the millionaire Louis Havemeyer, to purchase Degas' *Ballet Lesson on Stage* (1873–75) in 1875. Cassatt owned several pictures by Degas including *The Ballet Class* (c.1880) and a seated unfinished portrait of her. On encountering Cassatt's pictures, Degas said, "There is someone who feels like I do." He invited her to exhibit with him at the Impressionist shows, where she became a regular exhibitor, and they often spent time together visiting the Louvre, socializing and shopping.

Cassatt's pictures convey the influence Degas had on her and initially she was seen as his pupil. However, Cassatt soon created a distinctive direction of her own, albeit informed by Degas' example. Like Degas, her paintings focus on the milieu of women, sometimes depicted at the Opéra or socializing in domestic settings, but she also touched on subjects Degas rarely treated, such as women with children in everyday domestic settings. Though she never had children herself, these express with deep tenderness the

bond of mother and child in compositions that are novel, distinctive and far removed from treatments of the subject by her peers.

PORTRAITS OF CASSATT

Degas' depictions of Cassatt reflect his high regard and respect for her, presenting her as a studious and reflective woman. He emphasizes the intellectual qualities of his sitter, unusual in portraits of women at the time. In an unfinished interior portrait, dated 1884, she is shown plainly dressed and posed informally leaning toward the viewer. In

Above: Portrait of Mary Cassatt (1844–1926), by Degas, c.1880–84. *Unlike most of his images of women who are portrayed as types, Degas portrays Cassatt's inner character, individuality and intellectualism.*

another series of pictures Cassatt is shown studying in the Louvre. She is seen from behind looking at pictures on the walls, or, in a variant etching, gazing at Etruscan sculpture. Her fashionable, haute-couture clothing and rather unbalanced pose, pivoting on an umbrella, serve to convey her character

Right: In the Box, *by Mary Cassatt, 1879. These women are active onlookers rather than objects of another's gaze.*

Above: At the Louvre, Mary Cassatt (1845–1926), *by Degas. Though shown from behind, this image of Cassatt conveys a strong sense of personality.*

in the absence of any other information. Degas was obviously pleased with the composition, reworking it in a series of variations in different media.

A COMPLICATED RELATIONSHIP

The relationship between Degas and Cassatt was long, complex and tender, informed by mutual interests and respect for each other's talent. When Degas became bedridden Cassatt arranged for his niece to take care of him. While it was rumoured that Cassatt was Degas' mistress, late in life he remarked "I would have married her, but I could never have made love to her." Cassatt was curtly dismissive of such rumours, but this, combined with Degas' difficult behaviour in his final years, may have strained their relationship. After his death, Cassatt disassociated herself from the artist she had once revered as a modern master, burning his correspondence and in 1912 instructing Durand-Ruel to sell Degas' unfinished portrait of her.

Right: Mother and Child, *by Mary Cassatt, 1900. Cassatt's imagery of motherhood stresses the close physical contact between mother and child in a way that is unidealized.*

RE-INVENTING SCULPTURE

In addition to his paintings, pastels and drawings, Degas produced a large quantity of sculpture. These sculptures re-invigorated a tradition that many saw as in decline and led Degas to be acclaimed as one of the most important painter-sculptors of his generation.

It is not clear when Degas began making sculpture and the dates of individual works, and the role they played in his art remain matters of speculation. In an interview in 1897, Degas said he had been sculpting intermittently since the late 1860s, beginning by modelling equestrian statuettes as compositional aids for his racehorse pictures. The time he spent on sculpture undoubtedly increased as he got older and his eyes declined. Joseph Durand-Ruel, Paul's son, recalled: "Whenever I called on Degas I was almost as sure to find him modelling in clay as painting." The extent of his sculpture remains a mystery. The 74 models that survive show Degas worked predominantly in wax, and occasionally in clay and plaster, sometimes mixing these with other materials. The surviving works are probably only a fraction of what he produced. Manipulating pliable wax over improvized armatures, Degas explored movements in his sculpture that pushed the medium beyond its technical limitations; some sculptures simply fell apart. As Degas did not cast his figures, many of the dancers, bathers and horses he sculpted were left to crumble into dust in his studio.

In the 19th century sculpture was a tradition in decline. Cuts in state funding and the new market economy in the arts left sculptors vulnerable. Some critics, like Baudelaire, wondered whether, in an age of modernity characterized by flux, change and speed, sculpture could remain relevant. Nevertheless, Degas could look to his great contemporary Rodin's vibrant and animated work and, on a more minor note, the extraordinary wax sculpture of Medardo Rosso, which Degas admired.

DEGAS' ATTITUDE TO SCULPTURE

Though Renoir, who took up sculpture toward the end of his career, called Degas "the greatest living sculptor", only one sculpture, *Dancer Aged 14 Years* (1881), was exhibited in his lifetime. Prior to his death, knowledge of this secret and extensive body of work was

Left: The Dance, by Jean-Baptiste Carpeaux (1827–75), 1868. Carpeaux's classical bacchanal, originally sited on the façade of the Opéra Garnier, reflects the way sculpture struggled to adapt to the kind of modern life subjects that Degas would turn sculpture toward.

restricted to visitors to his studio. Degas modestly described his sculpture as only for his "own satisfaction" and "preparatory motions, nothing more". However, the relationship between his sculpture and his other work was more intimate and reciprocal than this suggests. Sculpture, like printmaking, allowed him the freedom to experiment and renew his art, and may account for the greater tactile quality of his later pictures.

Even before making sculpture Degas' pictures had often referred to antique bas-relief and free-standing sculpture. He made drawings and wax figures as studies in movement and kept them in his Montmartre studio, clustered on sculpture stands and on tables, so he could refer to them as he completed his paintings. Degas often drew sculptures from different angles, exploring the expressive possibilities of poses. Close correspondences between the poses of his sculptures and those of his pictures are very evident. Since antiquity artists had used mannequins and wax figures as models in conceiving their paintings, but Degas' sculptures were not merely made to assist in the completion of his

Above: Dancer Looking at the Sole of her Right Foot, *by Degas, c.1900. The mottled surfaces that betray the artist's hand, fragmentation and poses of Degas' sculpture owe much to Rodin's influence.*

Left: Torso, *by Degas, 1896–1911. Degas often made maquettes to use as models for his paintings. This one closely resembles some of his ballerinas.*

Below: Danaid, *by Auguste Rodin (1840–1917). Rodin's often angst-ridden sculptures dominated the medium in the later 19th century.*

oils and pastels, but to increase his understanding of the body's three-dimensional form and movement. Hence as his eyes declined, so his productivity as a sculptor increased. Later drawings suggest a progressive reliance on the

sculptures as models. His statuettes encouraged later generations of painters to experiment with sculpture and to create new dialogues between the media.

DEGAS THE SCULPTOR

Sculpture assumed a very special importance in Degas' work toward the end of his life. Often when his eyes were too poor to paint, he would turn to sculpting. François Thiebault-Sisson recalled visiting Degas in his later years: "In the dark cluttered room…the melancholy old man was modelling a figurine. Curled up in a studio Louis-Philippe armchair, a young woman, her upper body nude, made the gesture of wiping her neck. Scrutinizing her through his spectacles, Degas slowly, patiently, with little strokes of his sculptor's tool or his thumb, moulded and remoulded in red wax the projection of the shoulder."

LA PETITE DANSEUSE

Though Degas had apparently been making sculpture since the late 1860s, it was only toward the end of the 1870s that the work became truly innovative. With the *Little Dancer Aged Fourteen* Years (1881), Degas conceived a new contemporary form of realistic sculpture. The work caused a stir when first exhibited.

The catalogue of the Fifth Impressionist Exhibition in 1880 listed among Degas' entries a wax statuette entitled *La Petite Danseuse de Quatorze Ans (Little Dancer Aged Fourteen)*, though when the exhibition opened all that was visible was the glass vitrine Degas had made for it. It was not unusual for Degas to add work to exhibitions late and it seems he was keen to exhibit a work he believed was groundbreaking and would demonstrate a new direction in his art, but when the exhibition closed the polished case remained empty. The following year at the Sixth Impressionist Exhibition the statuette was listed again, and this time it appeared, quickly becoming the talk of the show. Admiring its ingenious technique and brilliant execution Mrs Havemeyer wrote, "[Degas'] name is on everyone's lips, his statue is discussed by all the art world."

Left: Woman with Two Little Girls, *by Degas, c.1889. Degas was to return to the theme of the young dancer in this affecting pastel.*

Above: Three Studies of a Nude Dancer, *by Degas, c.1878–80. Degas meticulously planned his* Little Dancer *making many studies from various points of view.*

THE MODEL

Marie van Goethen, the model, had just turned 14 when Degas began his studies for the sculpture around 1878. Degas initially modelled the figure nude, making many drawings from all angles and constructing wax maquettes to refine the pose and facial expression. He portrays her practising her exercises, her right leg extended forward with her foot turned out, hands clasped behind her back, chin raised and eyes closed in concentration. The statuette was about 1m (3ft) high and was modelled with exceptional accuracy. Degas took the unusual step of dressing it with a wax corset, a muslin and linen tutu and real ballet slippers, and added a satin ribbon to tie the hair, made from a horsehair wig. The wax had an extraordinary life-like sheen. After Degas' death, his estate made the decision to cast the figure in bronze.

CRITICAL RECEPTION

Though some critics found the figure "odious", "ugly" and "graceless", a "puny specimen" marked by a "profoundly vicious character", the work was generally well received. Many felt disturbed by the strange intensity of this statuette of an adolescent, but most acknowledged its powerfully realistic conception. Paul de Charry praised the sculpture's "truth to reality" and "extraordinary composition", hailing it as a "masterpiece", while Nina de Villars stated, "Before this statuette I experienced one of the most violent artistic impressions of my life" and went on to suggest the work would one day

figurines Tintoretto (1518–94), Poussin and Meissonier (1815–91) had used for their paintings. The wax museums of Madame Tussaud had also become a popular attraction and may have inspired him. As always, Degas was renewing the past and reworking it in the light of contemporary issues and art debates.

Despite many critics' belief that *La Petite Danseuse de Quatorze Ans* had inaugurated a new phase in sculpture, its real influence was on Degas himself. His sculpture over the past decade had been mainly equestrian statuettes. From now on he focused on the figure, and went on to make some of the most innovative and complex sculpture of his age. *La Petite Danseuse* remains an exceptional work in the history of art.

Above: La Petite Danseuse de Quatorze Ans, *by Degas, 1881. Degas conceived his sculpture in the round, making each angle interesting in its own right.*

perhaps be seen as "the first work of a new art". Huysmans concurred: "At the first blow...[Degas has] overthrown the traditions of sculpture, just as he had long ago shaken the conventions of painting". This was an understandable reaction, though not entirely true. Both Jules Claretie and de Villars noted Degas had given a very contemporary Parisian inflection to existing realist traditions of sculpture, comparing it to Spanish polychromatic statuary. At the 1869 Salon Jean-Baptiste Clésinger (1814–83) had adorned his painted marble Cléopatre with real jewellery and in 1876 Gustave Moreau wrapped a wax Salomé in a linen mantle. Degas may also have been aware that ancient Greek and Roman statuary was often painted and decorated, and knew of the model wax

Right: La Petite Danseuse de Quatorze Ans, *by Degas, 1881. The original 1m/3ft-sculpture had real hair tied in a ribbon as well as a silk bodice, tulle and gauze tutu.*

THE MODEL FOR LA PETITE DANSEUSE

Degas' model, Marie van Goethen, was a Belgian ballet pupil who made her debut at the Opéra eight years after posing for Degas' sculpture. By then she was already well known around artists' studios as a model and frequented the café Nouvelle-Athènes. She had lush, long black hair that she apparently insisted on wearing loose when she danced. Degas would make drawings that explored her physiognomy and anatomy from all angles, including some above head height, before beginning the sculpture itself.

AN ARTISTIC CRISIS

The mid-1880s might be described as a period of reassessment for many of the artists associated with Impressionism. During this period the artists redefined the range of subjects they tackled and their relationship with tradition. This was to lead to a period of revision and change for Degas.

During the 1870s, Degas, with Duranty as his chief spokesman, had set himself the project of portraying the types, manners and customs of modern life. His pictures from these years provide us with an enduring repertoire of images of contemporary Paris, its patterns of work and leisure and its spectrum of high and low forms of entertainment. Degas had begun as a history painter in the traditional sense, but in the late 1860s became a new kind of modern history painter, taking contemporary Paris as his "grand project". This change reflected a new recognition of the significance of the changes France was experiencing. Degas hoped modern Paris would provide him with subjects that would allow him to rival the ambition and achievement of the old masters, and believed that the grand tradition needed to be constantly renewed in relation to the spirit and

Below: The Laundresses, *by Degas, c.1884. These modern-life subjects were later to be abandoned by Degas in favour of more timeless motifs.*

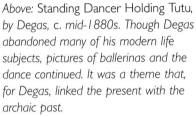

Above: Standing Dancer Holding Tutu, *by Degas, c. mid-1880s. Though Degas abandoned many of his modern life subjects, pictures of ballerinas and the dance continued. It was a theme that, for Degas, linked the present with the archaic past.*

sensibility of the age. His submissions to the Salon paired representations of the ballet and horse-racing with other images of the social and cultural world and established his reputation as a shrewd social observer.

A TIME OF REASSESSMENT

By the mid-1880s Degas was having doubts about the direction of his art. His work during these years is marked by a significant number of abandoned projects and pictures. The social observation that had prevailed in his art began to be replaced by new artistic preoccupations. Degas' later interest in the nude and the dance signalled a gradual withdrawal from the painting of modern life that had been central to his ideas from the late 1860s. In his later pictures of ballerinas there is a more exclusive focus on light and movement, and analysis of the social context of the ballet milieu disappears. His bathers are set in the interior world of the artist's studio and often make overt reference to traditional sources.

Degas was not alone in reassessing the direction of his art and turning away from representing the social world of

modern Paris. Renoir began to rethink his painting, journeying to Italy to study the old masters. On his return he, like Degas, became preoccupied with the nude and significantly altered his artistic style. There were subtle changes in the choice of motif of other Impressionists. In the late 1870s and 1880s Monet, now regarded as the leading landscapist of the group, replaced the ultra-modern Parisian and suburban motifs he had favoured in the 1870s with more remote landscape subjects, purged of figures, often producing seascapes that make much of the dramatic and monumental rock formations along the northern French coastline of Normandy and the countryside around Giverny. On settling in Giverny in 1883, Monet constructed a magnificent garden there that became his principal motif for the remainder of his life. Cézanne's landscape motifs also changed in this period. In the 1870s he had made many pictures of the modern landscape of L'Estaque, just outside the heavily industrial port of Marseille. In the late 1880s he turned his attention to more traditional and 'classical' motifs in Aix and the surrounding countryside, making the Montagne Sainte Victoire his major motif. Pissarro too reconsidered

Right: At the Café, by Degas, c.1875–77. *In the 1870s Degas sought to make modern life paintings that would rival the achievements of the old masters, though some of these remain unresolved.*

Above: The Bathers, *Pierre Auguste Renoir, 1887. Like Degas, Renoir began to reassess his work in the 1880s, drawing on the traditions of the Italian old masters.*

the path of his painting. Worried about the growing official acceptance and gradual absorption of Impressionism into the mainstream, albeit in diluted form, the most theoretically and politically minded of Impressionists temporarily abandoned it for the more scientific Pointilliste approach of Seurat's Neoimpressionism. Pissarro invited Seurat and Signac to exhibit with him at the final Impressionist exhibition in 1886, to the consternation of many of the other exhibitors, not least Degas.

A SUITE OF NUDES

In the 1880s the nude emerged as an important subject for Degas, giving rise to paintings that renewed this traditional subject in a distinctively modern fashion. Unlike nudes from earlier times, here the model is posed in a realistic setting, caught in a transient moment.

In the 1870s Degas was preoccupied with contemporary subjects such as ballet dancers, café-concert singers, race-horse scenes and the Parisian milieu. However, as he began to rethink his subject matter, he turned to the most traditional subject in art: the nude. This was not an entirely new direction. Degas had included nude studies in his submissions to the Impressionist exhibitions, but it was only now that he turned to the subject in earnest.

REMEMBERING INGRES
Not untypically, in turning toward the nude, Degas returned to earlier developments in his oeuvre. His unresolved *Young Spartans* was a picture he continued to reflect on. Yet it was the

memory of Ingres' masterpiece *The Valpinçon Bather*, a painting Degas particularly revered, that was continually revisited in his own nudes. Like Ingres' painting, most of these are bathers shown à la toilette and seen from behind or from an oblique angle that refers back to Ingres' example. The close proximity of the viewer to these figures provides a further parallel with Ingres' picture, creating a strong impression of intimacy and voyeurism. Gustave Geffroy wrote: "[The artist] wanted to paint a woman who did not know she was being watched, as one would see her hidden by a curtain or through a keyhole." Mauss remarked: "What Degas describes here is woman undressed, in her animal-like simplicity. ...He is solely

Above: The Tub, *by Degas, 1886. This painting, whose viewpoint is constructed from an unnaturally high perspective looking down on the nude below, creates a series of visual rhymes between the body and the props on the shelf.*

concerned with the woman who believes she is alone, absolutely alone, and who having discarded all coquetry, devotes herself...to the cares of her toilette.

RENEWING TRADITION
The nudes represent a renewed and more overt dialogue with traditional sources. *Woman in a Tub* (1884) alludes to a statue from antiquity, the *Crouching Venus* in the Louvre, while others refer to the nudes of Ingres, Rembrandt and

other old masters. As always, these traditional sources were reworked in an up-to-date fashion; his bathers are set in modern apartments or the artist's studio and refer to contemporary prints. This change in subject coincided with changes in media and technique that are typical of the synthesis of tradition and modernity in Degas' later work. Most of his bathers are pastels, but are often combined with oil paint and other materials to produce new technical effects.

From the 1880s on, the nude, along with ballet dancers, was his dominant subject. Nude figures and poses often reappear in his ballerinas and vice versa, revealing the close relationship between these works in his later oeuvre. Nudes formed the centrepiece of his pictures in the final Impressionist exhibition, listed under the title *Suite of Female Nudes, Bathing, Washing, Drying, Wiping, Combing Themselves and Being Combed.* He intended to show ten nudes, though only six or seven of these were included. This series was, however, a declaration of a change of direction and was followed, two years later, by a show of nine bathers at the Boussod & Valadon Gallery on boulevard Montmartre.

Contemporary critical reception recognized their originality, though was conditioned by his growing reputation

for misogyny and chauvinism. Their lack of idealization prompted one critic to describe them as "frank representations of the imperfections of the flesh". Octave Mirbeau was representative of the general reaction when he remarked

of them: "[These works] have not been done to inspire passion for women nor sensual desire. Degas has not sought beauty or grace…on the contrary there is a ferocity that speaks clearly of a disdain for women and a horror of love."

Below: Woman in a Tub, *by Degas, 1884. Many of Degas' nudes are seen from behind, thus increasing the intimacy.*

Above: After the Bath, *by Degas, 1895. Degas' technique builds up the surface from a range of pastel strokes.*

Below: Standing Nude, *by Degas, c.1886. Degas used this pose in several pictures, including some of the brothel monotypes.*

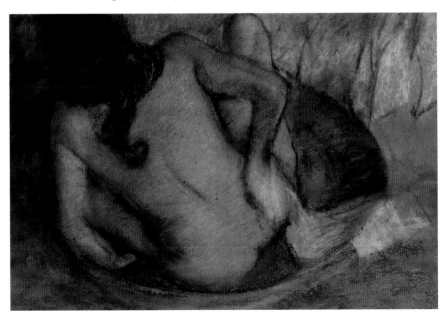

DEGAS THE TECHNICIAN

Degas was an artist at once more technically radical and more conservative than his Impressionist colleagues and his art was a continual, restless search for new techniques and methods. He once remarked, "Fortunately for me, I have not found my method; that would only bore me."

While Impressionist artists generally accepted the limitations of their relatively simple working methods and delighted in the spontaneity this afforded them, Degas revelled in experimenting with and discovering new techniques and technical procedures. At the same time he lamented the loss of the mysterious methods of the old masters and regarded his own period as one in which essential artistic knowledge and skill had disappeared irretrievably. We should remember the time in which he lived was one of fervent pursuit of technical progress, the desire for knowledge and the preservation of the past. There is something of the amateur scientist and connoisseur in Degas' passionate search for lost techniques. From the 1880s onward Degas progressively redefined his art around this restless experimentation with technique,

Right: After the Bath, Woman with a Towel, by Degas, c.1885–90. Degas became increasingly preoccupied with rediscovering the techniques of the old masters and uniquely developing his own.

sometimes ruining work as a result. Degas' desire for innovation also extended to rethinking the perceptual relationship of the viewer to the image. In Degas' work we are often made conscious of the position from which we view the picture. In exploring the possibilities of creating new and interesting viewpoints for his pictures, Degas assembled platforms around his studio so he could draw

Left: Danaë, by Tiziano Vecellio Titian, c.1554. The rich colour schemes, lush painterly technique and nudes of Venetian painters like Titian became increasingly important to Degas from the 1880s.

Above: Combing the Hair, *by Degas, 1892–95. The extraordinarily vibrant red tonality of this picture of a maid combing a woman's hair shows the strong influence Venetian painting exerted on Degas.*

the figure from an artificially high perspective. In his later years Degas' technique moved closer to the richly sensuous surfaces of Rococo and Venetian painters. Degas' late style parallels the loose, freely worked late manner of Titian, while his pastels owe much to the example of French Rococo artists.

A SELF-CONSCIOUS ART

Degas always emphasized the artifice of art. In the first part of his career, he was concerned with conveying a moment captured from the flow of the world around him, belying the fact that his art was the product of careful study and artistic contrivance. In his later years, his art revealed the technical processes of its manufacture, drawing the viewer into the act of making the image and the decision-making process it involved.

Degas' pastels and his monotypes from the 1880s reveal the physical intimacy of his working methods, bearing the imprint of the artist's hands smudging, smearing, rubbing the picture surface or printing plate, making and unmaking the image until he arrived at something satisfactory. The physical impression of the artist's manufacture of the work is also apparent in his sculpture. Many of the wax models show the gouging

marks of the various tools he used to model his figures but also preserve the fingerprints and impressions of Degas' hand working the surface of his materials. While testifying to Degas' way of working, these signs of fabrication also progressively become a theme of his painting.

THE ROCOCO REVIVAL

Degas' interest in Rococo art and 18th-century pastelists coincided with a reassessment of the French 18th-century tradition. Between 1856 and 1875, the Realist writers the Goncourt brothers published a series of well-researched articles on this period of French art that renewed their reputation. The richly sensual pictures of painters like Watteau (1684–1721) and Boucher (1703–70), and the delicate pastels of Quentin de la Tour (1704–88) and Jean-Baptiste Perronneau (1715–83), had been out of fashion in the first half of the 19th century but now received new attention.

Degas' earlier compositions refer to seminal paintings of artists he admired, or include paintings within paintings. His later works, in their re-working of repeated motifs or variations of particular compositions treated with different colour schemes, draw the viewer into reflecting on the artfulness of Degas' art.

Degas often drew on tracing paper and pieced multi-figure compositions together from a repertoire of stock figures whose poses he had successively refined over the years. Figures that first appear in his ballerina scenes later resurface in his bathers. "Make a drawing, begin it again, trace it; begin it again, and trace it again," is how he described his method, exemplifying his belief that "Art does not expand, it repeats itself." Degas also said: "Aren't all beautiful things made by renunciation?" His later pictures represent a paring away of the range of his artistic motifs to those most essential for his pursuit of movement and concern with the body.

Below: Jeanne Poisson (1721–64) the Marquise de Pompadour, *by Maurice Quentin de la Tour, (1704–88), 1755. Degas much admired and owned several of the exquisite pastels of the Rococo master Quentin de la Tour. These pastels inspired Degas to take up the medium.*

DEGAS' LANDSCAPES

After several years during which Degas exhibited no work, in 1892 he surprised the Parisian art world with an exhibition of landscapes at Durand-Ruel's gallery. The exhibition was thus an unexpected departure and reflected Degas' taste for unsettling expectations and reinventing himself.

Degas had been known as a painter of the figure, of Parisian scenes and more lately of nudes and dancers. He had shown an interest in landscape before: while in Italy in the 1850s, he had made many landscapes in watercolour documenting his travels around Naples and Rome. Landscape imagery had also featured as backdrops for his racing scenes and in the scenography of many ballerina pictures. *Beach Scene* (1869), which features several figures and yachts randomly scattered across a luminous landscape, had been the culmination of a series of small, limpid seascapes

Below: Beach scene: Little Girl Having her Hair Combed by her Nanny, *by Degas, c.1876–77. Though this picture compares with similar Monet and Boudin beach scenes of the 1860s, it was not executed en plein air, but posed in the studio.*

executed in the 1860s that reveal his interest in Eugène Boudin's (1824–98) impressionistic landscapes. However, this was the first time Degas had applied himself earnestly to a sustained series of pure landscape subjects.

Daniel Halévy claimed that Degas' landscapes were inspired by glimpses out of the window during train journeys. The broad, sometimes blurred, sweeping forms of many of these landscapes, devoid of any detail, suggest an instantaneous impression of a fugitive scene. Yet the range of effects Degas explored in these pictures indicates this was only a starting point. Many of these landscapes were small-scale, roughly worked monotypes overlaid with pastel. It may have been simply experimenting with the freely worked effects made possible by this flexible form of printing, which lent itself well to landscape.

Above: Landscape, by Degas, 1890–92. *Degas' landscapes often had an anthropomorphic quality, as in this picture.*

RESPONDING TO MONET

It seems likely Degas was inspired by Monet's hugely successful one-man shows at Durand-Ruel's gallery in the 1890s, where the painter showed only

one or two motifs in a series of variations. These emphasized the artist's range of responses, technical versatility and diverse tonal effects rather than the motif itself. Degas' exhibition of landscapes invited comparison with this new development in Monet's art. Nevertheless, despite technical similarities with Impressionist landscape painting, Degas' pictures were conceived very differently. Although often finishing his paintings in the studio, Monet travelled across the French countryside in search of suitable landscape subjects, basing his art on working directly in front of the motif and observing changes in the light and atmosphere.

Although Degas also travelled widely, journeying in the spring and summer of 1892 through the south-west of France and into Switzerland to visit one of his brothers in Geneva, as well as through the plains of Picardy and the valleys of Normandy, his landscapes were executed away from the motif and based entirely on memory. Degas did not make drawings during his travels and no notebooks or sketches of landscapes have survived from these years. Ingres had advised the young Degas: "Never work from nature, always from memory", advice Degas passed on to his own admirers. He had long been interested in Lecoq de Boisbaudran's memory-training techniques, designed to teach students to distil information

quickly from a motif and to enhance the artist's mastery of form.

VISUAL PUNS
These landscapes also show Degas' interest in the ethereal and evocative creations of a younger generation of Symbolist artists and writers, and won praise from critics associated with Symbolism. Some demonstrate Degas' love of visual puns and his interest in the tradition of anthropomorphic landscape, which was still very present

Above: Ravines of the Creuse at the End of the Day, *1889 by Claude Monet. This was one of a set of pictures of the ravines of the Creuse under different lighting conditions, exhibited together as part of Monet's series of one-man shows in the 1890s.*

in French art, literature and popular prints. Descriptions in the naturalistic novels of Zola and Maupassant often made great use of landscape imagery as metaphors for human feelings, imaginings and desires. *Steep Coast* (1892), which alludes to Monet's *Belle-Île* paintings, combines the undulating forms of the landscape with the contours of a recumbent female nude; Degas re-used the figure in *Woman Having Her Hair Combed* (1884–86), turning her body horizontally on her side. In *Landscape* (1890–92), the plausible naturalism of the pastures and dune-like horizon are combined with boulders that suggest the phallic form of a masculine body.

Left: Marine Sunset, *by Degas, c.1869. Though Degas criticized Impressionism's preoccupation with landscape painting, he had occasionally turned his hand to landscape and in the late 1860s produced a series of marines.*

LATE BATHERS AND BALLERINAS

From the 1890s onward ballerinas and bathers predominated in Degas' art. These works developed in close dialogue, with Degas often using the same figures for each subject. Making subtle variations to a standard array of poses, Degas explored the artistic possibilities of expression of the body in movement.

By the turn of the century Degas had become almost as famous for his nudes as his dancers. Women bathers à la toilette, mostly alone, though occasionally with a maid, became one of the great subjects of his art, one that allowed him to experiment with movement, colour and form. Degas' bathers, with their freely worked manner, richly saturated colour schemes and experiments with the point of view, drew critical praise as renewing the great tradition of the nude. Generally figures are seen from behind, unconscious of the painter's or viewer's gaze, washing and drying themselves,

Below: Seated Bather, by Degas, 1899. The pose of this bather recurs in a number of pictures, with the angle, viewpoint and colour scheme of the composition varied to obtain different effects.

Above: Woman Drying Herself, by Degas, 1889. The arched pose of this bather has a close relation to several figures that recur in his ballerina pictures.

or combing their hair. From a small number of careful poses Degas produces a diverse array of pictures. As with much of his later work, parallels are established between the application of the pastels to the surface of the paper and the movements of the bathers drying and rubbing their bodies.

LATE BALLERINAS

Degas made more than 200 pastels as well as many oil paintings, lithographs, charcoal drawings and sculptures of bathers in the last two decades of his working life, a total only exceeded by his depictions of ballerinas. Although he had painted ballerina pictures continuously since the 1870s, the pictures he produced from the late 1880s offer some distinctive features and reflect his artistic preoccupations of his later years. His earliest treatments had focused on the performance of the dancers on stage, and then of ballerinas in rehearsal. Though these subjects continued to interest Degas, the last phase of his ballerinas is marked by a new interest in the dancers waiting in the wings for the moment when they enter the stage. We see dancers expending nervous energy, fidgeting with their costumes, using their fans to keep cool, or watching the scene onstage in anticipation. However, such themes seem of less importance than the new decorative conception present in these pictures. Multi-figure compositions of groups of three or four figures, sometimes more, are arranged in compositional groupings in which figures are either presented in contrasting poses, or with subtly differentiated gestures that contain echoes and traces of each other. In many of these pictures ballerinas perform graceful dance steps in unison, their own individuality subordinated to the rhythm and movement of the dance. In others the effect is almost proto-cinematic, as a series of cascading gestures are threaded through a group of figures. In these compositions Degas explored how to suggest movement through slight adjustments of pose, and may have been influenced by Eadweard Muybridge's photographs of figures in movement, which he knew well.

COLOUR AND FORM

The sequential movement threaded through the dancers' choreography is also the movement of Degas' hand across the surface of the paper or canvas on which the dancers are given form. Continually we are made aware of the artist marking the picture surface and the "choreography" of the gestural vocabulary of his art. While in earlier ballet pictures Degas had also explored the social backgrounds of the dancers and the spaces of the Opéra in which the performance was viewed, later pictures eliminate such contextual information. Dancers are de-individualized and the sets in which they are depicted are reduced to generic scenography or decorative backdrops. Degas' attendance of the Opéra had

Above: Dancers in Blue, *by Degas, 1890. This was a favoured figure grouping of Degas' compositions during the 1890s and exists in a number of variations using different colour schemes.*

already peaked in the 1880s and he gave up his backstage pass. His later ballerinas show him increasingly working from memory and his own studies. As Gustave Geffroy said, the dynamics of colour and form gave direction to these compositions. Degas made several variations on particular motifs, exploring different tonal schemes and their expressive effects. In some his use of colour resembles the compositions of the Symbolist painters, with a cool, dominant blue or green tonality prevailing. In others he looked to the rich, warm tonality of Venetian artists.

Above: Dancer, *by Degas, 1882–95. This lightly worked pastel of a dancer adjusting her strap shows how Degas creates subtle variations of standard poses.*

CELEBRITY

By the 1880s Degas was recognized as a leading artist of his time and Impressionism began to receive official recognition and popularity. Degas once wrote "I want to be famous and unknown", but the art world was increasingly a world of celebrity where artists were marketed in terms of artistic personalities.

In a letter in the late 1880s, Pissarro noted: "Degas is without doubt at all the greatest artist of our time." This opinion was fast gaining ground. Degas did, though, have detractors. A heated comparison of the achievements of modern painters and novelists at a dinner party resulted in Degas being nominated as the only modern artist to have rivalled the achievements of the Naturalist novelists. Zola replied: "I cannot accept a man who shuts himself

Below: Dancers, by Degas, 1898. As Degas became more revered as an artist his work became more experimental, as illustrated by this stylized, loosely rendered scene of ballerinas backstage.

up all his life to draw a ballet-girl, as ranking co-equal in dignity and power with Flaubert, Daudet and Goncourt." Zola's response says more about his conservative views on art, but Degas' focus on a narrow subject range did lead some to question his achievement.

DEGAS THE SOLITARY

As Degas' art became more recognized, so he became more reclusive. Visitors and even old friends were made to feel unwelcome at his studio. Publicity and acclaim annoyed him. After reading a favourable article on him in *La Revue de Paris*, he said: "Is painting to be looked at? …One works for two or three friends and for others who are dead or

unknown, is it any business of journalists? …Painting concerns one's private life." Degas' comments reflected the way he felt art journalism created a taste for notoriety, inflating artists' reputations and prices for their work. From the mid-1880s onward he exhibited far less, turning down invitations to show at major exhibitions, including the Exposition Universelle of 1889. He also became more secretive, taking delight in contradicting expectations at times when he did exhibit.

Despite his apparent solitariness, Degas still led an active evening life, visiting the Opéra, the Théâtre des Variétés, Les Ambassadeurs and the Café Rochefoucauld. His reputation as an entertaining, if unpredictable, conversationalist meant he still received many dinner invitations such as from his old friends the Rouarts, with whom he shared a passion for collecting art. Henri Rouart had established an exceptional collection of Egyptian and antique sculpture and old and contemporary masters including 53 Corots, 15 Delacroixs and 15 of Degas' own works. Henri's brother Alexis had a collection of French and Japanese prints. Degas dined with him weekly. Degas' acute observation and occasionally cruel comments made him a fascinating but irascible companion, by turns charming, witty and malicious and apt to play up his reputation for misanthropy and spitefulness. For years Daniel Halévy kept a journal in which he noted Degas' witticisms. During a conversation with the dealer Ambroise Vollard he said: "I would have a brigade of gendarmes for keeping an eye on people who paint landscapes after nature".

DEGAS THE ART COLLECTOR

Commercial success allowed Degas to indulge a passion for buying art, assembling a collection of old and

Above: Rouen Cathedral, West Portal, Grey Weather, *by Claude Monet, 1894. Monet's series paintings shown in one-man shows met with international acclaim.*

Above: Four Dancers, *1903, by Degas. As Degas was increasingly celebrated as a painter of the ballet his pictures focused more narrowly on variations of stock compositions treated with different palettes.*

contemporary masters. He owned works by Tiepolo, El Greco and Jean-Baptiste Perronneau, as well as bronzes by Bayre and Bartholomé, and had a diverse collection of Japanese woodcuts. The majority of his collection was of 19th-century painters. As well as his 20 Ingres paintings, he owned 13 by Delacroix, seven Corots, seven Manets, eight Gauguins, seven Cézannes and two by Vincent van Gogh. He also had paintings by Bartholomé, Puvis de Chavannes, Renoir, Jeanniot, Legros, Lepic, Morisot, Pissarro, Daumier, Cassatt, Théodore Rousseau, Henri Rouart and Sisley. Monet was a notable omission. In addition, Degas collected Neapolitan puppets, and among his more unusual, and one suspects treasured artefacts, was a cast of Ingres' hand holding a pencil.

Right: Young Girls at the Piano, *by Pierre Auguste Renoir, 1892. The government bought this painting and one of Monet's Rouen Cathedrals for Musée Luxembourg.*

DEGAS AND LITERATURE

Degas had close relationships with some of the most important writers of his age and in later life wrote a number of sonnets. His work often shows affinities with the themes and imagery of contemporary novelists with whom he shared an artistically creative dialogue.

PAINTING AND LITERATURE

While the painter Odilon Redon once described Degas as having read "nothing, except some book or other of 1830", Degas appears to have cultivated a taste for French and Latin authors and was well versed in ancient and contemporary literature, with a particular penchant for the Romantic period. He could, nevertheless, be a fierce critic of the authors of his day, especially when they wrote about art, and also of literary references in painting. In abandoning his early career as an academic painter he was also abandoning the idea of literature and painting as sister arts, the informing idea of the classical tradition.

DEGAS AND THE NATURALIST NOVEL

As Degas moved toward Realism with depictions of the life and lifestyle of Paris, he was entering the terrain of Realist and Naturalist writers, like Zola, the Goncourt brothers, Alphonse Daudet and Guy de Maupassant. Degas knew several of these novelists socially, but seems to have shown little interest in their work. His personal dislike of Zola, who had come to notoriety in the 1860s in a series of novels that explored the seedier aspects of contemporary urban life, undoubtedly coloured his disdain of a writer whose work his pictures often seem to evoke. His art criticism also annoyed Degas, who described it as "puerile". Though Degas illustrated the Goncourt brothers' *The Prostitute Elisa* (1877) and perhaps secretly admired their elegant Realism, he regarded them as rivals, parodying and disparaging them in his letters. The work of Degas' close friend Edmond Duranty provides an exception; Degas shared Duranty's ideas of Realism and identified with his dryly ironical view of modern life.

DEGAS AND MALLARMÉ

Many of the younger Symbolist artists and writers who now came into contact with Degas admired him as an artist who shared Impressionism's experiments with form, without subscribing to its exclusive pursuit of nature. In Degas they found a more intellectually minded artist whose reverence of art echoed their own. Nevertheless, despite the admiration of leading Symbolist intellectuals like Paul Valéry (1871–1945), Octave Mirbeau (1848–1917), Gustave Geffroy (1855–1926), Joris-Karl Huysmans (1848–1907) and Camille Mauclair (1872–1945), Degas did not wholeheartedly embrace Symbolism, as demonstrated by his complex relationship with its leading poet Stéphane Mallarmé (1842–98). As early as 1876, Mallarmé had written an article indicating his admiration of Degas, whom he referred to as a "Master of drawing…and of a strange new beauty". Degas clearly

Left: Photograph depicting Auguste Renoir and Stéphane Mallarmé taken by Degas, (1895).

Above: Stéphane Mallarmé (1842–98), by Edouard Manet, 1876. Mallarmé was a close friend of both Manet and Degas and one of the leading writers associated with the Symbolist movement.

Right: A photograph of the naturalist writer Emile Zola taken by Eugene Pirou.

appreciated Mallarmé's reflective manner and subtle intelligence. In a photograph taken by Degas in 1895, which Valéry called the finest likeness of the poet he had ever seen, Mallarmé is shown leaning beside a mirror next to the seated Renoir; Degas himself appears as a spectral image reflected in the mirror alongside Mallarmé's wife and daughter. Despite the value Degas placed on their friendship, this did not prevent him from voicing his impatience with the complexities, hermeticism and super-subtlety of Mallarmé's thought and word play. When Mallarmé read his poignant tribute to the Symbolist writer

Villiers de l'Isle-Adam (1838–89), at a gathering at Berthe Morisot's studio, Degas alone stated he found it all too obscure and left before the end. On two separate occasions Degas agreed and then declined to provide images for an illustrated edition of Mallarmé's poems. Yet, despite artistic differences, it is clear Degas recognized the importance of Mallarmé's work, even if his poetry was not to his taste. One day, exasperated by his inability to finish a sonnet, he complained to Mallarmé: "It isn't ideas I'm short of…I'm full of them…I've got too many". In a response that one could imagine Degas himself making, Mallarmé replied: "But, Degas, you can't make a poem with ideas. …You make it with words."

DECLINING EYESIGHT

Degas' final years were blighted by the loss of his eyesight. Problems with his eyes had first become apparent in 1870, during his military interlude in the Franco-Prussian War and would influence the work he produced in the last two decades of his life.

If, as some friends suggested, Degas exaggerated the problems with his eyes in the 1870s, the gap between his "playing the role of the blind painter" and "the reality of it" was narrowing, according to the Degas biographer Roy McMullen. In photos from the last decade of his life Degas cuts a tragic figure, staring out of wounded eyes that appear hollow, like pools of darkness. Up until then, Degas continued to work, though his visual impairment affected both his working methods and the results. His pictures at the turn of the century could still be extraordinary. Etienne Moreau-Nélaton spoke admiringly of Degas' "vigorous, magnificent drawing" despite his "summary execution". His work from these years was less detailed, more lyrically abstract and vividly coloured. Dazzling bursts of coloured rain appear

to stream on to these canvases. This broader, more abstract quality of his work renewed his relevance to younger generations of painters, about whom Degas kept well informed.

While his damaged eyesight altered his style, it is difficult to know to what extent the increasingly strong colour in his pastels was the result of declining vision or a response to a current trend. Renoir, whom Degas valued above all other Impressionists, was heightening the colour of his pictures, to the point of garishness. The brilliance of the palette of artists associated with Fauvism, like Henri Matisse (1869–1954), and André Derain (1880–1954) and Symbolists like Gauguin, Odilon Redon (1840–1916), the Nabis and his friend Gustave Moreau, may possibly have encouraged Degas to push further in the direction of brilliant colour, which had already surfaced in his

Above: Five Dancers on Stage, *by Degas, c.1906–08. Degas captures the moment before the event begins, as here, where dancers limber up for performance.*

work in the mid-1880s. Degas' use of a predominant hue or prevailing tonality in many of his later pictures was certainly consistent with contemporary experiments in monochromatic effects often favoured by Symbolist painters to create a particular ambience or mood. To what extent Degas was responding to these tendencies or following the logical conclusions of his own course remains a matter of debate.

PASTEL AND SCULPTURE

Working in pastel helped maintain Degas' productivity. It encouraged a broad and less detailed way of working than oil painting and his pictures with their touches, smudges and streaks of pastel dragged across the picture surface suggest an ever more tactile method of working in these years. When his eyes were poor, Degas turned to sculpture, modelling in wax the subjects he had become accustomed to representing in

Left: Two Dancers at Rest *or,* Dancers in Blue, *by Degas, c.1898. Though the motif of dancers resting and nursing their weary limbs was a familiar one, Degas brought a more decorative, semi-abstract vision to the theme in his later work.*

Above: Before the Performance, *by Degas, c.1896–98. The elaborate choreography of the figures and rich and bold colour schemes of his later pastels are a marked feature of Degas' late work.*

his illustrative art. Though he complained of how time-consuming sculpture was, his work as a sculptor helped sustain him through the difficult years of his later life.

INCREASING BLINDNESS
Toward the end of the century Degas' productivity became fitful. At times his eyes were too painful to work, and he would become despondent. In a letter to Alexis Rouart, Henri's son, Degas wrote of long intervals when he was "unable to see" and feeling "guilty, stupid, unworthy" when he could not work. To Alexis' son Jean, he remarked on his difficulty in

Right: Four Ballerinas on the Stage, *by Degas, c.1897–1901. Degas' later ballet pictures show complex, de-individualized figure groupings where gestures are interlaced across the group to achieve harmony and decorative effect.*

managing to read or write and to Alexis he expressed his fears of going blind. By the time of a visit to the Ingres' retrospective in 1911, his eyesight had further declined. Degas remarked how he struggled to make out anything he was not already very familiar with. By this

point Degas was no longer travelling as he had in the previous decade, though he still delighted in taking streetcars around Paris until he became incapacitated. He was still drawing and producing works in pastel, though little of lasting value emerged after 1907.

THE DREYFUS AFFAIR

A long, drawn-out national crisis was sparked off by the notorious Dreyfus Affair in 1894, dividing opinion in France. Captain Dreyfus was accused of passing French military information to Germany. For Degas it was to have important consequences, ending close relationships that had sustained him throughout his life.

On 26 September 1894, a cleaner working at the German embassy in Paris turned over some papers to the French counter-espionage bureau. These included a bordereau of French military equipment for the Alsatian frontier and other confidential military information. Suspicion for the release of this information quickly settled on Captain Alfred Dreyfus, an Alsatian Jew, and an unpopular member of the general staff. Though no motive could be found, the press concluded Dreyfus' guilt. On 22 December 1894, a military court-martial, held in camera, sentenced Dreyfus to life imprisonment and he was deported to the coast of Guiana.

The Dreyfus Affair resonated in a context of growing political and economic uncertainty. Anti-semitism was strongly present in French society but acquired a new scale and intensity in a period of economic and political volatility. The rise of social Darwinism and new forms of dissenting patriotism informed by eugenics and fears of national decline gave pseudo-legitimacy to longstanding forms of racial prejudice. In 1886 the pamphleteer Edouard Drumont published a savage polemic against the influence of Jews in France, *La France Juive (Jewish France)*, which became a bestseller, and later published a newspaper, *La Libre Parole (Free Speech)*, that became notorious for its anti-semitic sentiment. Denunciation of Jewish bankers and the belief in the incompatibility of Jews and traditional French values were common on all sides of the political spectrum and grew more vocal in the wake of the humiliation of the Franco-Prussian war. French Jews were in general committed to assimilation, but many of the 50,000 French Jews were formerly from Alsatian Germany and bore German surnames, and this fuelled prejudice, as did the visible presence in Paris of many

internationally successful Jewish financiers. It was in this context of hypersensitivity to racism, militarism, nationalism and corruption that the events of the Dreyfus Affair took place.

DEGAS AND THE AFFAIR

Initially, Degas seemed little affected by the events of the Dreyfus Affair, though by November Daniel Halévy, Ludovic's son, noted in his journal: "Degas…has become a passionate believer in anti-semitism." Around this time, Degas had his maid Zoé read

Above: "Dreyfus est un traitre", *Publicity poster with the portraits of Dreyfus' accusers, late 19th century.*

La Libre Parole aloud to him along with Henri Rochefort's equally disreputable newspaper *L'Intransigeant*. The relationship with the Halévys, who were representative of France's assimilated Jews had deepened as a result of the many deaths of Degas' close friends. These included Manet, Caillebotte, Paul Valpinçon, Edmondo Morbilli, Berthe Morisot, his brother Achille and sister

Right: A Caricature of "J'Accuse", *the article written by Emile Zola (1840–1902) in defence of Alfred Dreyfus, 1898.*

Marguerite de Gas Fèvre, the latter an especially bitter blow.

By the summer of 1896 doubt about Dreyfus' guilt re-surfaced as suspicion fell on Major Marie-Charles-Ferdinand Walsin-Esterhazy as the real author of the bordereau, and the newspaper *L'Eclair* revealed irregularities in the process of the trial. By the following year, a number of influential people, including Clemenceau, began militating for a new trial. On 13 January 1898 Zola published his famous open letter to the President of the Republic, *J'Accuse*, which re-intensified the debate, dividing the nation into two camps, Dreyfusards and anti-Dreyfusards. Despite mounting evidence that eventually led to Dreyfus' exoneration in 1906, belief in the integrity of the military and blinkered patriotism, spurred by chauvinism and prejudice, encouraged many anti-Dreyfusards to hold fast to their position. Degas was one of them and remained intransigent. Valéry recollected: "Degas had political ideas. They were simple, peremptory, essentially Parisian. At the slightest indication he inferred, he exploded, he broke off. 'Adieu, Monsieur', and he turned his back on his adversary forever…. Politics in the Degas style were inevitably like himself – noble, violent, impossible". In the weeks leading up to the court-martial of Esterhazy and the publication of Zola's *J'Accuse*, Degas broke with the Halévys, as well as Pissarro and many other Jewish friends.

ZOLA'S *J'ACCUSE*

By the time of the publication of *J'Accuse*, Zola was recognized as one of France's greatest but most controversial contemporary writers. Besides his fame as a novelist, he had been a successful

journalist and his open letter, published on the front page of the Parisian newspaper *L'Aurore*, to the President of the Republic was designed for maximum impact. It was a brave gesture and an eloquent dissection and dismissal of the conduct of the case against Dreyfus. It was also widely seen as a manifestation of the new power of "intellectuals" (writers, artists and academicians), as Clemenceau named them, in shaping public opinion.

Right: At the Stock Exchange, *by Degas, c.1878–79. Degas portrays the world of the stock exchange as a place of corruption. The figure at the centre of the intrigue perhaps suggests Degas' anti-semitism.*

FINAL YEARS

Degas' final years were difficult and lonely ones, with diminishing productivity. He struggled with the limitations of his ill-health and was now an artist who had survived the failure of his powers and outlived his times. His last years saw him isolated, unhappy and in sharp physical and mental decline.

As Degas grew older his reputation for eccentricity, obstinacy and misanthropy increased. The critic Gustave Coquiot described him as a "skulking martinet and timorous bourgeois", and Degas is immediately recognizable as Hubert Feuillery, the hyper-sensitive, misogynistic painter of ballet dancers in Mauclair's novel *The City of Lights* (1903). His artistic reputation, however, continued to grow. In 1911, 19 of his pictures were accepted directly into the Louvre, an honour usually bestowed posthumously. The news did little to raise his mood. As his health declined, Degas, who was never satisfied by his past achievements, quick to anger when critics praised his work, or his pictures fetched high prices at auction, was robbed of the fundamental faith which sustained him, his belief in his future artistic progress.

DECLINING HEALTH

Degas was now troubled by bronchitis and intestinal and bladder problems. He was ageing rapidly, no longer recognizable as the elegant dandy who used to regularly attend the Opéra. In 1904 Daniel Halévy recalled after a visit to his studio, "I had a little shock at seeing him before me, dressed like a tramp, an emaciated man – another man." The ageing process hastened in 1910. Degas stopped trimming his beard and cutting his hair. Valéry around this time commented: "I reflected that this man had been elegant, that his manners, when he wished, had the most natural sort of distinction. …Here he was, a nervous old man, nearly always gloomy, sometimes inattentive in a sinister, perfidious fashion, given to sudden spells of anger or wit, to childish impatience and impulsiveness."

Above: The critic Thadée Natanson described Degas in his later years as looking like "an unemployable Montmartre model for God the Father".

In 1912 Degas was told his lease at 37 rue Victor-Massé would not be renewed and the building was to be demolished. He had lived and worked there for 20 years and this was a severe blow. Around this time he received news of his sister Thérèse's death, which hit him hard. The passing of old friends had left him more isolated and increased his awareness of his own mortality. Though friends rallied round, his refusal to move from the 9th arrondissement, where he had been brought up, made it difficult to find a suitable new home. After much delay Degas eventually moved a short distance to a fifth-floor apartment at 6 boulevard de Clichy. The vast accumulation of objects and artworks that were transported to the new home

Left: A portrait photograph of Edgar Degas and his maid Zoe by Roger-Viollet.

Above: Degas with his family and friends the Rouarts. From left to right, back to front row: Saint-Maurice, Lalo, Poujaud, Alexis Rouart (1869–1921), Julie Manet (1878–1966) wife of Ernest Rouart, Valentine Rouart, Madelaine Rouart, Edgar Degas (1834–1917), Loulou de Saint-Maurice, by Ernest Rouart (1874–1942), 1900–01.

remained mostly in their packing cases and, according to Vollard, Degas could sometimes be seen revisiting the location of his old apartment peering through the fence into the demolition site.

Unable to work or read, his mental faculties and health declined quickly and he became ever more indifferent and detached, even when at the end of August 1914 the distant boom of German artillery guns massed around

Right: A photograph of the forlorn Degas on his deathbed.

the Marne could be heard in Paris. At 80 he had long lost his enthusiasm for travel, but he continued to walk the streets of Paris. By 1916 he had become bedridden. Shortly after midnight on 27 September 1916, aged 83, he died of a cerebral congestion, after receiving

extreme unction from a canon of the Cathedral of Notre-Dame. A modest service attended by many of his friends and followers, including Cassatt, Forain, Zandomeneghi, Durand-Ruel and Monet, was held at Saint-Jean-L'Evangéliste, in Montmartre cemetery.

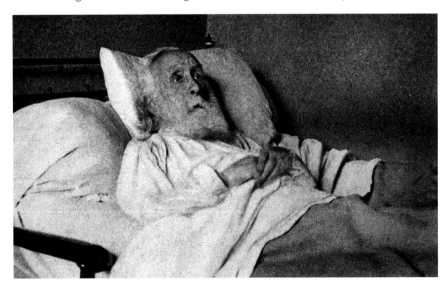

DEGAS' LEGACY

Even in his own lifetime Degas' art exerted a powerful influence on other artists. His legacy extends beyond this to the way his work imprints itself on how we view the world. Degas has remained one of the most influential of modern artists and his pictures still remain fresh and relevant today.

Degas' reputation as one of the great modern painters was assured by the end of his life. By the 1880s Degas' work had been discussed exhaustively in contemporary art magazines and his paintings disseminated internationally through reproductions. In 1886 several works by Degas included in the Caillebotte bequest of Impressionist paintings entered the Musée Luxembourg. One of the earliest histories of Impressionism, Camille Mauclair's *The French Impressionists* (1903), recognized the importance of his contribution to the modern tradition: "Degas has exercised an occult, but very serious, influence. He has lived alone, without pupils and almost without friends…. But all modern draughtsmen have been taught a lesson by his painting…and the young generation considers Degas as a master." By the mid-20th century Degas' paintings and sculptures had been collected by most major museums of art, consolidating his position in the history of modern art.

Above: Degas' View, by Nick Cudworth, (b.1947), 2006. Cudworth emphasizes the role of artistic dialogue with the legacy of Degas.

DEGAS' INFLUENCE

As younger artists in the 1890s began to react against the onus placed on appearances and nature in Impressionism and turn to a more cerebral approach, Degas was still held in respect. Symbolist artists admired the psychology of his portraits and his combination of technical innovation and knowledge of tradition. His nudes were emulated by younger artists. The paintings of Pierre Bonnard (1867–1947), Edouard Vuillard (1868–1940) and Suzanne Valadon (1865–1938), whose work Degas encouraged, admired and collected, owe much to his work. The nudes and interiors of Bonnard are unimaginable without Degas' example.

Likewise, Degas' exploration of Parisian life continued to be influential, especially on Toulouse-Lautrec. Lautrec was to become one of the foremost

illustrators and painters of his generation. His coloured lithographic posters advertising Parisian nightclubs and cabarets seem to define the belle époque. Lautrec was drawn to the bohemian life of Montmartre and his art documented this world of artists, dancers, nightclubs and prostitution. It was a world that Degas had already exhaustively charted and Lautrec's indebtedness is evident in his subjects, his unorthodox composition, vibrant colours and innovative draughtsmanship.

Degas' influence extended to other parts of Europe. In Britain he found a critical following in the 1870s. The artist William Quiller Orchardson (1832–1910) was an early admirer, but it was Walter Sickert (1860–1942), who was most affected by his art. Sickert shared Degas' love for the artifice and ambience of the theatre and responded to his interest in unusual lighting effects and surprising viewpoints, as well as his psychological portraits and nudes. Many Sickert paintings have specific references to Degas' works. Degas' *Interior* was the inspiration behind Sickert's *Ennui* (1914), which shares its claustrophobic ambience and alienated figures. Sickert was not alone in his admiration. The portraits and genre scenes of Walter Stott (1857–1900), Philip Wilson Steer (1860–1942) and James Guthrie (1859–1930) all reveal Degas' influence.

Today, Degas is recognized as one of the greatest artists of all time and his paintings, pastels and sculpture have continued to influence and inspire. His art has changed the way we see the world.

Below: At the Moulin de la Galette, *1899 and (Right)* The Hangover, *1889, by Henri de Toulouse-Lautrec, (1864– 1901). Lautrec's portrayal of the demi- monde of cafés and café-concerts indelibly identified him as a follower of Degas.*

THE GALLERY

Part two of this book examines the works of Degas broadly in chronological order and is divided into three sections. The first part deals with the paintings and pastels of Degas. The second section deals with his drawings, and the third with his sculpture. In comparing Degas' works as one looks through the gallery one can see how he developed and redeveloped certain motifs, his exacting method of working, and the fertile dialogue between his drawing and painting and his sculpture. Indeed, as with other artists associated with Impressionism, distinguishing between Degas' drawings, sketches and prints and his finished paintings and pastels becomes increasingly difficult in his later career from the 1880s on. Each aspect of Degas' work deeply informed and transformed the other. While Degas began as an oil painter, his later more hybrid and experimental pastel technique owed much to the art of drawing. Though Degas' themes in later life were relatively limited they were explored in an extraordinarily expansive and exhaustive fashion.

Left: Dance School, 1874, by Degas. Degas is best known for his ballet dancers, bathers and race-horse scenes.

PAINTINGS
AND PASTELS

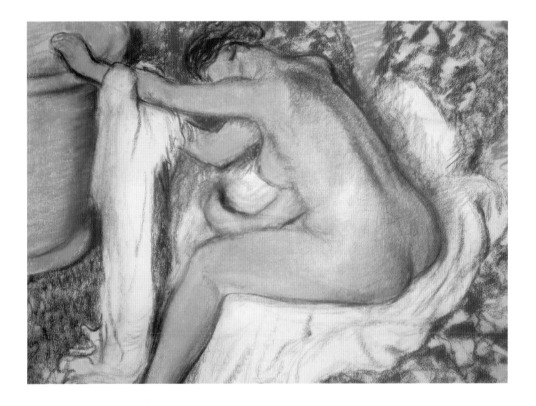

Degas was one of the greatest painters of the 19th century. A traditionalist by nature, he nevertheless produced an original and innovative body of work. From the 1880s onwards his oeuvre is characterized by a narrow group of themes and motifs that he continually explored in numerous variations. Degas' pictures from the first half of his career show him responding to the modernity of the new Paris, while his later work focused on movement of the body, and the expressive possibilities of painting and pastel unconstrained by the demands of realism and mimesis.

Above: Leaving the Bath (La Sortie du Bain), *1885.*
Left: Dancers, c.*1899, pastel on board, private collection, 53 x 39cm (21 x 15¼in).*

The Castel Sant'Elmo, Naples, from the Capodimonte, 1856, oil on paper laid down on canvas, Fitzwilliam Museum, University of Cambridge, UK, 20 x 27cm (8 x 10½in)

This view of the Castel Sant'Elmo was one of a number of landscapes Degas made while travelling through Naples. Most of the landscapes feature landmarks of historical interest. The castle was commissioned in 1329 by Charles of Anjou and was completed in 1343. Degas may have been attracted to it as a motif that expressed the historical ties between France and Naples.

Meadow by the River, c.1856, pastel, private collection, 23 x 38cm (9 x 15in)

During his prolonged stay in Italy during the late 1850s, Degas made more than 60 images of the landscape in a variety of media, including watercolour, pencil, ink, gouache, oil and pastel. These convey Degas' love of the Italian landscape and its classical ruins. Most of these pictures are small, minimal and closely follow the example of the Italian landscapes of the French painter Camille Corot.

Study of the Head of a Young Singer, after Luca della Robbia, *c.*1856–58, oil on canvas, Musée d'Orsay, Paris, France, 29 x 21cm (11½ x 8¼in)

This haunting painting, after a study of Luca della Robbia's (1400–82) remarkable *Cantoria* (singing gallery) (1431–38), was probably executed during Degas' time studying in Florence. Degas devoted much time to copying after Renaissance classical statuary. *Cantoria* would undoubtedly have attracted him for its naturalism and musical subject.

*David and Goliath, c.*1857, oil on canvas, Fitzwilliam Museum, University of Cambridge, UK, 64 x 80cm (25 x 31½in)

During his years studying in Italy, Degas worked on various projects but often struggled to bring them to fruition. His intention was to make his debut at the Salon with a history painting. This painting of *David and Goliath* shows his growing admiration for the bold compositions of Delacroix, Ingres' nemesis, in its loose drawing and painterly execution.

Portrait of Madame Ducros, 1858, oil on canvas, Musée Marmottan, Paris, France, 33 x 24cm (13 x 9½in)

Degas made this portrait of Madame Ducros, while in Rome, along with other portraits of her family. It is one of a number of such pictures of women posed next to a mirror, a compositional convention heavily influenced by Ingres' portraits of women. The handling of paint, however, shows the influence of Delacroix, whose work was beginning to have a strong attraction for Degas.

Self Portrait, c.1858, oil on paper, Musée de la Ville de Paris, Musée du Petit-Palais, France

This self-portrait of Degas, aged 24, is one of many portraits he made of himself in the 1850s. Although the summary modelling shows the work is unfinished, it indicates Degas' ability to convey the psychology of his subject and establish a strong mood. The pose of the figure turning toward the viewer enhances the picture's sense of intimacy.

René-Hilaire de Gas,
grandfather of the artist,
*c.*1859, oil on canvas,
Musee d'Orsay,
Paris, France,
25.5 x 25cm (10 x 9¾in)

This understated picture of René-Hilaire reading was made during Degas' stay at his grandfather's palazzo in Naples, shortly before his grandfather's death. A study in chiaroscuro (the depiction of light and dark in a composition), Degas allows the morning sunlight, streaming into the darkened room from the unseen left-hand window, to gently model the features of his grandfather's face. The soft brushwork is reminiscent of that of Venetian artists, while the artistic style shows his interest in Dutch 17th-century Realism.

Alexander and Bucephalus,
1859–61, oil on paper,
private collection

This is a preparatory watercolour for one of Degas' earliest history paintings, *Alexander and Bucephalus*. The theme, relayed in Plutarch, represents the guileful young Alexander at the court of his father Philip of Macedonia. Alexander is shown breaking in a wild steed after the failure of his father's trainers to do so. The picture was the first of several major history paintings by Degas in the 1860s to feature equestrian motifs.

The Finding of Moses,
after a painting by Veronese,
1860s, oil on canvas,
Fitzwilliam Museum,
University of Cambridge,
UK, 31 x 17cm
(12¼ x 6½in)

In the 19th century the
Venetian artist Paolo
Veronese (1528–88) was
considered one of the
greatest old masters and his,
much-copied *Wedding at
Cana* (1562–63) was one of
the highlights of the Louvre
collection. Veronese
produced several versions of
The Finding of Moses, one of
his finest compositions.
Degas copied only the left
section of the version from
the Musée des Beaux-Arts,
Lyons, France.

Calvary, after a painting by
Andrea Mantegna, *c.*1861,
oil on canvas, Musée des
Beaux-Arts, Tours, France,
69 x 92.5cm (27 x 36½in)

This is a copy of the
centre of the predella of a
monumental altarpiece
painted by Andrea Mantegna
(1431–1506) for the
Benedictine monastery of
San Zeno in Verona.
It was relocated in the
19th century to the Louvre,
where Degas copied it.
Mantegna was much admired
by Degas who had an
appreciation for early Italian
Renaissance masters.

At the Races: The Start, c.1860–62, oil on canvas, Fogg Art Museum, Harvard University Art Museums, USA, 33 x 47cm (13 x 18½in)

One of the first racing scenes Degas made, this small painting is based on a race he had witnessed in Normandy in the 1860s and shows a lake or bay in the background. The picture combines Degas' love of the races with his interest in the crowds who attended to watch. Many of Degas' pictures of racing capture the nervous energy at the beginning of the race.

Gentlemen Race, Before the Departure, 1862, oil on canvas, Musée d'Orsay, Paris, France, 48.5 x 61.5cm (19 x 24¼in)

Degas began this painting in 1862, but reworked it two decades later around 1882–83, when his dealer Durand-Ruel bought it. He altered some of the riders and probably added the hill and smokestacks. The initial painting was probably of the races at Argentan, near Ménil-Hubert, where his friends the Valpinçons had an estate. In reworking the painting Degas re-located the race to the gloomy, industrialized suburbs of Paris.

Portrait of Léon Bonnat,
c.1863, oil on canvas, Musée
Bonnat, Bayonne, France,
43 x 36cm (17 x 14in)

Léon Bonnat (1833–1922)
was a French naturalist
painter renowned for his
religious paintings and his
portraits of contemporary
celebrities and statesmen.
The critics Émile Zola and
Théophile Gautier were
among his many admirers.
He went on to become a
professor at the École des
Beaux-Arts in 1882 and was
awarded the Legion
d'Honneur. Degas had
known Bonnat since his
schooldays at the Lycée
Louis-le-Grand.

Thérèse de Gas (1842–95),
sister of the artist, later
Madame Edmondo Morbilli,
c.1863, oil on canvas,
Musée d'Orsay, Paris,
France, 89 x 67cm
(35 x 26in)

This elegant, though sombre
picture of the artist's sister
shows the influence of
Ingres as well as Bronzino in
its style and conception.
Bronzino's elegant female
portraits with their idealized
but understated
characterization and careful
attention to costume detail
left a strong and enduring
impression on Degas. It also
reflects his interest in austere
Spanish portraiture. Degas
depicts Thérèse, aged 23, in
the year of her engagement
to her first cousin, Edmondo
Morbilli, and would later
immortalize the couple in a
series of double portraits.

Portrait of Princess Pauline von Metternich, c.1865, oil on canvas, National Gallery, London, 40 x 29cm (15½ x 11½in)

This portrait demonstrates Degas' favourite presentation of his sitters in informal poses, turning either toward or away from the viewer.

The picture was based on a carte-de-visite photograph by André Disderi (1819–89) of Pauline von Metternich, whose husband had become Austro-Hungarian ambassador at the court of Napoléon III in 1859. Degas hoped that its exhibition at the Salon might attract wealthy clients.

Dead Fox Lying in the Undergrowth, 1865, oil on canvas, Musée des Beaux-Arts, Rouen, France, 173 x 92cm (68 x 36in)

The subject of this vigorously worked painting is unusual for Degas, but reflects his interest in the work of Courbet in the 1860s. Degas experimented with Courbet's colour, brushwork and palette-knife technique in several pictures around this time. Here he copies the recurring theme of hunting in Courbet's pictures of the period, which feature slain animals.

Portrait of a Man, c.1866, oil on canvas, Brooklyn Museum of Art, New York, USA, 85 x 64.5cm (33½ x 25in)

In the mid-1860s Degas began to shift his attention from history paintings to portraiture. In this portrait we see Degas posing his model in a relaxed manner with a sheet draped behind the sitter to neutralize the background. This indicates Degas was exploring the theme of the model posing for the artist. In this way the portrait becomes about the act of painting a portrait rather than simply about the sitter's identity.

Morning Ride, c.1866,
oil on canvas, Detroit
Institute of Arts, USA,
85 x 65cm (33½ x 25½in)

It is likely that Degas made
this sketch while visiting the
Valpinçons' estate at
Ménil-Hubert. The coastline
in the picture's background
suggests Normandy as a
plausible setting. The scale of
the picture indicates that
Degas intended to make an
ambitious painting structured
around a central grouping of
three riders with an intruder
entering from the left. The
painting was left in a
provisional state. The
ominous ochre sky is actually
only the underpainting.

The Collector of Prints, 1866,
oil on canvas, The
Metropolitan Museum of
Art, New York, USA,
53 x 40cm (21 x 15½in)

Inspired by Daumier's images
of collectors, Degas shows
his anonymous collector
rummaging through a
portfolio of prints. This
picture marks the advance
of Degas' portraits in the
mid-1860s, showing the
increasingly sophisticated use
of environmental settings in
his portraits, which serve to
define the status and
character of his sitters but
also have interest in their
own right.

Portrait of Joséphine Gaujelin, 1867, oil on mahogany panel, Hamburger Kunsthalle, Hamburg, Germany, 35 x 26.5cm (13½ x 10½in)

Joséphine Gaujelin was a dancer in the Paris Opéra's corps de ballet at the rue le Peletier during the Second Empire. Afterwards she became an actress at the Théâtre du Gymnase, a theatre renowned for romantic comedies and popular dramas. Degas portrayed her in several ballerina pictures including *The Dancing Class* (1870). Here, though, he portrays her as a demure and fashionable young woman.

Madame Gaujelin, 1867, oil on canvas, Isabella Stewart Gardner Museum, Boston, MA, USA, 61 x 45.5cm (24 x 18in)

Degas was fond of this rather sombre portrait commissioned by Joséphine Gaujelin and submitted it to the Salon exhibition of 1869. Joséphine is seated on a cream chair and red paisley shawl in her dressing room, following a performance. Dressed in black, she also wears a black bonnet that is decorated with grapes. The portrait shows her looking glum, bored and rather highly strung. Despite Degas' satisfaction with what was probably his first commissioned picture, Joséphine was furious and refused to pay for it

Study for a Portrait of a Lady,
1867, oil on canvas,
Hamburger Kunsthalle,
Hamburg, Germany,
75 x 84cm (29½ x 33in)

This unusual portrait of
an unidentified woman
conforms to Degas'
preference in his earlier
painting for poses that show
the figure turning toward the
viewer. The woman wears
very pale make-up and is
dressed in a way that
suggests she is about to
depart. Her gloved left hand
rests nonchalantly on the
back of the chair in a pose
that serves as much to
define her as does her rather
cool, reserved gaze.

Portrait of Paul Valpinçon,
c.1868, oil on canvas,
private collection,
32.5 x 24cm (13 x 9½in)

Degas had known Paul
Valpinçon since childhood
and they studied together at
the Lycée Louis-le-Grand.
Throughout his life, Degas
frequently visited Ménil-
Hubert, the Valpinçons'
country estate, in

Normandy. This portrait was
probably a study for a
portrait of Paul and his new
bride. Degas posed the
sitter in three-quarters
profile, conforming to the
traditional convention of
portraits of aristocratic
sitters, which emphasizes the
sitter's physiognomy and
creates an impression of
detachment.

Racehorses, c.1868, oil on canvas, The Barnes Foundation, Merion, Pennsylvania, USA

This oil sketch is one of Degas' earliest surviving horse-racing pictures showing riders preparing for a race. The landscape is sparse, as in many Degas landscapes of the 1860s, and the focus of the picture is the vibrant colour visible in the jockeys' tunics and the horses. The contrasting poses of the horses animate the picture and create a shallow sense of depth akin to bas-relief sculpture.

Racehorses (Leaving the Weighing) c.1868–72, oil on panel, private collection, 32.5 x 40.5cm (13 x 16in)

Degas' images of horse-racing show all aspects of the race, but many focus on the nervous moments leading up to the start. Here Degas shows the riders leaving the weigh-in and making their way to the starting line. The horses are posed naturally and randomly, with no impression of any artistic choreography. In the background a rider struggles to control his horse, a detail often present in Degas' pictures of the track.

The Laundress, c.1869, oil on canvas, Neue Pinakothek, Munich, Germany, 92.5 x 74cm (36½ x 29in)

Laundresses were a favourite subject of Degas in the late 1860s and early 1870s and formed part of his imagery of working class Parisian women. They were also a common motif of 19th-century visual culture and an object of erotic delectation on account of their customary state of deshabille while they worked. This scantily clothed laundress, staring at the viewer, draws on these associations. The motif also found expression in literature, notably in Zola's *L'Assommoir* (1877), which charts the rise and decline of a laundress called Gervaise Macquart.

Fishing Boats Moored at the Entrance to a Port, c.1869, pastel on paper, private collection, 23 x 33cm (9 x 13in)

Many of Degas' marine pictures were executed at the port of Dives-sur-Mer, near Houlgate on the Normandy coast. This picture of the harbour shows jetties and anchored boats in the near distance. Degas has suggested the beach by leaving the cream paper exposed, concentrating on the cloud formations in the large expanse of sky.

Marine Sunset, c.1869, pastel on paper, private collection, 21.5 x 30cm (8½ x 12in)

Degas' depictions of the sea often border on the abstract; a few notations on the horizon indicate some yachts on the far side of the bay. These landscapes are mood pieces that recall the critic Jules Champfleury's description of the landscapes of Antoine Chintreuil (1814–73): "One does not describe a landscape by Chintreuil; it is an emotion".

Beside the Sea, 1869, pastel, private collection 24 x 31cm (9½ x 12¼in)

In this extraordinary marine painting, attention focuses on the low skyline and the changeable climate of the sky, with figures reduced to mere staffage. Though modest in conception, such pictures pose the question of how great a landscape painter Degas might have been but for his prejudice against Impressionist landscapes. For the majority of his career he saw landscape merely as a background for his figures.

*Boat on the Beach, c.*1869, pastel on paper, private collection, 23 x 32cm (9 x 12½in)

Degas was one of many artists that made paintings of the beaches and resorts of the Channel Coast in the 1860s. Courbet worked at Etreat, while Boudin and Daubingy installed themselves in Trouville. Monet, Manet and Chintreuil also favoured the surrounding area. At Dives-sur-Mer and Villers-sur-Mer, Degas worked on many beach scenes informed by their example and the memory of the landscapes of Camille Corot. These small-scale, minimal landscapes with their broad expanses of space possess a tranquillity and subtle, understated poetry that reveals what a versatile painter Degas was.

Houses on the Cliff Edge at Villers-sur-Mer, 1869, pastel on paper, Wadsworth Atheneum, Hartford, Connecticut, USA, (bequest of Anne Parrish Titzell), 31 x 47cm (12¼ x 18½in)

Most of Degas' landscapes at Villers-sur-Mer take the bay and cliffs as their main motif. In some, Degas includes architectural features of the landscape, sometimes in isolation on the surrounding hills or, as here, in clusters around the cliffs. Though the picture is rendered in an atmospheric, softly brushed style, Degas individualizes the houses with their distinctive gables, chimney stacks and turrets. He was fascinated by the interface of nature and culture and the way the architecture echoes and contrasts with the varied forms of the landscape.

Mademoiselle Marie Dihau (1843–1935) at the Piano, c.1869–72, oil on canvas, Musée d'Orsay, Paris, France, 45 x 32.5cm (17¾ x 12¾in)

Marie Dihau was the sister of Degas' friend, the Opéra bassoonist and composer Désiré Dihau, and a talented musician in her own right. Here she is shown at the piano as if interrupted in the course of playing the musical score which rests on the piano lid. This was one of two portraits that Degas made of her. Marie was also painted years later by Toulouse-Lautrec, a distant cousin, and John Singer Sargent (1856–1925).

Orchestra Musicians, 1870–76, oil on canvas, Stadelsches Kunstinstitut, Frankfurt, Germany, 69 x 49cm (27 x 19in)

Degas' images of ballet performances often take unorthodox viewpoints that imply the location of the viewer within the Paris Opéra theatre. In this way Degas intensifies the viewer's absorption into the picture space. The picture is divided in two halves, with the scene on stage, in the top half with its artificial light, contrasting with the naturalism of the depiction of musicians in the lower half.

Violinist and Young Woman, c.1871, oil and crayon on canvas, Detroit Institute of Arts, USA, bequest of Robert H. Tannahill, 46.4 x 56cm (18 x 22in)

During the late 1860s and early 1870s Degas executed many paintings on musical themes. This unfinished picture also coincides with the numerous double portraits or genre portraits he made at this time of alienated male and female figures. The woman, possibly Degas' sister Marguerite, appears to be holding open a book of sheet music while the man tunes his violin. Both seem to be distracted and distant.

Jeantaud, Linet and Lainé, 1871, oil on canvas, Musée d'Orsay, Paris, France, 38 x 46cm (15 x 18in)

Charles Jeantaud, Pierre Linet and Edouard Lainé were industrialists who all served in the same unit of the Garde Nationale as Degas during the Franco-Prussian War. Degas painted this a month after their demobilization. Degas paints them as confident, wealthy young bourgeoisie. Jeantaud, on the left, was an engineer and Degas also painted a portrait of his wife. In the centre is Linet, a building material's merchant, shown holding a cylinder, and Lainé, also an engineer, reading a newspaper.

Portrait of Henri Rouart
(1833–1912), 1871, oil on
canvas, Musée Marmottan,
Paris, France, 27 x 22cm
(10½ x 8½in)

Stanislas-Henri Rouart was a
close friend of Degas. They
studied together at the
Lycée Louis-le-Grand, after
which Rouart went into the
military, before becoming a
successful engineer and
industrialist. Rouart was also
a part-time painter and art
collector who showed with
the Impressionists. After the
Franco-Prussian War, in
which Degas served under
him, they dined together
weekly and Degas produced
three portraits of him.

*Young Woman Arranging
Flowers,* 1872, oil on canvas,
private collection,
100 x 137cm (39 x 54in)

This painting is part of
several domestic genre
scenes of women from the
1870s. Flower arranging was
one of the accomplishments,
alongside needlework,
playing the piano and
watercolour painting, that
young women were
encouraged to learn in
preparation for future
marriage. Degas' interiors
sometimes feature the
elaborate arrangements of
flowers that a married
woman composes here.

Woman with the Oriental Vase, 1872, oil on canvas, Musée d'Orsay, Paris, France, 65 x 54cm (25½ x 21in)

Painted while in New Orleans, this extraordinary portrait shows Degas experimenting with decentralized composition. The figure is pushed back into the background behind the table and flower arrangement. The orange-red flowers, purple-blue vase and jade green walls give the picture a tropical and exotic ambience. It has been speculated that the sitter is René's wife Estelle or alternatively Madame Challaire, a family friend of the Mussons.

Alice Villette, 1872, oil on canvas, Fogg Art Museum, Harvard University Art Museums, USA, Gift of C. Chauncey Stillman, in memory of his father, James, 45 x 30.5cm (17¾ x 12in)

In the 1870s Degas experimented with pictures that show the model posed alongside an elaborate backdrop, which acquires interest in its own right. Here Alice Villette holds a tapestry in her lap while she patiently poses in front of the window of Degas' studio in the rue Blanche in the 9th arrondissement. Through the window we see a half-rendered view of the city.

*The Rehearsal, c.*1873–78, oil on canvas, Fogg Art Museum, Harvard University Art Museums, USA, bequest from the Collection of Maurice Wertheim, Class 1906, 45.5 x 60cm (18 x 23½in)

The Rehearsal shows Degas experimenting with the distribution of the figures and compositional asymmetry, evident in the looming empty space extending across the right-hand side. This use of empty space owes much to the example of Japanese prints, a fertile influence on Degas. Dancers practise a step in unison to the musical accompaniment of a violinist, while others go through their routines. The mute and harmonious colour schemes are a notable feature of these works.

The Dance Foyer at the Opéra on the rue Le Peletier, 1872, oil on canvas, Musée d'Orsay, Paris, France, 32 x 46cm (12½ x 18in)

Degas' early depictions of the rehearsal room often show dancers practising their exercises under the gaze of the ballet master. Here the choreographer Louis François Mérante instructs a dancer, while others watch on, stretch their limbs, rehearse or are distracted. The asymmetrical composition shows the influence of Japonisme. The open door is a device associated with Dutch painting.

The Pedicure, 1873, oil on paper laid on canvas, Musée d'Orsay, Paris, France, 61 x 46cm (24 x 18in)

The Pedicure is an unusual subject for Degas. Set in a domestic interior, with its striking acid green walls, the painting is a touching but understated scene of ordinary bourgeois life. Though still-life painting held no attraction for him, Degas masterfully used such still-life details to great effect. It is notable for its unusual compositional arrangement, which shows Degas placing objects or still-life elements in the foreground. The absorption of the father in his occupation finds a mute echo in the way his daughter watches him performing his task.

Two Dancers Resting, 1874, pastel on paper, private collection, 46 x 32cm (18 x 12½in)

During the mid-1870s Degas began to shift his attention from domestic genre pictures that feature double portraits, to the portrayal of two dancers, whose contrasting poses and attitudes are the focus of attention. This picture shows two of his most characteristic poses for ballerinas, a dancer seen from behind scratching her back and one adjusting the strap of her ballet slipper.

Ballet Rehearsal on Stage, 1874, oil on canvas, Musée d'Orsay, Paris, France, 65 x 81cm (25½ x 32in)

This monochromatic painting is one of three works that Degas executed between 1873 and 1874 of dancers rehearsing on stage. Attentive to both the elegance and the gaucherie of the dancers, Degas creates a contrast between the figures attentively practising their choreography on the right and the group of dancers stretching, scratching and yawning on the left.

Dancer in Front of a Window (Dancer at the Photographer's Studio) c.1874–77, oil on canvas, Pushkin Museum, Moscow, Russia, 65 x 50cm (25½ x 20in)

Degas made several pictures that reflect his interest in contre-jour effects of figures posed before windows, in which the backlighting affects the quality of light and dark in the image. *Dancer in Front of a Window* appears to be a rehearsal scene, but shows a dancer posing for a photographer, the edge of whose tripod can be seen on the right-hand side. The distorted perspective of the dancer's left leg as she forms her pose, appears as it would do in a photograph taken from this viewpoint.

Ballet Practice, 1875,
gouache and pastel, private
collection, 56 x 68cm
(22 x 26½in)

Though most of Degas'
ballerinas of the 1870s are
set backstage in the
rehearsal room, a group of
pictures show dress
rehearsals on stage. Degas
again uses contrasts of
elegant poses with gaucherie,
juxtaposing the dancer
performing on the right with
the one who is bent over.
The rehearsal is presided
over by the ballet master
Jules Perrot, while a stage
manager or an abonnée
watches from the right.

Dancers at Rehearsal,
1875–77, pastel on
cardboard, Pushkin
Museum, Moscow, Russia,
50 x 63cm (20 x 25in)

This delicate and carefully
worked pastel is one of
several that feature a spiral
staircase, which in this
instance crops off the final
figure on the left, as in a
Japanese print. The ballet
dancers on the left are
shown practising a step in
unison, which allows Degas
to use their pose to unify
this group of figures with
those on the opposite side
of the picture. Ever the wit,
Degas introduces a dissonant
note in the kicking leg of the
dancer on the extreme right.

At the Races, 1876–87, oil on canvas, Musée d'Orsay, Paris, France, 66 x 82cm (26 x 32in)

At the Races brings together many of the characteristic elements and motifs of Degas' horse-racing pictures. Here he employs a number of Japanese print conventions – these include use of asymmetry, compression of space, random distribution of figures and riders, and the use of empty spaces in the composition. A carriage of wealthy spectators is also present, and in the background a train can be seen cutting through the landscape. The speed of the train is juxtaposed with that of the horses.

Place de la Concorde, 1876, oil on canvas, Hermitage Museum, St. Petersburg, Russia, 80 x 117.5cm (31½ x 46in)

Degas painted his friend the Vicomte Ludovic-Napoléon Lepic, a member of a Napoleonic aristocratic family and amateur painter, on two occasions with his children. This extraordinary painting, with its empty space, extreme compositional cropping and ostensibly disorganized grouping of figures, shows Lepic distracted by some chance sighting that has aroused his curiosity. The figure compares with Manet's arbitrary slice-of-life compositions.

The Ballet Scene from Meyerbeer's Opera, Robert le Diable, 1876, oil on canvas, Victoria & Albert Museum, London, UK, 76.5 x 81cm (30 x 32in)

As in *Orchestra Musicians* (1870–76), Degas takes a vantage point close to the musicians in the orchestra pit, looking up toward the ethereal performance on stage. However, in this painting the viewer is located in the stalls. The scene is from Meyerbeer's gothic romance *Robert the Devil*, where under Bertram's orders, the nuns are brought back to life to haunt his son, Robert. Degas contrasts the rapt concentration of the performers with the distraction of the audience, none of whom are watching the performance.

Le Foyer de l'Opéra, c.1877–82,
pastel on board,
Art Gallery and Museum,
Kelvingrove, Glasgow,
Scotland, 70 x 95cm
(27½ x 37½in)

Many of Degas' pictures of
ballerinas rehearsing feature
the mothers who chaperone
the young dancers, some of
whom had been dancers in
their youth. In this intricate
and crowded composition we
see two mothers and
daughters interspersed
between the dancers, who are
shown adjusting their
costumes, practising or resting
from their toil. A mother and
daughter embrace, while
another pair look out of the
window to the city beyond.

*The Duchess de Montejasi
and her Daughters Elena and
Camilla*, 1876, oil on canvas,
private collection,
66 x 98cm (26 x 38½in)

Degas executed several
portraits of his Aunt Fanny,
the Duchess de Montejasi
and her daughters,
exhibiting one at the 1867
Salon, which won him
praise from the critic Jules
Castagnary. In this portrait
the figures are dressed in
mourning and presented
as individualized
psychological studies, with
the presence of the
widowed mother, who is
absorbed by her loss,
dominating that of the two
sisters who are seen in
contrasting poses.

Dancer with Bouquet, Curtseying, 1877, pastel on paper, Musée d'Orsay, Paris, France, 72 x 77.5cm (28 x 30½in)

In the mid- to late 1870s Degas made several pictures of dancers on stage that contrast in ambience and tone with his rehearsal room pictures. In comparison with the latter's delicate harmonies and subdued tonality, these intensely coloured pictures show Degas fascinated by the distorting effects of artificial stage lighting from the pits. While the dancer holding her bouquet takes her applause with a delicate curtsey, other dancers are portrayed less elegantly.

The Ballet Class, c.1878–80, oil on canvas, 82 x 77cm (32 x 30in)

This painting is a good example of the combination of high and low visual art traditions in Degas' ballet pictures. Though attentive to the graceful arabesques of the dancers in the background, whose intertwining poses express the harmony of the choreography, their decorousness is combined with the caricatured physiognomies of the foreground figures, showing the influence of the popular illustrators Degas avidly collected, such as Daumier and Gavarni.

Louis Marie Pillet, 1877, oil on canvas, Musée d'Orsay, Paris, France, 61 x 51cm (24 x 20in)

Louis Marie Pillet was a violoncellist at the Opéra. Degas depicts him in his study, distracted from composing an arrangement by something he has seen out of the window. Degas often shows figures whose curiosity is aroused by something the viewer does not see, creating a sense of mystery. The composition with its cramped space, foreground objects and print on the wall is reminiscent of Dutch 17th-century pictures. The wall print shows some of the illustrious musicians of the day.

Dancers at the Barre, 1877–79, pastel on paper laid down on board, private collection, 66 x 51cm (26 x 20in)

Degas' rehearsal scenes sometimes involve large groups, but more occasionally he focuses on a few figures shown in contrasting poses or in unison. Here two figures practise their battement at the barre. While Degas mostly presents the dancers as types, here the figure on the left is individualized. The figure on the right remains incomplete as the face is blank. Clearly Degas was attracted to the rigorous repetitive training of the dancers, finding in it an echo of his own working methods.

Les Pointes, c.1877–78, oil on canvas, private collection

Movement emerges as a theme of Degas' art in his racehorse and ballet pictures. Here the soft blurry quality of his painterly style and impressionistic brushwork accentuates the sensation of movement. In many pictures Degas connects figures across an empty expanse of space. Here, the dancer projects her arm into the distance where a male dancer is located.

End of an Arabesque, 1877, oil and pastel on canvas, Musée d'Orsay, Paris, France, 67.5 x 38cm (26½ x 15in)

Closely related to *Dancer with Bouquet, Curtseying*, and executed around the same time, the picture shows a star dancer performing an arabesque as she takes her applause. In this picture we view the dancer looking down on to the stage from a steep angle from one of the exclusive loges, or opera boxes, located to the side of the stage. Executed in mixed media, oil and pastel, it again shows Degas' interest in the effects of stage lighting.

Dancer in her Dressing Room, c.1878–79, pastel and gouache on cardboard, private collection, 60 x 40cm (23½ x 16in)

Degas' art is often an art of quiet, personal moments and apparent seclusion, an effect which intensifies the viewer's voyeuristic sense of intimacy with and distance from what is shown in the picture. Here a prima ballerina prepares herself for performance. Degas' attention to the detail of her comportment shows how even when offstage the dancer's body customarily assumes the elegant poses of her art.

Jockeys Before the Race, c.1878–79, oil, essence, gouache and pastel, The Barber Institute, Birmingham, UK, 107 x 74cm (42 x 29in)

This extraordinarily bold composition shows the influence of Japanese prints on Degas. The picture is painted with diluted oil paint to give a watercolour effect. The composition is divided into unequal halves, with the starting pole on the right cutting the composition in two, cropping the horse's head and the body of the horse immediately behind it. The jockeys prepare for the race against a transitional sky that shows the sun breaking through the clouds.

Cafe-Concert Singer, c.1878, pastel on joined paper over monotype, private collection, 17 x 16cm (6¾ x 6in)

In his portraits of performers at the café-concerts, Degas sought to capture the distinctive, signature gestures that distinguished the performers from each other. Here he shows a singer at the Café des Ambassadeurs motioning towards the audience as she delivers her song.

Green Dancers, 1878, pastel on paper, private collection, 72.5 x 39.5cm (28½ x 15½in)

Green Dancers anticipates Degas' more decorative late ballerina pictures, with its group of three dancers set against the scenography of a painted-landscape backdrop. The dancers are portrayed elegantly and gracefully and without irony. Degas subtly conveys the movement of the figures by slight adjustments of the pose. The figures could possibly be one dancer seen in successive motion. Degas captures the rapt attention and concentration of the dancers as they perform their choreography.

Dancer in her Dressing Room,
pastel, *c.*1878, private
collection, 58 × 44cm
(23 × 17in)

The love life of the dancers
at the Opéra was a subject
of much intrigue in the 19th
century. Ballerinas were
portrayed as 'gold-diggers'
ensnaring wealthy lovers.
Degas usually avoided
this theme, occasionally
obliquely alluding to it,
but here he shows a dancer
with her attendant in her
dressing room with an old,
wealthy admirer.

*Portrait of Henri Michel-Levy
in his Studio*, 1879,
Museu Calouste
Gulbenkian, Lisbon,
Portugal, 40 × 28cm
(16 × 11in)

This exceptional portrait
shows Henri Michel-Levy in
his studio, set against two of
his picnic pictures. Michel-
Levy was a close friend of
Degas and exhibited in the
Impressionist group shows.
Degas casually poses him
staring back at the viewer,
with his palette and paint-
box in the foreground. On
Henri's left, seated on the
floor, is a mannequin the
artist has used for his
pictures, her pose echoed by
the figure in the artist's
The Regattas (1876) that is
seen on the left.

La Farandole, 1878–79, gouache on silk with silver and gold laid on board, private collection, 31 x 61cm (12¼ x 24in)

At the Fourth Impressionist Exhibition several impressionist painters showed eventails, or fan-shaped paintings. These designs tended to be made for commercial purposes and were mainly decorative. In this example Degas presents a delicate and intricate ballet design, with a star dancer receiving a tribute of flowers on the left and the corps de ballet departing stage right.

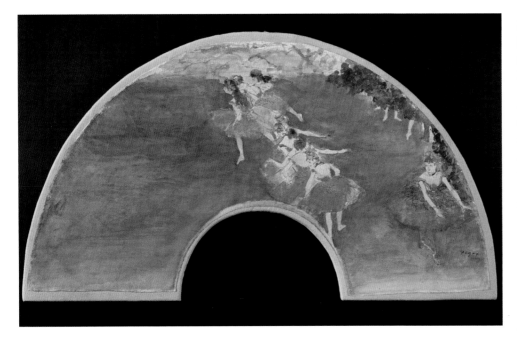

Ballet Dancers, design for a fan, 1878–79, gouache on canvas, private collection, 31 x 61cm (12¼ x 24in)

One of the attractions of these semi-circular fan designs for Degas was the opportunity they gave him to adapt the 'floating world' imagery of Japanese prints to the contemporary world of Parisian entertainments. The asymmetrical composition, with figures located on the centre right and empty space on the left, closely echoes the conventions of Japanese painting.

The Dance Lesson, c.1879,
pastel, Metropolitan
Museum of Art, New York,
USA, 65 x 56cm
(25½ x 22in)

The Dance Lesson is one of
several pictures that show
dancers rehearsing to the
musical accompaniment of a
violinist. Here the violinist
occupies the foreground,
while the young dancer
practises at the barre,
intently watching the
musician who seems in
reverie and far removed
from the activities around
him. The upward-tilted
perspective of the floor
creates an impression
of instability.

*Mademoiselle La La at the
Cirque Fernando,* 1879, oil on
canvas, National Gallery,
London, 117 x 77.5cm
(46 x 30½in)

Degas enjoyed the
performances at the Cirque
Fernando, located close to
his apartment in the
9th arrondissement.
Mademoiselle La La created
a sensation when she
performed there at the
beginning of 1879. Here she
is shown in an arresting
pose, dangling from the
rafters of the circus dome by
a rope gripped in her teeth,
seen from the perspective of
the audience looking up at
the performer.

Dancer on a Stage, c.1879,
gouache on silk,
Samuel Courtauld Trust,
The Courtauld Gallery,
London, UK, 24 x 14cm
(9½ x 5½in)

Unusually painted on silk, this
is one of many images of
dancers seen from the loges,
looking down on the stage.
Normally, Degas emphasizes
the artifice of the stage,
portraying the scenography
as if it was a painting within a
painting. Here the landscape
appears as a convincing
landscape scene, only the
artificial lighting making clear
it is a stage performance.

The Duet, 1877–79, pastel
on monotype, private
collection, 11.5 x 16cm
(4½ x 6in)

Degas' taste included comic
opera, shown here in a
scene set in the old opera
house. Most of his pastels on
this theme focus on the
performance of the dancers
and singers of such
establishments. Here the
viewer looks out from the
exclusive opera boxes
positioned at the side of the
stage beyond the performers
toward the orchestra
and audience. Degas'
indebtedness to popular
caricaturists and illustrators is
evident in the schematic
drawing of the figures.

Race Horses c.1879–82, pastel, Pushkin Museum, Moscow, Russia

While most of Degas' equestrian scenes are of horse-racing, he also made a series of pictures on the theme of riding and hunting. Many of these compositions are characterized by a simplified landscape with a thin skyline and a frieze-like arrangement of horses and riders decoratively distributed across the picture in a shallow spatial setting. While the tone is subdued and sedate, the horse on the extreme right rears up, interrupting the otherwise quiet procession.

Dancers in the Green Room, c.1879, oil on canvas, Detroit Institute of Arts, Michigan, USA, 41 × 87.5cm (16 × 34½in)

Painted in a vibrant colour scheme of yellows, greens and reddish browns, this ballet picture is in the frieze format, which Degas often favoured in his rehearsal scene paintings. In the distance figures rehearse, but Degas focuses our attention on the rather gauche movements of the three ballerinas in the foreground adjusting their costumes, one of whom rests on the cello lying on the floor to tie her ballet slippers before she begins rehearsing.

Dancers Bending Down, 1879–80, oil on canvas, private collection, 36 x 49cm (14 x 19in)

In this delicately executed frieze-like composition Degas uses a stooping pose for the two dancers occupying the foreground plane. In the background, dancers are interlaced, holding hands in a circle. In the shimmering light of the stage the two main dancers' tutus appear golden and pink, encircling their bodies like auras.

On Stage, 1879–81, pastel on paper, private collection, 58.5 x 45cm (23 x 17½in)

In this version of a dancer taking her applause, Degas has given more attention to the dancers around her. The crisper drawing of the central figure reinforces her hierarchical presence in the picture. Degas uses a range of different types of pastel touches in articulating the picture's space and compositional focus.

Dancers in the Classroom, c.1880, oil on canvas, Sterling and Francine Clark Art Institute, Williamstown, USA, 39.5 x 88.5cm (15½ x 35in)

Exceptionally inventive in his compositions, Degas, as in many similar pictures, balances looming, empty spaces with figures distributed across the tableaux. In this case, an arabesque connects the foreground to the figures in the distance, unifying an otherwise arbitrarily dispersed set of figures. Degas' frieze-like compositions may have been influenced by the long, thin, horizontal format of panoramic photographs, which became popular in Paris in the 1870s.

Three Dancers in the Wings, c.1880–85, mixed media, private collection, 54.5 x 65cm (21½ x 25½in)

Degas' pictures of the 1880s show him at his most experimental as he tried out a range of different styles, palettes and techniques. In this bold and loosely worked painting, he shows three ballerinas at the side of the stage set with an abonné. Two of the dancers compete for his attention, while the third seems withdrawn and melancholy.

The Bow of the Star, *c.*1880, gouache on paper, private collection, 61 x 42.5cm (24 x 17in)

This is one of several variations of ballerinas taking a bow. We see the dancer in extreme foreshortening from the vantage point of one of the exclusive loges. In this version the dancer is shown close to the picture edge. The pose has a mute echo in the painted tree of the scenery behind her.

Pink Dancer, *c.*1879–82, pastel, private collection, 71 x 39cm (28 x 15in)

A dancer prepares to take her bow, while other dancers and extras remain in the background in oriental dress. In this picture Degas gives full force to the artificial illumination of the stage that fascinated him. His novel portrayal of the distortive effects of this new modern lighting is something that critics continually mentioned and saw as part of the artist's modernity.

Dancer Against a Stage Flat, *c.*1880, tempera and pastel on paper, private collection, 66.5 x 47cm (26 x 18½in)

Dancers waiting in the wings to enter the stage became an important motif for Degas from the 1880s onward. He uses bold compositional cropping in the foreground figure to suggest the impression of a moment captured. The informality of the picture is continued in the pose of the dancer adjusting her slipper.

La Toilette, c.1880, pastel,
private collection

In *La Toilette*, we see Degas using different kinds of pastel stroke, including directional striations, squiggles, zébrures and hatching strokes to build up the surface of the picture and define its forms. The combination of these techniques economically creates a densely worked surface. In this picture we also see Degas using visual analogies to unify and harmonize his picture but also to give it a touch of visual wit and comic humour. A corseted woman stretches in front of a mirror. Degas draws a visual analogy between her figure and pose and the jug on the chest of drawers in front of her.

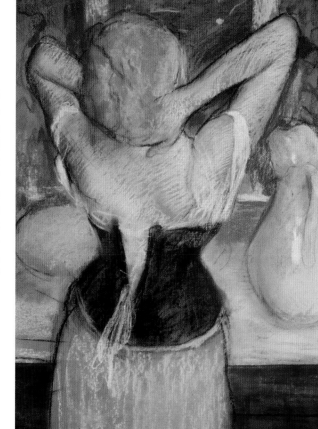

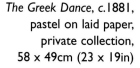

Dancer Resting, c.1880,
pastel and black chalk on
board, private collection

Most of Degas' images of dancers focus on the movement of the dancer's bodies, although some capture the quiet moments between rehearsals. In the sketchy pastel and black chalk style Degas sometimes employed, this picture shows a more intellectual portrayal of the dancer, who is shown reading the newspaper while she warms herself next to a stove.

The Greek Dance, c.1881,
pastel on laid paper,
private collection,
58 x 49cm (23 x 19in)

Degas saw dance as containing traces of the irretrievably lost beauty, grace and harmony of antiquity. In this elegant portrayal of ballerinas, the majestic movements of the dancers are echoed in the trees behind. The poses enhance the impression of movement, but also draw contrasts between the beauty of the central figure and the Parisian physiognomy of the figure to her left.

Seated Dancer, c.1881–83,
pastel and chalk on paper,
Musée d'Orsay, Paris,
France, 62 x 49cm
(24½ x 19in)

The image of a seated
dancer bending to rub her
ankle was a recurring motif
in Degas' oeuvre in the
1880s. He reused this
compositional motif in
several pictures featuring
dancers either alone, in
groups, or with their mother.
Degas' portrayals of the
physical strain the dancers
had to endure in training
sets his pictures apart from
those of his contemporaries.

Dancer with Tambourine,
c.1882, pastel on paper,
private collection,
97 x 65cm (38 x 25½in)

Degas was exceptionally
knowledgeable about the
dance positions of the ballet
and shows precision in his
portrayal of them, attending
to the exact attitude and
co-ordination of the arms
and legs. In this picture he
shows a ballerina dancing
with a tambourine. Degas
uses different pastel strokes
within the picture, using
cross-hatching strokes for
the stage and softer,
blurred strokes, smudged
with his fingers, for the
landscape backdrop.

Two Women, c.1882,
pastel on paper,
private collection,
76 x 85cm (30 x 33½in)

Degas was fascinated by the
different ways that gender
affected behaviour in
modern society. The casual
intimacy of women's physical
exchanges, for example,
differed markedly from the
more protective and
assertive qualities of men.
In this picture, a milliner's
assistant adjusts the position
of a hat that a customer is
trying on. Degas attends
carefully to the details of the
figures' clothing and the
design of the hat. The
customer looks inquisitively
at her reflection in a mirror
located out of the picture.

*Three Dancers in a Diagonal
Line on the Stage*, c.1882,
pastel, private collection,
63 x 50cm (25 x 20in)

Using the black chalk and
pastel style that is present in
several pictures of the early
1880s, Degas shows three
figures performing their steps
in unison. Though Degas
was always appreciative of
the elegance and majesty of
the dance, he also had an
eye for the clumsy execution
of some dancers. In this
picture the dancers' lack of
grace is quite evident.

At the Milliner's, 1882, pastel on grey paper, The Metropolitan Museum of Art, New York, USA. H. O. Havemeyer Collection, bequest of Mrs H. O. Havemeyer, 1929, 76 x 86.5cm (30 x 34in)

Degas took pleasure in shopping at dressmakers and milliners with his friend Mary Cassatt. His interest in pictures of millinery shops where women try on the latest fashions probably arose from such outings. Using a tonal scheme of yellows and reddish browns, this well-observed cameo of modern life shows Cassatt admiring herself in a mirror while trying on a range of hats.

Two Women Leaning on a Gate, 1882–85, pastel, private collection,

Degas made a series of pictures of women conversing at rural racetracks. This theme was closely related compositionally to the pictures of casual exchanges and conversations of women in his milliner pictures dating from the early 1880s. As with these, the focus is on foreground elements. In many of Degas' genre pictures the viewer is left to speculate about the subject of the women's conversation – as in this case, where the tone of the picture remains unclear.

Breakfast After a Bath,
*c.*1883, pastel on paper,
private collection,
121 x 92cm (47½ x 36in)

Most of Degas' bathers are
shown alone, heightening the
impression of intimacy.
In some he introduces a
maid bringing tea or
combing the bather's hair.
The use of a vibrantly
contrasting palette, pairing
colour oppositions such
as red and green, and
yellow and violet, gives
this otherwise quiet,
understated composition a
heightened sensation.

Bedtime, *c.*1883, pastel over
monotype on paper,
private collection

This erotic image of a
woman wearing only her
bed cap climbing into bed is
closely related to Jacob van
Loo's (1614–70) *Young
Woman Going to Bed* (1650),
which Degas probably knew
through an engraving made
after it by Charles-Antoine
Porporati (1740–1816). As
in the van Loo, the subject is
probably intended to be of
prostitution, or at least
implies an erotic encounter.

After the Bath, *c.*1883, pastel on joined paper, private collection, 52 × 32cm (20½ × 12½in)

Degas often used the same poses in his studies of ballerinas and bathers. In this picture the pose of a woman drying herself echoes many of those shown in the ballet rehearsal rooms. The decoration and furnishings suggest a humble apartment or cheap hotel. Working on paper allowed Degas the freedom to alter pictures as he developed them – he would often extend the size of the picture's dimensions, as he has here, adding a strip of paper to the lower edge to amplify the space.

La Toilette, 1883, pastel and chalk on paper, private collection, 30.5 × 24cm (12 × 9½in)

La Toilette recycles the pose of *After the Bath* (1883), but to different expressive effect. In this version the figure is placed close to the right-hand edge and is shown washing rather than drying herself. The interior is executed in vibrant warm reds and yellows. Degas was fascinated by the way small compositional adjustments and different styles, techniques and palettes could alter his motifs.

Woman in her Bath Sponging her Leg, *c.*1883, pastel on paper, Musée d'Orsay, Paris, France, 20 × 41cm (8 × 16in)

Most of Degas' bathers use portable, round metal tubs. In some he shows women submerged in enamelled bathtubs. The bowed edge of the bathtub here mirrors the arched chair back.

Danseuse a l'Eventail,
c.1883–86, pastel on paper,
Art Gallery and Museum,
Kelvingrove, Glasgow,
Scotland, 62 x 87cm
(24½ x 34in)

Fans were an essential
accoutrement of fashionable
women in the 19th century.
In his later ballerina pictures
Degas often shows dancers
cooling themselves with
decorative fans. In this
delightful picture, with its
bold red tonality, two
dancers in contrasting poses
converse between a
performance. One fans
herself, while the other
holds a fan closed in her
extended left arm.

The Bath, c.1884–88, pastel,
David David Gallery,
Philadelphia, USA

Most of Degas' images of
bathers show them washing
or after the bath. Here
Degas appears to show a
bather rather tentatively
climbing into a modern
metal bath. The colour
scheme of the picture is
subdued with cooler tonality
than is typically found in his
bathers of this period. The
picture is rendered very
economically and the figure
is shown in *profil perdu*,
which places the visual focus
of the viewer on to the
curvaceous forms of
her body.

Woman Drying Herself,
c.1884–86, oil on canvas,
Brooklyn Museum of Art,
New York, USA,
150 x 214cm (59 x 84in)

This large, almost
monochrome, painting
returns to the familiar motif
of bathers' pictures that first
emerged in monotypes and
drawings of the late 1870s
and early 1880s. This shows
Degas' continuing interest
in contre-jour effects. The
large number of Degas'
pictures left 'unfinished' by
traditional standards raises
a question of what the
artist considered a complete
painting in his later career.

Woman in the Tub, 1884,
pastel and black chalk on
paper, private collection

This picture, executed in
pastel and black chalk, shows
Degas reducing his palette to
achieve a dominant blue
tonality, which establishes the
subdued and rather
introspective mood. Degas
has chosen a high vantage
point and has severely
cropped the picture, so we
see only the hands and part
of the lower body of the
maid who holds the towel.
The soft curves of the
woman's body echo the
form of the tub in which she
washes herself.

After the Bath, 1884, pastel on paper, Hermitage, St. Petersburg, Russia, 50 x 50cm (20 x 20in)

This picture of a woman kneeling, drying herself on a sofa draped with towels focuses on the pose and movement of the body rather than the bather herself. Generally, Degas' bathers are de-individualized; their faces withheld from the viewer, who sees them either from an oblique angle in foreshortening or from behind. The decorative conception of the picture is evident in the pink flower-patterned wallpaper on the back wall.

Woman Drying her Arm, c.1884, pastel on buff paper, private collection, 54.5 x 65.5cm (21½ x 26in)

This tender and understated picture of a woman drying herself shows Degas using a variety of pastel techniques. The green chair on which she sits is modelled with thick, broad strokes, while the woman's body is more crisply worked with a combination of diagonal lines of alternating length and thickness, with more broadly worked and smudged areas. The white towels on the chair and in her hand are rapidly rendered and the background is more diffusely brushed in, using diluted pastel.

Femme au Tub, 1884, pastel on paper, Art Gallery and Museum, Kelvingrove, Glasgow, Scotland, 59 x 83cm (23 x 33in)

This is one of several pictures showing a figure stooping while washing herself. The viewer looks down on the figure from above eye level, probably using one of the raised platforms Degas placed in his studio. It may have been exhibited as part of the *Suite de Nudes* Degas showed at the Eighth Impressionist Exhibition (1886) and at the art dealers, Boussod et Valadon (1892). Degas' composition focuses attention on the body pose, which some critics found indecorous.

Reading a Letter, 1884, pastel on paper, Burrell Collection, Glasgow Museums and Art Galleries, Glasgow, Scotland, 63 x 45cm (25 x 18in)

Degas' early images of laundresses tend to be single figures ironing. However, in the 1880s these give way to groups of two figures in contrasting attitudes and poses set in the humid atmosphere of the workplace. Although Degas' treatment of this theme was influenced by Daumier, his pictures rarely focus on the hardship and toil of the laundresses. Here one laundress reads a letter to another, who may have been illiterate.

Woman Putting on Gloves,
1884–86, oil on canvas,
private collection,
61 x 47cm (24 x 18½in)

Degas' interior scenes are
often distinctive for their
vantage points, in this case
from the threshold of a
doorway looking into an
interior where a woman
sits, unaware of being
observed. This quiet,
understated picture
illustrates Degas' desire to
make details expressive in
communicating. The sitter's
hand gestures arguably
convey as much about her
as her face. Degas' pictures
often allude to an imminent
moment. The sitter is putting
on her gloves, a sign that she
is about to depart.

Two Women in Conversation,
1884, pastel on paper,
Nationalgalerie, Berlin,
Germany, 65 x 86cm
(25½ x 34in)

Degas was a close observer
of mannerisms and gestures
and sought to give form to
modern comportment in his
paintings. The informal range
of unguarded gestures
demonstrated by women
while shopping fascinated
him. Though known as
Two Women in Conversation,
the women are inspecting
watermarked silk in a shop.
The women's poses closely
echo each other and are
shown from different
points of view.

Woman Ironing, 1885, oil on canvas, The National Gallery of Art, Washington, DC, USA, Collection of Mr and Mrs Paul Mellon, 81 x 66cm (32 x 26in)

Some of Degas' works depicting laundresses have parallels with the way women were portrayed in realist novels. Others, such as this study, show Degas' attention on the movements of the laundresses' bodies as they carry out their work. The motif, which Degas made several variations of, also shows an exploration of the ambience of a laundry room and the portrayal of contre-jour lighting.

Dancers, 1884–85, pastel on paper pasted on cardboard, Musée d'Orsay, Paris, France, 75 x 73cm (29½ x 29in)

This, one of Degas' more naturalistic representations of the ballet, portrays ballerinas dressing themselves. Degas captures the somewhat claustrophobic atmosphere of the ballerinas' dressing rooms. The contre-jour lighting sets the tone of the picture, which is built up using discrete incidental cameos. One figure adjusts the strap of her dress, another ties the straps of her slipper while resting on a chair and another gazes distractedly out of a window. Her gaze on to the world outside intensifies the claustrophobic feeling of the room.

Ballerina and Lady with a Fan, 1885, pastel on paper, Philadelphia Museum of Art, Pennsylvania, USA, 66 x 51cm (26 x 20in)

The figure of the star receiving applause shows a female spectator holding binoculars and a fan while seated in the lower front loge near the stage. The composition is de-centralized and the space is compressed with bold compositional cropping present in all the figures. Degas again shows his interest in the strange distortions of the artificial stage illumination.

After the Bath, 1885, pastel on paper, private collection, 48 x 87cm (19 x 34in)

A woman dries herself by rolling on a towel on the floor in a picture that brings to mind Degas' statements about women being closer to their animal nature than men. However, the poses of Degas' bathers also often allude to specific and generic types of classical art, retaining mute resonances of more dramatic nudes associated with the narrative paintings of Poussin and the Venetian masters. The figure is reminiscent of one of the dead women in Degas' *Medieval War Scene*.

After the Bath, Woman Drying her Left Foot, 1886, pastel on cardboard, Musée d'Orsay, Paris, France, 54 x 52.5cm (21 x 20½in)

Degas positions the vantage point of the viewer just to the side of a screen behind which a nude woman dries her feet. Degas may have had Rembrandt's *Bathsheba* (1654) in mind when making this and other similar nudes, though the figure's pose is very different. Her arm is pressed between her torso and thigh and her body is compressed into a snail's shell-like whorl.

Jockeys in the Rain, c.1886, pastel on paper, Burrell Collection, Glasgow, Scotland, 47 x 63.5cm (18½ x 25in)

Degas' ballerina and race-horse scenes often bear compositional similarities in terms of the distribution of figures in space. In this pastel we see Degas representing jockeys lining up for the start of a race in the pouring rain. The figures are arranged across the picture in a frieze-like format, with subtle variations of pose threaded through the composition. The randomness enhances the impression of the nervous moments before the race. Degas uses directional pastel strokes to suggest the textures of grass and the rain pouring down.

Dancers Ascending a Staircase, c.1886–88, oil on canvas, Musée d'Orsay, Paris, France, 39 x 89.5cm (15 x 35in)

The frieze-like arrangement of figures entering the rehearsal room from a lower staircase, brings to mind similar compositions

by classical masters, such as Domenico Ghirlandaio's (1449–94) fresco *The Confirmation of the Rule of the Order of St. Francis by*

Pope Honorius III (c.1480–85), which Degas would have seen at the Sassetti Chapel during his time in Florence.

Two Bathers on the Grass,
*c.*1886–90, pastel on paper,
Musée d'Orsay, Paris,
France, 70 x 70cm
(27½ x 27½in)

Though the majority of
Degas' nudes are set in
interiors, a few return to the
classical convention of

bathers in rural settings. In
doing so they bring a new
incidental and banal quality
to the traditional arcadian
theme. The modernity of
this large picture lies in its
bold simplification of form
and its use of accumulated
pastel strokes to build up
the picture's textures.

Harlequin and Colombine,
*c.*1886–90, oil on canvas,
Musée d'Orsay, Paris,
France, 33 x 23.5cm
(13 x 9in)

By the 19th century the
Italian tradition of *Commedia
dell'arte* had fallen into decay,
but nevertheless proved
popular in various
adaptations to musical hall,

pantomime and ballet.
Degas shows a ballet
adaptation featuring
Columbine and her suitor
and servant Harlequin. In
treating this theme, Degas
would have had in mind the
18th-century French artist
Antoine Watteau's
(1684–1721) portrayals of
the *Commedia dell'arte.*

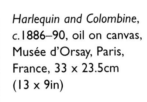

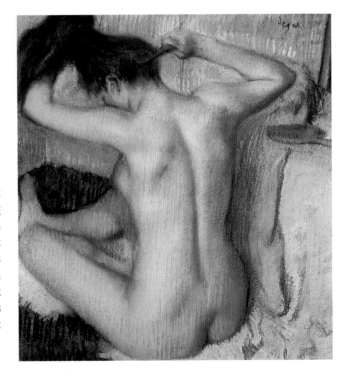

Woman Combing her Hair,
*c.*1886, pastel on
cardboard,
Hermitage, St. Petersburg,
Russia, 53 x 52cm
(21 x 20½in)

Images of women combing
their hair became a
common Degas motif from

the mid-1880s on, though it
first appeared in his painting
in the mid-1870s. In this
pastel, one of Degas' most
erotic bathers, the woman is
seen crouched on the floor,
the nape of her neck
exposed as she backcombs
her thick tresses of red hair.

Portrait of Hélène Rouart, 1886, pastel on paper, private collection, 49 x 32cm (19 x 12½in)

Hélène Rouart was the daughter of his friend Henri Rouart and features in several Degas pictures. Degas charted the family's development for almost 30 years, beginning in 1871 with his portrait of Henri. This may have been executed as a study for the large double portrait of Hélène and her father painted in the same year.

Seated Woman, 1887, pastel on paper, private collection, 50 x 50cm (20 x 20in)

Though the identity of the sitter remains a matter of speculation, it is probably a portrait of Mary Cassatt, whom Degas painted on several occasions, always presenting her stylishly dressed and in idiosyncratic poses. Here she is seated and wearing a fashionable hat. She looks away from the viewer, as though her attention is caught by something out of the picture that the viewer can only speculate about.

**Woman Washing Herself,
c.1887, pastel on card laid
down on board, private
collection**

Closely related to the same
series as *Woman Washing
Herself*, Degas focuses our
attention on the movement
of the body in the act of
ablution rather than the
identity of the woman. As in
many Degas pictures of
ballerinas and bathers, visual
puns abound. The woman's
body is analogized to the
shapes of the sponge, bowl
and jug she washes with. She
is scrutinized dispassionately
as one object among others.

**Woman Combing her Hair,
1887–90, pastel on paper,
Musée d'Orsay, Paris,
France, 82 x 57cm
(32 x 22½in)**

The series of pictures of
women combing their hair
show Degas experimenting
with different poses, vantage
points and colour schemes.
In contrast to the warm and
vibrant tonality of the *La
Toilette*, here Degas uses a
cool tonal harmony of
pinkish whites, lime greens,
soft blues and violet. The
figure is viewed from
the side and seen below
eye level. She is shown
dragging her comb through
her long brown hair.

Vicomte Le Pic and his Daughters, 1888, oil on canvas, private collection, Zurich, Switzerland, 66.5 x 81cm (26 x 32in)

This portrait of Vicomte Ludovic Napoléon Le Pic shows him with two of his daughters, Eylau and Janine. It presents a more traditional image of family life than in Degas' earlier depiction of the vicomte, where he is portrayed as a nonchalant man about town at the Place de la Concorde. A year after this was painted Le Pic was dead.

Before the Ballet, 1888, oil on canvas, The National Gallery of Art, Washington, DC, USA, 40 x 89cm (15½ x 35in)

Before the Ballet belongs to the series of frieze-like arrangements of ballerinas rehearsing that emerged in the 1880s and features the motif of the dancer rubbing her foot. The picture is a study in movement, with the viewer's eye led across the picture from left to right, a reversal of the western way of reading a picture. The pointing leg of the ballerina adjusting her stocking bridges the gap between the two groupings of figures.

Woman Drying Herself, c.1888–90, pastel on paper, private collection

Woman Drying Herself draws comparison with *Two Bathers on the Grass* in its bold simplification and economical realization. The figure is allowed to occupy the entirety of the space, which creates a strong sensation of compression and also intimacy. Degas often used brown or green paper, as is the case here. A few strokes of pastel represent the background, while the body is more carefully modelled.

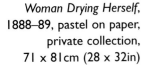

Woman Drying Herself, 1888–89, pastel on paper, private collection, 71 x 81cm (28 x 32in)

This nude is a good example of Degas' pastel technique, with its shimmering surface made up of varied pastel strokes. The dazzling multiple layers of coloured pastel are composed of different types of striations, squiggles, zébrures and crisscross hachures, which create a rich texture and establish a dense network of coloured touches.

Woman Drying Herself, 1888–89, pastel on paper, National Gallery, London 104 x 98.5cm (41 x 39in)

In this vibrantly coloured and densely worked pastel of one of Degas' standard motifs, he shows light suffusing the darkened room through the drawn curtain, using his pastel technique to suggest the sumptuous textures of drapery and furnishings. The lines of pastel colour along the figure's back suggest the action of the towel rubbing against the body's surface.

Reader Lying Down, c.1889,
pastel on paper, private
collection, 99 x 67cm
(39 x 26in)

Degas captures a child's
perspective well in this
picture of a young girl lying
on a rug reading a large and
imposing tome. She is shown
turning a page, but seems
momentarily distracted from
her reading by something
outside of the picture. The
pastel, executed on brown
paper, is loosely worked,
using a range of different
pastel strokes to build up
the surface.

In Front of the Mirror, 1889,
pastel on paper,
Hamburger Kunsthalle,
Hamburg, Germany,
49 x 64cm (19½ x 25in)

In this picture Degas brings
together two themes of his
work in the 1880s, women
at their toilette and women
trying on hats in millinery
shops. Degas used the same
red-headed model that
appears in many of the
nudes in the mid-1880s. On
the table we see the hair
extensions that also appear
in some of the bathers'
pictures she features in.

Portrait of Michel Manzi,
1889, pastel on paper,
Musée d'Orsay, Paris,
France, 70 x 70.5cm
(27½ x 27¾in)

Michel Manzi was an
engineer, engraver, art
collector and dealer. Here
he is shown looking at a
copper plate for an
engraving he has just
immersed in a bath of acid.
The picture is set in his
studio in the rue Forest in
the back streets of the place
de Clichy. Manzi fought
alongside Zandomeneghi for
the unification of Italy and
eventually, on coming to
Paris, became head of the
art dealer Goupil's print
workshop.

*Group of Dancers, c.*1890s,
oil on paper, National
Gallery of Scotland,
Edinburgh, Scotland,
47 x 62cm (18½ x 24½in)

By the late 1880s Degas was
redefining his art and
developing a more
decorative approach. Now
aesthetic concerns were
replacing the social content
of his pictures of the
previous decade. *Group of
Dancers* illustrates this with
its rich peppermint-green
and silvery-white tonal
scheme laid over a chestnut-
red ground and its more
decorative conception of the
figure grouping.

Coastal Landscape, 1890–92, pastel on monotype on coloured paper, Galerie Jan Krugier, Geneva, Switzerland

Degas' unexpected return to landscape painting in the 1890s saw him taking on many of the stylistic attributes and characteristic types of motifs of his Impressionist colleagues. Yet these landscapes are witty exercises in anthropomorphic landscape painting. The body of a female nude can be seen sprawled across the mountainous form of the landscape, her flowing red hair streaming along the left-hand edge of the cliff face.

Woman Drying Herself, c.1890–95, pastel, National Gallery of Scotland, Edinburgh, Scotland, 65 x 63.5cm (25½ x 25in)

Though many of Degas' images of the nude convey an impression of objective detachment, others are highly eroticized, fetishizing the nape of the neck, breasts and buttocks of his models. The sitter's apparent lack of self-consciousness or awareness of the viewer's gaze heightens the picture's voyeurism. Degas once said, "In former times I would have painted Susannah in her bath."

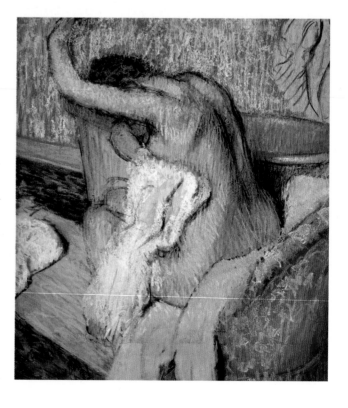

After the Bath, Woman Drying Herself, c.1890

This vibrantly coloured and densely worked composition features one of Degas' favourite bather motifs. Degas produced numerous versions and variations using this pose, experimenting with different colour schemes and pastel techniques. It is also a motif closely related to the ballerina pictures. Degas draws us into an absorbing and intimate relation to the tactile experience of the woman's action of dragging the towel across her body to dry her skin.

The Ballet Dancer, 1891,
oil on mahogany panel,
Hamburger Kunsthalle,
Hamburg, Germany,
22 x 16cm (8½ x 6in)

Unusually painted on a
mahogany panel and
executed in a very rapidly

worked and loosely painted
style, *The Ballet Dancer*
depicts a dancer against a
maritime landscape theatre
backdrop. In the foreground
we see the tops of two
violoncellos, which shows
the viewer's vantage point to
be within the orchestra pit.

Two Dancers, c.1891, pastel
on paper, private collection,
79 x 45cm (31 x 17¾in)

In some of Degas' ballerina
pictures of the 1890s figures
seem almost to merge into
each other, as though their
individuality was entirely
subsumed into their bodily
movement. Degas may well
have had the example of
Leonardo in mind where
figures often merge in a
similar fashion. The two
figures here are shown
tending to their aches and
strains after a performance.

*Billiards Room of Ménil-
Hubert*, 1892, oil on canvas,
private collection,
50.5 x 66cm (20 x 26in)

Though an interior, *Billiards
Room of Ménil-Hubert*, might
be considered a portrait of
sorts, evoking the personality
and taste of the occupants
by the furnishings. Ménil-
Hubert was the Valpinçon
family estate and the painting
shows some of their fine-art
collection. The picture was
inspired by Delacroix's *The
Comte de Mornay's
Apartment* (1833), that
Degas owned and
considered one of his most
prized works. Delacroix's
picture features a similarly
empty room with furnishings
and paintings. The viewer
is tacitly invited to
reconstruct a portrait of the
missing owner from the
clues in the picture.

Woman Washing Herself,
c.1892, pastel, private
collection, 63 x 48cm
(25 x 19in)

Despite Degas' love for the
classical tradition, evident in
both his bathers and
ballerinas, he continued to
be committed to
representing the body
naturalistically, even when
this resulted in ungainly and
inelegant gestures. Degas
placed the principle of 'truth
is beauty' over the notion of
'beauty is truth' that
informed the idealism of the
masters he most admired.

The Brown Dress, c.1893,
pastel on paper, Whitworth
Art Gallery, The University
of Manchester, UK,
65 x 49cm (25½ x 19in)

In the 1890s Degas'
portraiture was much less
prolific and those he made
were for his own pleasure.
Degas no longer needed to
accept portrait commissions,
but had also become
disenchanted with the
informing idea of his earlier
portraiture, namely that
inner truth was reflected by
outward appearance. His
later portraits tend to be
mood pieces. Degas uses
the 'interior portrait' to
explore the sitter's
subjectivity or inner
psychological reality, which is
left undefined and open for
the viewer to reflect on.
The result is a more 'open-
ended' picture, which offers
the viewer less certainty but
more room for personal
judgment. The sitter of this
portrait is probably the
same one as in *Bust of a
Woman With Her Left Hand
on Her Chin.*

*Before the Race, c.*1893, pastel, private collection, 65 x 72cm (25½ x 28in)

Though ballerinas and bathers were to dominate Degas' oeuvre in the 1890s, equestrian subjects continued to strongly interest him. This picture incorporates some of the features of the simplified landscapes Degas was making in this period. It shows two groupings of jockeys aligning their horses for the start of the race, with an expectant crowd in the distance.

*Seated Woman Drying her Feet, c.*1893, pastel laid on board, private collection, 55 x 62cm (21½ x 24½in)

This loosely worked picture using broad swathes of pastel strokes, shows a woman sitting on a bed drying her left leg with a towel. The figure is drawn only slightly more crisply than the fabrics and furnishings of the room. The claustrophobic impression of the room is increased by the vantage point, which is located considerably above head height looking down on to the figure from a slightly oblique angle.

Breakfast After the Bath (Young Woman Drying Herself), c.1894, pastel on paper, private collection, 98 x 60cm (38½ x 23½in)

In the 1890s Degas began increasing the scale of his pictures, producing larger versions of his motifs. He also continually explored different ways of presenting his favourite motifs. Here the maid in the background bringing the bather tea is shown with her head cropped off at the picture's edge. We look down on the scene from a high vantage point. Degas creates spatial depth in the compressed space through the oblique angle of the furnishings.

Morning Toilette, 1894, pastel on paper, private collection

Most of Degas' images of women *à la toilette* are nudes, but a few show women dressed, grooming themselves in front of a mirror, as in this picture of a young woman in her chemise braiding her hair. This quiet, understated interior scene set in a modest apartment, is enlivened by the rapid, sketch-like pastel technique that picks out the flowered wallpaper and the pattern of the carpet.

Seated Dancer, c.1894, pastel on paper, private collection

Having established a motif, Degas worked through its expressive possibilities in a series of variations over many years, drawing from different angles and vantage points, with subtle adjustments in style, drawing and colour scheme. This variation of a woman rubbing her swollen foot turns the body outward toward the viewer, with her tutu encircling her in a fan-like shape.

Jockeys, 1895, oil and pastel on canvas, private collection, 26 x 38cm (10 x 15in)

This picture was developed from a drawing Degas made approximately five years before for a new interpretation of horses at the track. It is closely related to other similar pictures of horse-racing in the 1890s. The painting incorporates various individual motifs, like the balking horse that Degas had been working on for many years, but also includes some new ones like the horse stooping in the foreground.

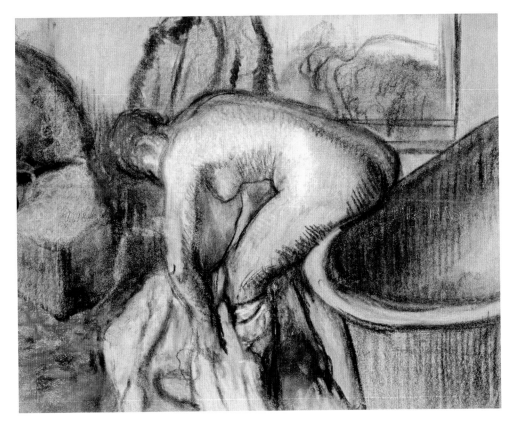

After the Bath, c.1895, pastel on paper, The Dayton Art Institute, Dayton, Ohio, USA, 45.5 x 59cm (18 x 23in)

Though many of Degas' bathers have rich, sensual and deeply saturated colour schemes, this bather has a subdued pastel tonality. Degas creates space in this otherwise cramped composition by placing the bathtub diagonally. The figure is modelled in rudimentary cross-hatched strokes in black chalk. The background seems to show a reflection of the bather, but it is so sparsely rendered that it could also be a landscape.

Woman at her Bath, c.1895, oil and pastel on canvas, Art Gallery of Ontario, Toronto, Canada, 71 x 89cm (28 x 35in)

Degas' bathers reveal an intricate dialogue between drawing and painting and constant adjustments of media, poses and compositional effects. Here Degas changes the orientation of the bather to the left and the maid is shown pouring water over her back, rather than bringing tea or holding a towel. The vibrant colour scheme with its pinks, violets, oranges and greens creates a strong sensation.

Group of Three Dancers, c.1895, pastel on paper, The Barnes Foundation, Merion, Pennsylvania, USA

This variation of the motif of the ballet dancer rubbing her foot shows Degas introducing other supplementary figures that seem to be consoling her or conversing with her. There is little differentiation between the figures with the hair and dress almost identical. In these works from the 1890s Degas' pastel technique becomes ever more overt, drawing the viewer's attention to the method of marking the surface.

After the Bath, c.1895, pastel and gouache on paper, Hermitage, St. Petersburg, Russia, 82 x 72cm (32 x 28in)

The colour scheme of this picture is more delicate than many of Degas' bathers of this time. The pastel technique displays the dense network of pastel strokes Degas used to build up and model his surfaces. The striations of pastel chalk across the surface of the body serve to define the model, but also parallel the action of the model in rubbing the towel across her body.

Dancers in Violet, c.1895–98, pastel on paper, Musée du Docteur Faure, Aix-les-Bains, France, 45.5 x 20.5cm (18 x 8in)

In his ballerina pictures Degas explored various contrasting or complementary figure groupings. In this picture the poses of the two figures seem almost to echo each other but for the gestures of the arms. Degas captures well the scintillating effects of the stage lighting in the subtle and harmonious tonal scheme of violet, pink, blue, green and yellow.

Ballet Scene, 1895–98, pastel
on canvas, private collection

The extraordinarily rich, hot
palette of some of Degas'
later works shows him
adopting some of the tonal
schemes of the Venetian
painters and establishing
parallels in his colour use
with French Symbolist
contemporaries. Here we
see the performance from
the wings of the stage,
looking beyond two dancers
waiting at the side
of the platform.

Dancers at Rehearsal,
1895–98, pastel on paper,
Van der Heydt Museum,
Wuppertal, Germany,
70.5 x 100.5cm
(28 x 39½in)

Dancers at Rehearsal displays
the rich and lively colour
schemes that typify Degas'
later work, with its use of
crimson reds, pinks,
peppermint and silvery-
white. The ballerinas
rehearse and rest, with
many familiar recurring
motifs present. The room
is divided into pools of light
and deep shade.

*Bust of a Woman With Her
Left Hand on Her Chin*,
c.1895–98, pastel on paper,
private collection

This simple but affecting
interior portrait of an
unidentified sitter is a good
example of the way Degas
increasingly turned his
attention from the social
status of his subjects to
artistic issues of
representation. While Degas
communicates the
introspective mood of his
sitter, little information about
her class or occupation is
given. The viewer's attention
is deflected from such
thoughts to attending to
Degas' style of rendering
with its densely worked and
very visible pastel strokes.

Woman Drying her Hair After the Bath, c.1895–98, pastel on paper, Brooklyn Museum of Art, New York, USA, 84 x 105.5cm (33 x 41½in)

The motif of a woman drying her neck and hair seen from an oblique angle to the rear became one of Degas' favourite motifs of the 1890s. The monumental conception of the figure connects the picture to the tradition of Rubens' nudes, while maintaining plausible naturalism. Degas has added strips of paper to the top and bottom of the picture to amplify the space.

Dancer with a Fan, c.1895–1900, pastel, private collection, 70.5 x 52cm (28 x 20½in)

Degas made numerous versions of this motif of a dancer holding a fan. Some show her waiting in the wings, but others incorporate her into varied, larger ensembles of dancers. Degas traced and re-traced his figures, altering and reworking their poses and enlarging and reducing them. He also made many adjustments while he worked on pictures, as can be seen in the pentimenti, (meaning something that has been painted over or covered) around the dancer's legs, where he has successively revised the pose and contour.

Dancers, 1895–1900, oil on canvas, private collection

This subdued picture of dancers in the rehearsal room shows how Degas, like Manet, employs selective focus in his pictures. The foreground figures are rendered legibly, while in the background the dancers entering the room through a door are blurred. Degas shows a dancer putting on her slippers, while another, cloaked in shadow, ties the sash of the central dancer.

Three Dancers, c.1895–98, pastel on paper, private collection

Essentially a study in choreographed movement, *Three Dancers* makes little differentiation between the figures, except for slight adjustments of pose. Degas always sought to animate his compositions. Here, the diagonal position of the figures and their ascending arm gestures creates a strong sense of progressive motion through the picture space, which is depicted with broad and freely rendered pastel strokes.

Woman at her Toilette, c.1895–1900, oil and pastel on canvas, private collection, 82.5 x 77cm (32 x 30in)

Degas' colour schemes became progressively more brilliant and deeply saturated towards the latter part of his career and are unconstrained by the demands of Realism present in his early work. In this picture of a woman brushing her hair before a dressing table, he transforms a quotidian scene by his rich piquant colour which he owes both to contemporary artists and to his study of the Venetians. The woman's pose is echoed in the jug on the dresser.

Dancers in the Wings
*c.*1895–98, pastel on paper,
private collection,
29 x 26cm (11½ x 10in)

This is a variation of the motif of dancers waiting at the side of the stage, showing two dancers in pale yellow dresses set against almost abstractly rendered landscape stage scenery. Degas economically suggests differences between the figures through pose, hairstyle and makeup, but almost merges the figures, making the neckline of the two dancers' dresses continuous. The viewer is left to speculate about what they are watching and thinking.

Dancers Wearing Green Skirts, *c.*1895, oil and pastel on canvas, private collection, 140 x 80cm (55 x 31½in)

Degas was constantly searching for expressive, modern poses. In the 1890s he developed several pictures featuring the motif of a dancer with her hands on her hips leaning forward either in isolation or in multi-figure groupings. This vibrantly painted picture, with its rich juxtapositions of acid oranges and peppermint greens, appears unresolved. Degas intended to introduce a third figure between the other two, but only traces of the figure's bodice and legs are evident.

Dancers with Hair in Braids,
*c.*1895–98, pastel on paper,
The Barnes Foundation,
Merion, Pennsylvania, USA

The title given to this painting draws attention to the long sinuous lines of the braids of the dancers, which are echoed in the movements of their arms. This picture is one of a series of works featuring three or more dancers in similar poses waiting in the wings. The acid yellows and lime greens contrast with the violet blues and reds to create a strong colour sensation.

Dancers Rehearsing,
c.1895–98, pastel on paper,
Bridgestone Museum of
Art, Tokyo, Japan,
38 x 80cm (15 x 31½in)

This gloomily lit scene of
rehearsal shows an untypical
motif of a dancer leaning
against a column. It is loosely
worked with directional
pastel strokes and uses a
restricted green, yellow and
violet tonality. The pentimenti
shows how Degas adjusted
poses as he went along.

At Saint-Valéry-sur-Somme,
c.1896–98, oil on canvas,
Ny Carlsberg Glyptothek,
Copenhagen, Denmark,
67.5 x 81cm (26½ x 32in)

Degas' affection for the
town he visited with his
parents as a child is
captured in several pictures
from late in his career.
The town must have held
fond memories for him.
The landscape paintings
Degas made vary greatly.
Here an overgrown track
flanked by walls leads to a
distant cottage.

Return of the Herd, 1896–98,
oil on canvas, New Walk
Museum, Leicester, UK,
73 x 92cm (29 x 36in)

An unusual subject for
Degas, this is one of several
paintings executed in the
Saint-Valéry district in
the mid-1890s. It was a small
resort to the west of
Abbeville in Picardy where
the Degas family had often
vacationed. This rather
lugubrious picture of the
herd returning at the end of
the day shows the influence
of Gauguin, whom Degas
much admired.

*After the Bath, c.*1896, pastel
on paper, Philadelphia
Museum of Art,
Pennsylvania, USA,
89 x 116cm (35 x 45½in)

This extraordinary canvas
painted in a deep red, almost
monochrome tonality
reminiscent of Venetian
painting, creates a rich visual
sensation. Though Degas had
experimented with mono-
chrome in his early versions
of *Young Spartans*, in the
1890s he began to explore
its expressive possibilities
more rigorously. Degas had a
photograph taken of the
model's pose as an aide
memoire, as the model
would not have been able to
hold the pose for long.

Woman Drying Herself,
1896–99, pastel on paper,
private collection

Closely related to *After the
Bath, Woman Drying Herself*
narrows the space so the
figure occupies the entire
length of the picture surface,
as though it was a close-up
of the earlier picture. Degas
has also added washing
utensils and a sponge in the
foreground, drawing visual
analogies between the figure
and the jug on the extreme
right. The green and red
patterned wallpaper creates
a heightened visual sensation.

*Three Dancers, c.*1896–1905, pastel on paper, Art Gallery and Museum, Kelvingrove, Glasgow, Scotland, 51 x 47cm (20 x 18½in)

The motif of a woman with her hands on her hips was employed by Degas in several compositions of the 1890s to varying effect. These figures pay rapt attention to something that is happening on the stage but which the viewer does not see. In the 1890s, Degas was experimenting with different levels of completion in his work. Though unfinished by traditional 19th-century standards, Degas clearly liked the impression achieved by a sketchier finish.

*Three Dancers (Yellow Skirts, Blue Blouses), c.*1896, pastel and charcoal on paper laid down on thin card, private collection, 56 x 51cm (22 x 20in)

This version of the *Three Dancers* illustrates how Degas would vary the treatment of his motifs. Despite its similarities of conception, Degas adjusts the poses, lighting, palette and background to convey an entirely different impression. The densely worked and deeply saturated colour of these later paintings often recalls the works of artists like Titian, Veronese and Tintoretto, whom Degas greatly admired.

The Green Skirt, c.1896,
**pastel on paper,
Art Gallery and Museum,
Kelvingrove, Glasgow,
Scotland, 45 x 37cm
(18 x 14½in)**

The writer Joris-Karl
Huysmans, an admirer of
Degas, spoke of him as an
artist who worked against
the grain of his talents as a
draughtsman. In his later
career Degas often gave
greater emphasis to colour,
and his drawing style
becomes less finely
rendered, no doubt as a
result of his declining
eyesight. Here the line
drawing orders
the composition.

La Toilette, **1897, pastel on
paper, private collection,
61 x 50cm (24 x 20in)**

In the 1890s Degas
explored a motif of a
woman washing herself with
a bowl of water, viewed
from an oblique frontal
angle. In this example the
woman converses with her
maid who has warmed fresh
water for the washbowl.
In these pictures there is
often little interaction
between the maids and the
bathers, but in some a more
intimate relationship
between the two is shown.
As in several pictures of the
period, visual puns are made
between the woman's body
and the sponge and jug she
washes with.

Woman at her Toilette,
**c.1897, pastel on paper,
private collection**

Though closely connected to
La Toilette, the impression is
markedly dissimilar. The
almost monochromatic dark
ochre tonality, relieved only
by subtle white, blue and red
inflections, creates a different
ambience. Degas also
introduces more detail into
the background, while
de-personalizing the figure,
whose proportions and
nakedness bring a more
classical inflection to the
subject. The absence of the
maid creates a more intimate
relation to the bather.

Four Dancers on Stage, 1897,
pastel, private collection,
65.5 x 65.5cm,
(26 x 26in)

Another of Degas' most
favoured motifs of the 1890s
is a group of ballerinas in
dress rehearsal or waiting at
the side of the stage for their
entrance. Degas produced
many versions of this motif
using different tonal schemes
and making various
adjustments of pose and
expression. The intricate
interlacing of the figures,
shown stretching and
adjusting their costumes
and hair, reveals Degas'
command of compositional
figure grouping.

Dancer with a Tambourine,
c.1897, oil and pastel on
canvas, private collection,
33 x 40cm (13 x 16in)

Degas' borrowing of motifs,
themes and allusions from
the classical tradition have
been well explored, but
his references to the art of
his contemporaries have
received less attention.
Degas enjoyed
experimenting with different
styles and techniques. This
exuberant ballet scene,
featuring *Commedia dell'arte*
characters, shows him
loosely adopting the
Pointilliste style of
Neoimpressionists like Seurat
and Signac.

Dancers Wearing Salmon-Coloured Skirts, c.1898, pastel, private collection

Degas shows three ballerinas in contrasting poses, signifying other contrasts between them through the details of comportment, gesture and other minor inflections. Changes to the position of the figures are evident in the lower part of the picture. Degas used the compositional cropping of figures both to suggest an arbitrary, indiscriminate slice of life but also to imply continuity between the actual world of the viewer and the fictive world of the picture.

Dancers on a Bench, c.1898, pastel on paper, Art Gallery and Museum, Kelvingrove, Glasgow, Scotland, 54 x 75.5cm (21 x 30in)

Closely related to other rehearsal pictures such as *Dancers in the Classroom* and *Dancers at Rehearsal,* this variation focuses on dancers taking a break. The picture shares three figures with *Dancers at Rehearsal,* but also includes a figure fanning herself. The cramped format adds to the sense of fatigue expressed by the dancers.

The Hatmaker (detail), c.1898, pastel, private collection

Degas' pictures set in millinery shops began to disappear in the mid-1880s, as he reassessed his artistic priorities and focused his attention on less immediately contemporary subjects. This rare millinery scene shows him adopting a style similar to the Nabis artists, such as Vuillard and Bonnard, Symbolists inspired by Gauguin's paintings.

After the Bath, Woman Drying her Neck, 1898, pastel on mounted paper, Musée d'Orsay, Paris, France, 62 x 65cm (24½ x 25½in)

In this version of a woman drying herself, Degas places the figure on the edge of the tub rather than seated in a chair. He unifies the picture through harmonious colours. The white towel is picked up in the linen screen, while her orange dress, draped on the chair, is picked up in the wall, and the pattern of the wallpaper is echoed in the upholstered chair.

Two Dancers Relaxing, c.1898–1900, pastel, Suzuki Collection, Tokyo, Japan, 73 x 105cm (29 x 41in)

Dancers are shown tending their sore legs and feet. Degas would make many variations of this motif using different colour schemes and adjustments to the poses, exploring the relationships between the figures. Here the extraordinary yellow, green and orange tonality seems to merge the figures into the background. In his later pictures Degas often harmonized figures with the background.

Two Dancers, c.1898–99,
pastel and charcoal on
paper, Hermitage, St.
Petersburg, Russia,
48 x 36cm (19 x 14in)

This is an unusual picture for
Degas. The dancers are
mature and full figured
rather than the lithe young
girls who usually populate
his ballerina pictures, and he
has gone to some lengths to
differentiate the figures. The
contrasting poses, each
preparing themselves for an
imminent performance is a
recurring motif in the 1890s.

Three Russian Dancers, 1899,
pastel on paper,
Nationalmuseum,
Stockholm, Sweden,
62 x 67cm (24½ x 26in)

In this pastel Degas
emphasizes the co-ordination
of the dancers' bodies in
unison. The dancers are
shown from different angles.
Degas differentiates them by
their physiognomy and floral
crowns, but unites them
through their billowing pink
skirts. The two figures
nearest the picture edge
seem almost joined at the
hip, while the skirt of the far
dancer echoes that of those
nearest the viewer.

Three Dancers, *c.*1899, pastel on paper, private collection, 65.5 x 65.5cm (26 x 26in)

This is one of a major series of pictures featuring three or four dancers adjusting their costumes before the performance. Set against a painted landscape backdrop, the poses of the figures are picked up in the trees and hills of the stage scenery. In earlier ballerina pictures, dancers were often seen from distant, detached perspectives. Later pictures like these bring the viewer close to the figures in a way that is comparable to the bathers' pictures.

Blue Dancers, *c.*1899, pastel, Pushkin Museum, Moscow, Russia, 65 x 65cm (25½ x 25½in)

Blue Dancers provides an interesting comparison with *Three Dancers*. Executed on the same scale, but with an additional figure, it demonstrates how Degas varied his motifs. Minor and major adjustments of poses, palette, stage setting, space, vantage point and style are evident, and result in a more dramatic, animated and vibrant picture.

Four Dancers in the Wings,
c.1899, pastel, private
collection, 80 × 110cm
(31½ × 43¼in)

In this late picture of dancers
waiting at the side of the
stage, Degas brings together
various motifs in a striking
new arrangement. On the
right two figures in pink are
deep in conversation; on the
far left a dancer peers on to
the stage, while the central
figure prepares herself for
her performance. The
picture is loosely worked
with varied techniques in the
handling of the dancers and
the scenery.

Dancers in Lemon and Pink,
c.1899–1904, pastel,
Solomon R. Guggenheim
Museum, New York, USA,
99 × 71.5cm (39 × 28in)

Degas often represents
figures completely absorbed
in something that falls
outside the picture, a
compositional convention he
would have noted in the
work of the 17th-century
Dutch masters he and
Duranty admired. Here, the
focus is only broken by the
figure bending to tie her
slipper. The concentration of
the figures forms a parallel
with the attention of the
viewer to the picture itself.

Russian Dancers, c.1899, pastel on paper, private collection, 48 x 67cm (19 x 26in)

The series of images of Russian dancers form an unexpected departure in Degas' late work. Located in open-air landscape settings, they show Degas' interest in the contemporary vogue for folk art. Troupes of foreign dancers regularly performed in the cabarets near Degas' studio in Montmartre. These are among the most exuberant and energetic pictures of Degas' career.

Three Dancers in Peasant Costume, 1899, pastel on paper, private collection, 62 x 67cm (24½ x 26in)

Degas' images of Russian dancers convey the energetic choreography of the dances, allowing the brightly coloured skirts to expressively animate the pictures. In making these pastels, Degas may well have drawn on Henri de Soria's illustrated *Histoire Pittoresque de la Danse* (1897), in which the frenzied performances of Balkan and Russian dances are documented. Such performances were also documented by film-makers and it is possible that Degas saw images of dancers like these at the cinema.

Two Dancers, c.1900–02, pastel and black chalk, private collection, 81 x 67cm (32 x 26in)

In this simplified and loosely drawn picture, two identically dressed and similarly posed dancers sit astride a bench, resting after a performance. Degas only distinguishes between them by their hair colour and the somewhat absent-minded pose of the dark-haired dancer, who plays with her hair. Both figures tend to the sore foot of the red-headed dancer.

Two Blue Dancers, c.1900, pastel on paper, Van der Heydt Museum, Wuppertal, Germany, 79 x 51cm (31 x 20in)

This is one of several variations on a pose of two dancers with their hands raised, which Degas returned to many times in the 1890s. The tree in the foreground echoes the dancers' gesture. Degas added a strip of paper across the left-hand and lower margins to give the composition more breadth.

Two Dancers in the Foyer, c.1901, pastel on paper, private collection, 74 x 60cm (29 x 23½in)

In this picture are two familiar motifs of the 1890s being used in a new way. This is another example of the way Degas structures his pictures of dancers around states of absorption, unaware that they are an object of interest. Their attention to something outside the picture space creates a corresponding impression of curiosity for the viewer.

Dancer Arranging her Hair,
c.1900–12, pastel on paper,
private collection,
37 x 28cm (14½ x 11in)

Degas' bathers and
ballerinas were made in a
close and mutually informing
dialogue and reflect the
concentration of his later

oeuvre. In this picture,
reminiscent in pose and
subject of many of Degas'
pictures of women *à la
toilette*, we see a dancer
pinning a decorative flower
headpiece in her hair.
A yellowish green tutu hangs
on the wall before her.

Ballerinas in Red Skirts,
c.1901, pastel on paper,
Gallery and Museum,
Kelvingrove, Glasgow,
Scotland, 81 x 62cm
(32 x 24½in)

This picture is closely related
to *Dancers with Hair in
Braids*, though Degas has
altered the poses of two of

the figures and made
changes to their position,
placing them closer to the
picture threshold. The
picture has a higher level of
finish than its sketchier
counterpart, but the most
dramatic change is in the
palette with its vibrant red
tonality and decoratively
patterned scenery.

*Three Dancers with a
Backdrop of Trees and Rocks,*
1904–06, pastel, private
collection, 84 x 59.5cm
(33 x 23½in)

This picture has a close
relationship to others in the
series of three ballerinas
waiting in the wings, though
here Degas takes a more
distant vantage point, allowing

more scope for showing
contextual features of the
stage. The dancer with her
hands on her hips is now
placed in the centre instead
of the front. Degas seems to
suggest that even when
waiting offstage the dancers'
bodies naturally fall into the
positions their bodies have
been conditioned through
training to adopt.

Woman Combing her Hair,
1905–10, pastel on paper,
Kunsthaus, Zurich,
Switzerland, 70.5 x 70.5cm
(28 x 28in)

This rhythmic version of a
woman combing her hair is
one of the most decorative
and abstract of Degas'
treatment of the motif. The
visual rhymes between the
arabesque of the woman's
long, wavy, black back-combed
hair and the undulating curves
of her hips and back are
obtrusive. Other subtler
symmetries are to be found
in the form of her body.

Ballerinas Dancing, c.1907,
pastel on greenish tracing
paper, National Gallery of
Washington, Washington,
DC, USA, 77 x 111cm
(30 x 44in)

The last two decades of
Degas' working life were
characterized by increasing
experimentation with style
and technique. The bold
colour and looser manner of
rendering of his later
pictures gives rise to some
of his least constrained
compositions. Some of
Degas' ballerinas adopt
natural poses but others,
as here, are more stylized
and make clear allusions to
classical poses. The
decorative conception of
the figures is enhanced by
the stage scenery.

DRAWINGS, PRINTS AND OIL SKETCHES

Degas' drawings show him exploring and experimenting with the expressive possibilities of his motifs. Drawing served not only as preparatory sketches for paintings but as an expressive medium in its own right. Though rightly considered one of the great draughtsmen of his time, Degas' drawings show that he was as active in exploring the potential of colour as that of line, and many of his sketches are studies in colour. Printmaking was also an important feature of Degas' oeuvre and provided him with another opportunity to try various media.

Above: Profile of a Dancer Upright, charcoal, pastel and chalk on paper, c.1877–80, private collection

Left: Dancer Fixing her Slipper, c.1885, charcoal on paper, Musée Bonnat, Bayonne, France, 31 x 24cm (12 x 9½in)

Portrait of a Young Man,
*c.*1859–60, thinned oil on
blue-grey cardboard,
private collection

This portrait of Degas'
younger brother René is one
of many of his family in the
1850s and 60s. It shows
Degas mastering the art of
capturing a likeness and hints
at the deeper character of
his brother. René would later
marry his first cousin, Estelle
Musson, in New Orleans and
set up in the family cotton
business, but was never
successful. His borrowings
from his father left the family
with huge debts from his
failed enterprises.

*Self Portrait, c.*1857, oil on
paper laid down on canvas,
private collection

In Degas' early portraits we
see him exploring various
aspects of his identity. In
this rather reserved and
unfinished portrait he
appears melancholic and
introverted, using the amber
lighting to divide his face and
model his features. It is
unusual for Degas to portray
himself frontally and this
suggests the portrait was
made using a mirror to
reflect his appearance.

Venus, after Mantegna, *c.1855*, pencil on paper, Ashmolean Museum, University of Oxford, UK

This fine pencil study is of the central figure of Andrea Mantegna's *Pallas Expelling the Vices from the Garden of Virtue* (1497). It is one of several copies he made of Mantegna's representation of Venus, which he studied in the Louvre. From the beginning of his career Degas admired this austere Quattrocento painter, a taste that would last a lifetime.

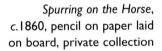

Spurring on the Horse, *c.1860*, pencil on paper laid on board, private collection

In addition to his many pictures of horse-racing Degas made many sketches and several paintings of gentlemen riding. These were mainly in response to his visits to the Valpinçon estate in Ménil-Hubert, Normandy, whose elegance left an enduring impression on him. The Valpinçons owned stables and rode for recreation and hunting. This study places emphasis on the powerful body of the thoroughbred horse, seen from the rear.

Study of Hands, 1859–60, oil on canvas, Musée d'Orsay, Paris, France, 38 x 46cm (15 x 18in)

This elaborate study of hands for the portrait of *The Bellelli Family* shows Degas' technical mastery. Though only a study, the picture leaves a strong and perplexing impression on the viewer. The inclusion of details such as the table and clothing encourage the viewer to search for a subject and try to reconcile these two hands with a body that might possess them. They are each treated with different degrees of detail.

Twelve Studies of Women in Costume of the Second Empire, c.1875, pen and ink on buff paper, Louvre, (Cabinet de Dessins), Paris, France, 46 x 32cm (18 x 12½in)

This series of studies of fashionable Parisian women suggests a composition rather than a set of individual studies. Though some figures are isolated, the majority fall into two coherent groupings of women interacting and conversing. This may indicate Degas was intending to make a painting in the style of Tissot, whose genre pictures of fashionable women won him great success in England.

Young Spartan Girls Provoking the Boys, 1860, oil on canvas laid down on board, private collection

Young Spartans was Degas' first major picture, though one he felt ambivalent about. He kept it in his apartment and never exhibited it, despite considering doing so at various points in his career. Degas made many preparatory studies of the painting's main figures. Though the poses of these two girls remained relatively unchanged, Degas altered the physiognomy, hairstyle and expression of the right-hand figure and also gave both figures skirts.

Study for a Portrait of Manet,
1864–65, black chalk,
Metropolitan Museum of
Art, New York, USA,
32.5 x 23cm (13 x 9in)

Degas made many sketches
and several paintings of his
close friend and artistic ally
Édouard Manet. Degas'
imagery and technique owed
much to Manet's example
and his personality was
congenial for the young
artist. In turn, Manet
recognized Degas as a
unique talent. This sketch
captures a good likeness,
not only in the face, but in
the characteristic pose,
allowing Manet to casually
define himself.

Portrait of Edouard Manet,
c.1864–65, pencil on paper,
private collection

In this study Degas
concentrates on Manet's
facial features and powerful
head, seen in three-quarters
profile, emphasizing the
artist's strong intellect. As in
some of Ingres' pictures the
face is worked up in far
greater detail than the bust
and clothing, signifying the
special emphasis traditionally
placed on the face to define
the personality of the sitter.

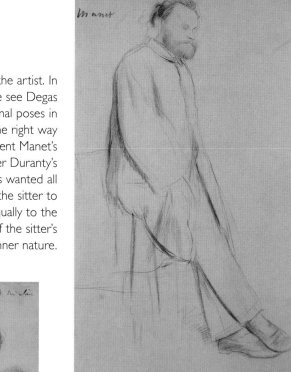

Portrait of Édouard Manet, c.1864–65, pencil on paper, Musée Marmottan, Paris, France, 40 x 26cm (15½ x 10in)

In some of Degas' studies of Manet he concentrates on the artist's face, using his physiognomy and expression to convey the inner character of the artist. In other studies we see Degas exploring informal poses in order to find the right way to present Manet's personality. Under Duranty's influence Degas wanted all aspects of the sitter to contribute equally to the expression of the sitter's inner nature.

Study for a Portrait of Edouard Manet, c.1864–65, pencil on tinted paper, private collection, 41 x 28cm (16 x 11in)

These studies of Manet refer back to earlier work. Degas has redrawn the previous study of Manet's head, added more detail in the costume, and redrawn the head of the Musée Marmottan study. He has also returned to the seated format of the drawing in the Metropolitan Museum of Art, though dispensing with Manet's long coat and posing him more informally. Manet's top hat lies on its side, an allusion to Manet's inclusion of such isolated details in his pictures.

Elizabeth de Valois (after Anthonis Mor or Moro), c.1865–70, charcoal on paper, Fitzwilliam Museum, Cambridge, UK, 40.5 x 27.5cm (16 x 11in)

Degas' copies allowed him to enter into an intimate dialogue with the work of other artists. Degas was especially attracted to copying the drawings of Raphael, whom Ingres considered the greatest artist, but also Mannerist court portraiture, as here in this copy after the Netherlandish painter Anthonis Mor (c.1516–75).

Jockey on Horseback, c.1866,
crayon on paper, The
Barnes Foundation, Merion,
Pennsylvania, USA,
16 x 21.5cm (6 x 8½in)

Degas' equestrian pictures
explore many aspects of the
world of racing. One of the
persistent underlying themes
is the struggle of man to
harness and control the
wildness of nature. This was
a theme Degas encountered
in Géricault and Delacroix
and which he continued into
his own work. Often, as
here, we see jockeys
struggling to bring rearing
horses under their control.

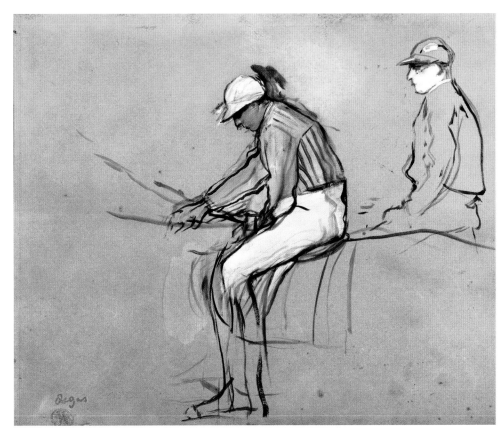

Jockeys, c.1868, gouache
on paper

The majority of Degas'
equestrian studies are of
horses, often without riders,
but Degas also produced
studies of the jockeys
showing them in contrasting
poses and attitudes. These
vary considerably, showing
the jockeys confident and in
control or struggling to
master their horses. Here,
Degas' rapid notational
drawing gives a nervous
energy to the rather
tentative-looking jockeys.

*Man and Woman, c.*1869, oil
on canvas, private collection

This is one of the studies for
Degas' *Interior,* also known
by the title *My Genre Picture.*
Degas retained the pose of
the man holding his hands in
his pockets, but little else.
In the final picture the figure
is placed against a door not
a window and stands on
wooden floorboards.
However, the most
important change is the
transformation of the
conception of the female
figure into a seated and
partially undressed figure at
the far side of the
composition.

Lady with a Parasol, 1870–72, oil on canvas, Samuel Courtauld Trust, The Courtauld Gallery, London, UK, 75 x 85cm (29½ x 33½in)

This aborted painting suggests Degas planned a large picture of a woman with a parasol, perhaps a beach scene. The woman is dressed in fashionable clothing as though *en promenade*, yet it is an unusual composition that leaves open what the subject is. The woman is seen from an oblique sideways angle, offering little information about her identity, and there is little space for contextual detail. This may be why Degas abandoned it.

Mademoiselle Malo, c.1875–77, pastel on buff paper, Barber Institute, University of Birmingham, UK, 52 x 41cm (20½ x 16in)

Thérèse Mallot, a former dancer, was the wife of Victor-Georges Legrand and mistress of Achille, Degas' brother. Mademoiselle Malo, sat for Degas for four portraits around 1877. These portraits are varied portraying her looking distinctly younger and older, leading to speculation that one of the portraits may be of her mother.

The Ballet Master, 1875, pastel, Philadelphia Museum of Art, Pennsylvania, USA, 48 x 30cm (19 x 12in)

This was a study for *The Dance Class*, which Degas made two versions of. Degas admired Perrot, the most successful male dancer of the mid-1830s. He featured as ballet master in four paintings of rehearsal scenes, though by the time Degas depicted him he was retired. Degas sought him out and he agreed to pose for several drawings.

The Song of the Dog,
1876–77, crayon lithograph,
private collection,
51 × 42cm (20 × 16½in)

In this lithograph of *The Song of the Dog,* reworked with crayon, Degas places more emphasis on the singer, whose song is embodied in the pose with its raised forearms accentuating drooping hands. Her chin is raised and eyes closed in total immersion in the song. Degas has animated the sky, roughly working the plate to achieve a highly animated effect that serves to amplify the mood of the song.

Three Girls Bathing (Peasant Girls Bathing in the Sea at Dusk), 1875–76, oil on canvas, private collection, 65 × 81cm (25½ × 32in)

As Degas redefined himself as a painter of contemporary life in the late 1860s and 1870s, he temporarily stopped painting the nude. This is a rare example from the 1870s. Although the title suggests an observed scene, social protocols about public bathing make this almost certainly an imaginary composition.

The Café-Concert, or *The Song of the Dog,* 1875–77, gouache and pastel on paper, private collection, 52 × 42.5cm (20½ × 17in)

In this version of a picture that he reproduced in various media, Degas captures the luminous glow of the gaslights, which were still considered a novel feature of the new Paris. The lights hang from trees or stand on columns. The strange light illuminates the face and arms of the singer, possibly the celebrated Thérèsa or one of her lesser competitors.

The Star, c.1878, pastel on paper, Philadelphia Museum of Art, Pennsylvania, USA, 38 x 28cm (15 x 11in)

This is one of several studies for the many pictures of star dancers taking their applause. In these sketches and paintings, Degas shifted the position of the dancer across the picture surface and made various adjustments to her pose. Here, adding a comical note, her grand curtsey is obscured by the branches of the scenery. Degas boldly compresses the perspective between the main figure and the ballerina on the right.

Mademoiselle Bécat at the Cafe des Ambassadeurs, 1877–78, print, lithograph on white woven paper, private collection, 20.5 x 19cm (8 x 7¾in)

Of all the stars of the café-concerts Degas represented, he made more images of Emélie Bécat than any other, making five separate prints of her, including one with three individual prints. Here she is seen at the Ambassadeurs with her arms spread in a gesture imploring the audience. Bécat's act was notable for its eccentric, frenzied movement and engagement of the audience.

Lady with Opera Glasses, 1875–76, oil on paper, Galerie Neue Meister, Dresden, Germany, 48 x 32cm (19 x 12½in)

During the mid-1870s Degas was preoccupied with the idea of an image of a woman with binoculars gazing out of a picture, in a reversal of the usual structure of observation in his work. Typically, Degas located the viewer as the bearer of an unreciprocated gaze, straying only from this in his portraits. The sketches remain all that was realized of this aborted project.

Girl Looking Through Opera Glasses, 1874–75, oil on panel, Art Gallery and Museum, Kelvingrove, Glasgow, Scotland, 32 x 18.5cm (12½ x 7in)

Comparison with *Lady with Opera Glasses* shows Degas making changes to the clothing and palette, as well as minor adjustments to the figure's pose. It is interesting to speculate why Degas abandoned the picture. It seems likely the reversal of the structure of looking proved impossible to reconcile with his painting, but it may also have concerned the image of a woman, for once empowered with the gaze normally reserved for the spectator.

Three Ballet Dancers, c.1878,
monotype on paper,
Sterling & Francine Clark
Art Institute, Williamstown,
USA, 20 x 41.5cm
(8 x 16½in)

Degas tended to reserve his
monotypes for his more
satirical and caricatured
images. This monotype of
ballerinas performing on
stage falls into that category.
The dancers' poses seem
comical and a little absurd.
The heavy proportions and
imbalance of the two
ballerinas on the right leave
an impression of clumsiness
rather than grace.

*Study of a Violinist Seen from
the Back, c.1878–82,*
black chalk touched with
white chalk squared in
black chalk on grey paper,
Ashmolean Museum,
University of Oxford, UK,
48 x 31.5cm (19 x 12½in)

This charcoal study of a lone
violinist seen from the rear
was probably done in the
opera rehearsal rooms. This
motif features in several
ballet rehearsal scenes.
Though seen from the back,
Degas conveys a strong
impression of the musician.
The page has been squared
up to keep the drawing in
proportion and white chalk
added to provide highlights.

*Girl Dancer at the Barre,
c.1878,* black chalk,
Fitzwilliam Museum,
University of Cambridge,
UK, 31 x 24cm
(12 x 9½in)

This quickly rendered pencil
drawing shows a young
dancer practising at the
barre. Though roughly
drawn, the picture
nevertheless captures the
struggle of the dancer to
learn her positions. It shows
Degas' awareness of the
expressive possibilities of the
naive drawing style of
popular illustrators and
cartoonists and a desire to
incorporate aspects of
popular art into his pictures.

*The Brothel, c.*1879, pastel and monotype on paper, private collection
14 x 20.5cm (5½ x 8in)

The majority of the brothel monotypes that survived Degas' death are scenes of the prostitutes socializing and relaxing or interacting with clients, though some have sexually explicit content, as in this lesbian scene. The fact that some of these brothel monotypes were posthumously destroyed suggests many more may have shown explicit sexual acts.

Mademoiselle La La at the Cirque Fernando, 1879, black chalk and pastel on paper, The Barber Institute, University of Birmingham, UK, 47 x 32cm (18½ x 12½in)

In planning his picture of the sensational acrobat Mlle. La La, who performed at the Cirque Fernando in Paris to great acclaim, at the beginning of 1879, Degas made several preparatory studies in pencil and in pastel. Always seeking out ultra-contemporary subjects Mlle. La La's act, which involved being suspended from a rope between her teeth, provided Degas with a daring and spectacular subject.

*Le Cirque Fernando –
architectural study*, black and
red chalk and pencil on two
sheets of joined paper,
1879, The Barber Institute
of Fine Arts, University of
Birmingham, UK,
48 x 31cm (19 x 12in)

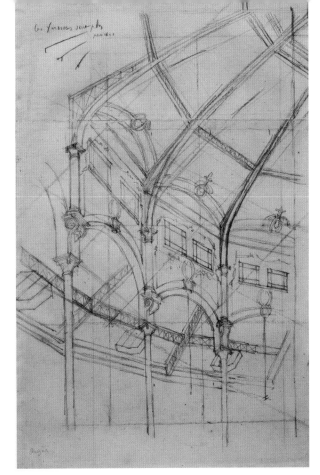

This is an architectural study
for his painting *Mlle. La La at
the Cirque Fernando*. It shows
how keen Degas was to
incorporate an accurate
representation of the
environment of the circus,
with its distinctive dome.
Degas extended this sketch
by adding two pieces of
paper to the central section.

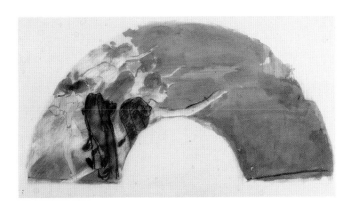

Sketch for a Fan, c.1879,
pastel, turpentine and chalk,
private collection,
36 x 65cm (14 x 25½in)

Degas produced several
designs for fans for the
Fourth Impressionist
Exhibition. In this example
the right-hand space is left
vacant as in Japanese prints,
while on the left a group of
dancers perform arabesques.
In the foreground the
headstock and tuners of two
violoncellos can be seen.
The design has been left in a
provisional state, as on the
right the diluted pastel has
bled beyond the edges.

Portrait of Diego Martelli,
1879, chalk on paper,
private collection,
42 x 30cm (16½ x 12in)

This black-and-white chalk
drawing on brown paper
was a study for Degas'
portrait of the Florentine
engraver and critic, Diego

Martelli (1838–96). A
leading advocate of the
Italian Macchiaoli group who
were strongly influenced by
Courbet, Martelli struck up
a close and affectionate
friendship with Degas during
his time in Paris. Degas liked
to drop into his studio and
speak Italian with him.

Mary Cassatt at the Louvre, The Paintings Gallery, 1879–80, etching, Sterling & Francine Clark Art Institute, Williamstown, USA, 30.5 x 12.5cm (12 x 5in)

Degas printed around 20 versions of this etching, the second largest number of any of his prints. The motif, which exists in various states and versions, shows Mary Cassatt admiring works in the Louvre, accompanied by her semi-invalid sister, Lydia, shown seated reading a catalogue in the foreground. Degas intended the work to contribute to a journal he was hoping to found entitled *Le Jour et la Nuit (Day and Night)*, which was to include literary texts and prints.

Mary Cassatt at the Louvre, c.1879–80, pastel, private collection, 64 x 48cm (25 x 19in)

This is a sketch for the pastel version of *Mary Cassatt at the Louvre,* concentrating on the physiognomy of Cassatt's back and her idiosyncratic pose. In the various versions of this motif, she is shown either in the paintings gallery or observing an encased Etruscan sculpture. For the final pastel version, Degas moved her sister to the right to give an unimpeded view of Cassatt, whose character is defined through her pose and dress.

Ballerina Viewed from the Back, c. late 1870s, charcoal on paper, private collection, 31 x 23cm (12¼ x 9in)

This simple but affecting charcoal drawing on tinted paper shows Degas looking for symmetries in the dancer's appearance. Her feet, turned outwards, create a visual rhyme with the line of her tutu. The compact alignment of her arms creates a roughly tubular form that continues through the position of her legs. Only her head, turned to the side in profile, breaks with this rigid harmonization.

Study of Dancers, c. late 1870s, pencil on paper, private collection, 47.5 x 30cm (19 x 12in)

This undated sheet of sketches of ballerinas was probably made while studying dancers at the rehearsal rooms in the Opéra. These pictorial notations rapidly put down on paper, show various poses, intended as aide memoires for later compositions. The style of the drawings is quite naive, showing the strong and enduring influence of caricaturists and cartoonists on Degas.

Study of a Girl's Head, late 1870s, oil on canvas, National Gallery of Scotland, Edinburgh, Scotland, 57 x 45cm (22½ x 17¾in)

This is an unusual work for Degas, coming at a time when his portraiture had already receded. The way the figure is dressed suggests this was a portrait of a ballerina, though it is rare for Degas to portray a ballerina in a portrait. The way her straps have fallen below her shoulders gives an erotic inflection to the painting.

*Prostitutes Waiting for a Client, c.*1877–79, monotype, private collection, 13 x 20cm (5 x 8in)

This brothel monotype shows the broad, naive style of drawing this medium favoured. As in *Waiting for a Client*, the prostitutes seem alerted to the presence of a customer; the central figure adopting a vulgar pose to try and lure him. The figure on the far side lies flat out on the sofa, perhaps asleep or exhausted, while the middle figure has an almost rodent-like physiognomy.

*Waiting for a Client, c.*1879, pastel and charcoal on paper, private collection, 16.5 x 12cm (6½ x 5in)

Degas occasionally coloured the second, fainter impressions of some of his brothel monotypes with pastel, as he has done here. The prostitutes look toward a client, whose profile can just be made out cropped at the left-hand margin. Degas' images of the brothel depart from the idealized portrayals of courtesans at the Salon, adding a note of realism into contemporary images of prostitution. However, their brutish and rather bestial imagery speaks to common 19th-century notions of prostitutes as sexually depraved.

Dancer Viewed from the Back, c.1880–85, pencil, charcoal and chalk on yellow paper, private collection, 50 x 39cm (20 x 15in)

The motif of a woman supporting her back with her arms first emerges in the mid-1870s and continued to be used by Degas until the end of his career. Here we see a dancer turned to her left, gazing at a scene withheld from the viewer, a typical trait of Degas' compositions. The figure is drawn in brown ink with green modelling to the costume and flesh.

Three Prostitutes on a Sofa, c.1879, pastel on monotype on beige paper, private collection, 16 x 21.5cm (6 x 8½in)

In one of the more subdued images of the brothel monotypes, Degas shows three barely covered prostitutes seated on a couch, awaiting clients. Their expressions suggest different states of mind or mindlessness. Degas, like many men of his time, believed prostitutes were sexually deviant by nature, rather than drawn to prostitution through impoverishment.

*Three Dancers, c.1880,
pastel and charcoal on
paper, private collection,
46.5 x 51cm (18¼ x 20in)*

Many of Degas' drawings
show him developing an
image repertory of poses
to populate his multi-figure
ballerina compositions. Here
we see him developing
contrasting poses of dancers.
These sheets of drawings
testify not only to his desire
to find a variety of poses,
but to establish coherent
groupings between the
figures. Visual rhymes as well
as differences are present in
the relationship of the figures
to each other, allowing subtle
unities and contrasts to
co-exist harmoniously in
his compositions.

*Two Ballet Dancers Resting,
c.1880s, pencil, chalk and
pastel on green paper,
Kunsthaus, Zurich,
Switzerland*

Comparison with *Study of
Dancers* shows how Degas
varied his drawing style for
particular effect. This
drawing shows a familiar
motif of dancers resting.
Degas often explored his
motifs from different points
of view and here we see the
dancers from an oblique rear
angle. A crimson colour note
is introduced in the
hairbands of the dancers and
subtle violet shading on the
dresses and floorboards.

*Jockeys, c.*1880,
pencil on paper,
private collection

Degas was an artist who
continually sought to
challenge himself, and
believed that only by doing
so could he make genuine
artistic progress. In this
elegant but modest drawing
of three jockeys riding their
horses to the starting line,
he sets himself the task of
communicating contrasting
attitudes among the jockeys
exclusively from their poses
seen from the rear.

*At the Theatre, Woman with
a Fan*, 1880, pastel and
charcoal on paper laid down
on paper, private collection,
70.5 x 47cm (28 x 18½in)

In this study for *Ballerina and
Lady with a Fan,* Degas
concentrates on the pose
for the woman located in
one of the front loges at the
opera. In the final picture
more space was accorded
to the stage and the
ballerinas; the figure was
moved closer to the edge of
the picture and seen in
stricter profile. Greater
prominence was also given
to her decorative fan.

Dancer Seated, Readjusting her Stocking, c.1880, pencil on paper, private collection

The erotic motif of a ballerina pulling on her stocking appears in *Before the Ballet* (1888), though this study may have been made several years before. The dancer's coarse features and posture, turning her head away, seem slightly anomalous. Is she distracted, perhaps in conversation with another unseen dancer? The picture seems to carry a curious undercurrent of disquiet, even perhaps disgust.

Dancer Adjusting her Tights, c.1880, pencil and charcoal on paper, Fitzwilliam Museum, University of Cambridge, UK, 24 x 31cm (9½ x 12¼in)

Closely related to the pose of *Dancer Seated, Readjusting her Stocking*, the position of the dancer's head more closely resembles the ballerina in *Before the Ballet*, though her facial expression and hairstyle are different. In this drawing we see Degas harmonizing the ballerina's pose through visual similarities in the drawing of the arms and the legs. On the right-hand side, we see the redrawing and refining of the position of the arm.

Dancer, c.1880, pastel on laid paper, private collection

Though Degas' imagery of the ballet often de-personalizes the ballerinas, portraying them as types rather than individuals, some of his drawings convey a strong impression of their character. The pose of this solidly built dancer, looking down at her feet to check her position, conveys something of the personality of the model.

A Dancer in Profile, c.1880s, chalk and charcoal on tinted paper, private collection

This economically rendered portrait of a red-headed dancer shows Degas studying the ballerina's posture in mid-dance. The revisions around the legs and arm reveal Degas searching to find a way of being true to the precision of the choreography of the body, while also suggesting its movement. The successive lines enliven the picture aiding the impression of animation.

Study of a Dancer,
c.1881–85, chalk on paper

In this curious sketch, we see Degas drawing a ballerina poised on one knee with her right arm raised, perhaps a study for a dancer taking her applause. Degas has redrawn the arm enlarged on the same sheet, studying the hand gesture in more detail. This is not unusual, as artists' sketchbooks are full of such supplementary studies, though the effect here is, intentionally or not, comical and curious.

Jockey at a Canter, c.1881,
red chalk over counterproof
on paper

Eadweard Muybridge's photographs of horses in motion changed the understanding of how horses move. Degas' early pictures of horses galloping show them with all legs off the ground. After seeing Muybridge's work, Degas began to correct the faults of his earlier work and represent more accurately the movement of horses.

In the Bath, c.1883, pastel and charcoal on paper, private collection, 26.5 x 31.5cm (10½ x 12½in)

Degas' bathers often look tentative as they lower themselves into the bathtub. The simplified context of the picture places attention on the body. Degas often drew his models leaning forward and in relaxed positions. Unusually the model in this study has short hair, perhaps having dispensed with the hair extensions often seen in Degas' toilette scenes.

Female Nude, c.1883, charcoal, private collection, 110 x 60cm (43¼ x 23½in)

This study of a woman who appears as a maid in several bathers' pictures, shows how carefully Degas worked out her careworn appearance and simian-like features. The age of the model varies in his pictures, but the pose remains constant, sentry-like and hieratic in comparison to the informality and varied, flexible motions of the bathers she is customarily juxtaposed with.

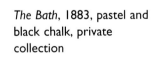

The Bath, 1883, pastel and black chalk, private collection

This study of a woman climbing into her bathtub places the emphasis on the articulation of the woman's body. The figure, with its realistic proportions, suggests references to Rubens and Courbet, whom Degas admired greatly. Both artists favoured heavier, more monumental depictions of the female form. Degas makes the contouring and musculature of the woman's back and buttocks the visual focus of the work, using rapidly worked strokes in black chalk to give the body form, depth and volume.

*Dancer c.*1882–84, charcoal
and pastel, private
collection

This image of a ballerina
stooping to fix the strap
of her slipper is a good
example of the artistic
dialogue between Degas'
ballerinas and bathers.
A similar pose can be found
in pictures from the mid- to
late 1880s, showing some of
the bathers washing in a tub.
Here we see Degas
harmonizing the contour
lines of the back across the
whole of the dancer's body.

Female Standing Nude,
undated, charcoal and
pastel, Galerie Daniel
Malingue, Paris, France,
55.5 x 36.5cm (22 x 14in)

Some of Degas' drawings
carry an undercurrent of
disquiet and pathos
underneath their banal
exterior. This drawing may
well belong to Degas'
imagery of bathers, however,
the pose suggests allusions
to representations of Eve
being cast out of the Garden
of Eden. The successively
revised lines around the
contours of the body serve
to animate the figure, who
struggles to cover herself
while staring at something
outside the picture.

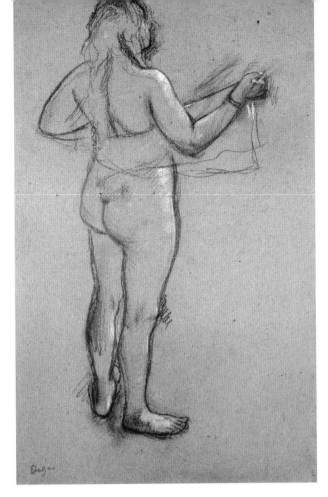

Nude Woman Drying Herself, 1884–86, charcoal heightened with white on paper, Ashmolean Museum, University of Oxford, UK, 43 x 48cm (17 x 19in)

Related to the group of works that includes *Woman Drying Herself*, this is one of several drawings Degas made of a woman posed in this fashion with her back to the viewer. Sometimes he reversed the position, reflecting his practice of tracing and retracing his drawings to refine and subtly alter their appearance. Degas also considerably varied the body, hair and features of the woman, who is shown to be more heavily set in this version.

Young Woman in Blue, c.1884, pastel over charcoal on paper, Indianapolis Museum of Art, USA, 64.5 x 47cm (25½ x 18½in)

The motif of a woman stretching her back with her arms on her hips is a familiar feature of the ballerina pictures by the 1880s and, more occasionally, of his bathers. Here, however, Degas has adapted it to a domestic interior scene of a fashionable middle-class woman seated on a red sofa. Degas adjusts the pose to make it into a rather affected gesture that tells us something about the personality of the sitter.

Seated Woman Adjusting Her Hair, c.1884, chalk and pastel on paper, Samuel Courtauld Trust, The Courtauld Gallery, London, UK, 63 x 60cm (25 x 23½in)

This picture may be a preparatory study for an oil version of the same subject. It belongs to the millinery shop series of the early 1880s. Degas often used pastels when preparing his oil pictures. As in many of his drawings, marked changes are evident in pose and other parts of the composition, which is made out of two joined pieces of paper.

Nude Getting Out of the Bath,
*c.*1885–90, pastel on crayon,
private collection,
93 x 78cm (36½ x 31in)

Degas was at his most
technically experimental in
the latter part of his career
and sought to rediscover
lost techniques and invent
new ones. Often he worked
with mixed media. Here he
combines pastel and wax
crayon to striking effect,
with its prevailing green
tonality, heightened by red
accents in the naked
woman's hair and the chair
she leans against.

Woman at her Toilette,
*c.*1885, pastel on cardboard,
Hermitage, St. Petersburg,
Russia, 56 x 59cm
(22 x 23in)

Closely related to the
painting of the same title,
and executed around the
same time, the model is
viewed from a sideways
angle and from a high
vantage point looking down
on to the woman. This is
another example of Degas
using the raised platforms in
his studio to create novel
viewpoints. Here the tonal
scheme has been changed,
including the colour of the
model's hair.

Dancer, c. mid-1880s, charcoal heightened with white chalk on paper, private collection

The twisting pose of the ballerina creates a complex dynamic to the body, as she turns to scrutinize her position in a mirror in the rehearsal room. The bold lines of the skirt and successively revised lines around the body also accentuate the impression of momentary movement and studious poise.

Dancer Fastening her Pump, c.1880–85, pastel and black chalk on buff paper, private collection, 47 x 43cm (18½ x 17in)

This extraordinary picture shows Degas' ability to confer artistic value on an otherwise banal scene.

Degas animates the fan-like form of the dancer's tutu as she bends to tie her slippers. The viewer is positioned looking down from a high vantage point on to the dancer, which dramatizes and makes strange a familiar, everyday action.

*Dancer at the Barre, c.*1885, charcoal with pastel and chalk on paper, Fred Jones Jr. Museum of Art, University of Oklahoma, USA, 31 x 23.5cm (12¼ x 9in)

This drawing of a dancer at the barre shows many successive revisions of the pose. Degas has altered the general position of the figure, adjusted its length and also made several changes to the position of the dancer's arms. These revisions are partly motivated by a desire for accuracy, but also by Degas' attempt to harmonize and bring symmetry to the dancer's pose.

Seated Woman in a White Dress, c.1888–92, pastel on board, private collection, 72 x 49cm (28 x 19½in)

Though genre pictures and portraiture receded in Degas' oeuvre after the mid-1880s, Degas remained committed to the idea he shared with Duranty of finding gestures which would communicate the spirit and sensibility of the age. Taking a high vantage point, which results in the model's face being covered by her hat, we nevertheless obtain a strong impression of the personality of the sitter from her costume, comportment and hand gestures.

La Danseuse, c.1888, pastel on paper, Art Gallery and Museum, Kelvingrove, Glasgow, Scotland, 45 x 23cm (17¾ x 9in)

Realism in France was predominantly associated with a picture in which the viewer's presence was not acknowledged. In the vast majority of Degas' pictures, with the exception of some portraits, we are drawn into a world in which figures are deeply absorbed in some activity, oblivious that they are being observed. The intense state of absorption in some activity, in this case a dancer watching from the wings, establishes a correlative for the viewer's attention to the picture.

Dancer Adjusting her Shoe, c.1890, pastel and charcoal on paper, private collection

This familiar motif of the ballerina adjusting her slipper is seen here from an oblique perspective and high vantage point. Degas gives more emphasis to the flamboyant bell-like shape of her tutu than the dancer herself, who is seen in *profil perdu*. The folds and form of the skirt have an almost flower-like appearance. The modelling and shadows, achieved with the use of charcoal and white pastel, suggest a strong sense of three-dimensionality despite being notational.

Kneeling Nude Woman, c.1889–95, pastel on paper, private collection

Some of Degas' bathers are closely related to the brothel monotype series, presenting figures in erotic and uninhibited poses, as in this pastel and charcoal sketch. This has led to broader speculation about the identity of these bathers. Regulations for registered brothels required prostitutes to wash before having sex with their clients. Are these bathers therefore prostitutes or simply middle-class women à la toilette? Degas leaves the question of their identity unanswered and ambiguous.

Seated Dancer Adjusting her Shoes, c.1890, charcoal and pastel on paper, Hermitage, St. Petersburg, Russia, 47 x 30.5cm (18½ x 12in)

Degas has made several adjustments to the pose of this motif, portraying the dancer rubbing her sore ankles. We are placed closer to the dancer than in comparable works such as *Dancer Adjusting her Shoe*, and the perspective lines of the floorboards draw us into a less detached engagement with the ballerina. Close proximity, however, is met with objectivity and psychological distance, a common feature of the Dutch 17th-century painting Degas admired.

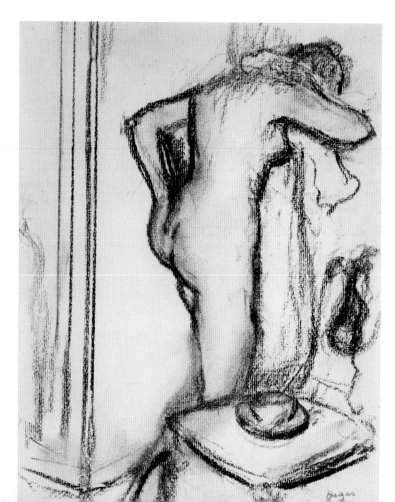

Woman at her Toilette, c.1890, charcoal on paper, Fitzwilliam Museum, University of Cambridge, UK, 32 x 25cm (12½ x 10in)

Closely related to the woman drying herself in *Breakfast After the Bath*, Degas has reversed the vantage point and altered the position of the left hand, as well as the setting. Although compact, the picture creates a strong impression of shallow space, through overlaps and the slanted walls that project outwards toward the front of the picture, suggesting a modest and cramped apartment setting.

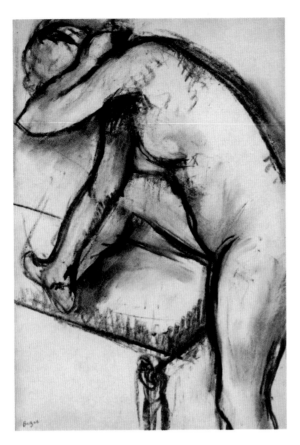

*Study of a Dancer, c.*1890, charcoal on paper, private collection, 52 x 34cm (20½ x 13½in)

This figure stepping out of a bathtub while drying her hair draws attention to the close dialogue between the bathers and ballerinas, as the pose resembles that of ballerinas adjusting the straps of their slippers or rubbing their weary limbs. The inelegance of the foreshortening of the leg seems deliberate, communicating the awkwardness of the action.

Studies of the Nude, c.1890–95, pastel on paper, The Barnes Foundation, Merion, Pennsylvania, USA

By any standards *Studies of the Nude* is a bold work, with its compositional cropping of the standing figure in the foreground, whose position masks the head of the prone nude in the centre with her legs crossed. Though a traditional pastoral theme, the picture is made contemporary by the clothing and fabrics on the ground, as well as by the modern technique Degas has used in applying the pastel.

Group of Dancers, c.1890–95, charcoal with traces of blue pastel on buff paper, private collection, 38 x 43cm (15 x 17in)

Like Baudelaire, Degas saw himself as living in an age in which art had fallen into a state of decrepitude and culture had decayed. The great themes and artistic licence that had sustained the grand masters were no longer available to painters of the contemporary world. In the ballet, he found poses and ways of grouping his figures that approximated to the multi-figure 'choreography' of the once great tradition of history painting.

After the Bath, c.1891–92, charcoal on yellow tracing paper, Sterling & Francine Clark Art Institute, Williamstown, USA, 35 x 25.5cm (13½ x 10in)

This standing nude is vigorously modelled, showing how Degas varied his drawing style to achieve different kinds of effect. The model's cascading hair is echoed in the draped towel she dries herself with. Degas' succesful revision of lines around the figure's contours draws the viewer's attention to the deliberations and decisions the artist has taken in revising his conception of the figure. In this respect, the picture becomes not only about the nude represented, but the artist's act of representation.

Woman Washing in the Bath,
c.1892, pastel on card,
Musée d'Orsay, Paris,
France, 32 x 47.5cm
(12½ x 19in)

This compact motif recurs in
several pictures of the 1890s.
Sometimes Degas adapted
the pose to include a maid
pouring water on to her
back, while she holds her
hair out of the way. Degas
uses similar pastel strokes to
model the body as well as
for the bathtub and wall,
although their size is varied.
The woman's back is
illuminated, contrasting with
the shadows in her
lowered head.

Bather Drying Herself,
c.1891–92, pencil on paper,
The Barnes Foundation,
Merion, Pennsylvania, USA

Degas exhaustively explored
the expressive possibilities
of his motifs. However,
some motifs proved more
fertile than others. This lithe
and elongated figure is
reminiscent in its proportions
to some of Ingres' nudes
and has a relation to
other standing figures, such
as *After the Bath*, but
despite this it remains an
isolated and relatively
unexplored motif.

Woman Drying Herself,
c.1893–98, charcoal and
pastel, private collection,
78.5 x 79cm (31 x 31in)

In Degas' depictions of
women washing and drying
themselves, the focus of his
attention is often on the
articulation of the body, not
merely its movement. In this
sketch of a familiar Degas
motif, visual harmonies are
established throughout the
body, most notably in the
triangular shapes of the arms
and the curves of the
woman's hips, buttocks, spine
and hair.

Two Dancers Resting,
c.1892–95, charcoal on
paper, private collection,
78 x 81cm (31 x 32in)

Degas' exploration of the
artistic possibilities of his
motifs shows him varying
the relationships between
figures. Sometimes the two
dancers in the *Dancers in
Repose* series seem distant
from each other, but here
they seem intimate. Degas
brings them into closer
proximity and uses visually
similar and rhyming lines to
suggest, in an understated
fashion, affinities between
the women.

*Woman at her Toilette,
c.1894, pastel, private
collection*

Degas' bathers convince
the viewer the figures are
unaware of being observed
as they express themselves
naturally in the activities of
their toilette. Close attention
to this informally posed
figure, however, shows how
Degas has carefully arranged
the body to create a series
of visual symmetries in the
representation of her body,
and visual puns with the
objects she washes with.

*Woman Drying, c.1893–98,
charcoal on paper,
private collection*

Closely related to *Woman
Drying her Arm*, this sketch
shows how Degas could
change the feeling and mood
of a picture by varying his
drawing technique, colour
and lighting. In this case, the
darker lighting makes for a
more sombre picture,
though the lines delineating
the folds of the towel
and the striations of
charcoal across the
woman's back enliven and
animate the picture.

Dancers, 1895, pastel and charcoal on paper, private collection, 86 x 63.5cm (34 x 25in)

Degas is rightly celebrated as one of the 19th century's most innovative draughtsman, but he was also one of its greatest colourists. His pictures from the 1880s onwards experiment with different tonal palettes in a way that is informed by tradition but not restricted by it. Degas' use of pastel fused his two talents. In using pastels Degas was, in effect, drawing with colour.

Half Length Nude Girl, *c*.1895, charcoal heightened with white on tracing paper, Fitzwilliam Museum, University of Cambridge, UK, 54 x 39cm (21 x 15in)

Though Degas seems to have seen his early history paintings as a 'false start' he sometimes worked on motifs that have similar poses to those of his earlier paintings. This figure is closely related to one that appears in *Medieval War Scene*, as if Degas was reaching back into the past and appropriating earlier work.

Dancer, 1896, pastel on
paper laid down on board,
private collection,
40 x 26.5cm
(15½ x 10½in)

This pastel sketch exemplifies
the mixing and matching of
motifs in Degas' later work.
The foreground dancer is
related to the motif of
dancers adjusting their
shoulder straps, although
seen from a different vantage
than normal. The pose of
the dancer behind her is
taken from *Two Dancers in
Repose*, although Degas has
altered her physiognomy to
make her appear older.
The picture's subtext
becomes the transition from
youth to maturity.

Two Dancers Resting, 1896,
pastel on paper,
private collection,
80 x 104.5cm (31½ x 41in)

This sketch of two dancers
in repose takes a simplified
frontal vantage point of its
subject. The figures at rest
are carefully choreographed,
as though their movements
were still part of a
performance, which, in the
sense that they are modelling
for Degas, they are. Degas
was drawn to the idea of an
art of apparent naturalism
that concealed within it the
truth of art's artifice.

Group of Dancers, c.1896–99,
pastel on paper, The Barnes
Foundation, Merion,
Pennsylvania, USA,
59 x 49cm (23 x 19in)

Degas once remarked that
painting required all the
cunning of a crime. The
impression of having
captured a natural and
informal pose, he argued,
concealed the artist's careful
contrivance to make it
appear as such. This pastel
is a good example.
It appears as though Degas
has captured a passing
instant, but this ostensibly
incidental scene is carefully
composed. The position of
the main ballerina's arms
creates a subtle symmetry,
echoed in the bodies of
the other figures.

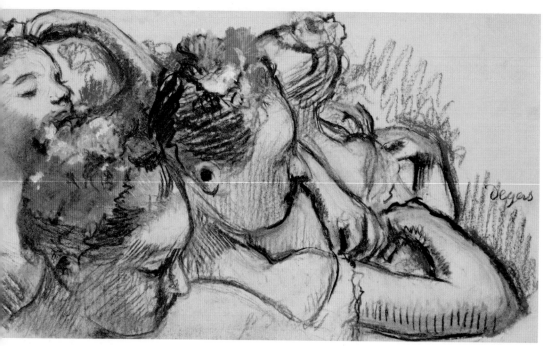

Dancers, c.1896–98, pastel
and charcoal on paper,
Hermitage, St. Petersburg,
Russia, 30.5 x 55cm
(12 x 21½in)

In this charcoal and pastel
drawing of four dancers,
Degas intricately links the
figures into a coherent
grouping through the
repetition of pose and
similarity of the dancers'
physiognomy, especially the
two dancers nearest the
viewer. The introduction of
colour accents in the flowers
in the dancers' hair adds a
decorative note.

Two Dancers, 1896–99, pastel and charcoal on tan board, private collection,

In most of the versions of two dancers waiting in the wings, the dancers are completely absorbed in attending to the performance or in adjusting their costumes. In this variation, the figures are shown interacting and conversing with each other. The pose of the front figure turning slightly to listen to what the figure behind her is saying, captures this ephemeral moment.

Woman Combing her Hair, 1896–99, charcoal and pastel, private collection, 58.5 x 81cm (23 x 32in)

Degas' many drawings and paintings of women combing their hair explore the possibilities of this motif from different angles and vantage points. In this instance, the figure is seen frontally from a sideward angle. Her long red hair tumbles down in front of her body, echoed in the linear folds of her nightdress. Degas has made successive revisions to the arms to create a strong sense of symmetry to the figure.

Two Dancers Adjusting their Shoulder Straps, c.1897, pastel on paper laid down on board, private collection

Degas developed this motif of ballet dancers adjusting the straps of their dresses in paintings of groups of two, three and four dancers, to great effect. He could create subtle differences between individual figures while still conveying strong affinities between those in the group. The last-minute adjustments to costumes creates a strong sense of expectation; in a moment the dancers will enter the stage.

*The Russian Dancer, c.*1899, pastel and charcoal on joined paper laid on board, private collection, Sara Lee Corporation, 63 x 54cm (25 x 21in)

Degas was obviously delighted by the Russian dancers who visited Paris, and made many pictures of their vigorous folk dancing. In this study, as in many of the ballerinas, we see Degas harmonizing the pose, drawing out the symmetry between the shape of the arm resting at the back of the head, with the shape of the dancer's legs and red skirt.

*Russian Dancers, c.*1899, charcoal and pastel on paper, Berwick-upon-Tweed Borough Museum and Art Gallery, UK, 67 x 47cm (26 x 18½in)

This study for the front and middle figure of *Three Russian Dancers* establishes physiognomy and poses that Degas would use across the series. The more detailed front figure, for instance, appears as the central figure in *Russian Dancers* (1899). The naturalistic landscape setting belies the fact that the dancers actually performed on stages with scenery backdrops.

Nude Woman Drying Herself After the Bath, c.1898, pastel and charcoal on canvas, private collection

Here Degas returns to a motif that he had treated in the original *suite de nudes* in 1886, which publicly announced his renewed engagement with the nude.

In this version the figure is seen from a higher viewpoint. These self-absorbed nudes are intensely private works and Degas' long fascination with the theme of private experience perhaps expresses something of his own deeply private nature.

Dancers in Repose, c.1898, pastel and charcoal on woven paper, Detroit Institute of Arts, USA, 57 x 43cm (22½ x 17in)

Dancers in Repose revisits a familiar motif of two dancers resting after the exhausting rigours of rehearsal. In this version, Degas has cropped the figure on the left, focusing attention on to the right-hand ballerina. Though in close proximity, the two figures seem remote from each other; the left-hand figure napping, while the right-hand figure stretches her foot on the bench.

Study of Dancer, c.1898, pastel and charcoal on yellow tracing paper on laid board, private collection

Though some of Degas' drawings present the dancer in a graceful fashion, many suggest the plainness, ordinariness and even gaucherie of the dancers. Most, like this drawing, contain elements of both. Though Degas saw in the dance the continuation of the traces of a lineage that led back to ancient Greece, he also regarded that lineage as contaminated by the inelegance of his own age. This ambivalence gives depth and complexity to Degas' portrayal of the ballerinas.

Three Dancers, c.1900,
charcoal on paper,
Musée Bonnat, Bayonne,
France

In a variation of his motifs,
this 1900 charcoal sets
some of the figures usually
shown waiting in the wings
in the 1890s pictures of
the rehearsal room. The
figure seated on the bench
converses with someone
out of the picture, while
the other two figures look
on. Successful revision of
lines are visible where Degas
has altered the pose of the
right-hand figure to bring her
closer to the margin.

Nude, c.1902, pastel on
translucent paper, Brooklyn
Museum of Art, New York,
USA, 64 x 70cm
(25 x 27½in)

The contemporary settings
in which Degas' women
bathers are located places
them unequivocally in the
context of modern France.
Yet these bathers often
suggest something of the
ancient world, too. Their
bodies, especially when the
head is obscured as here,
recall fragments of the
ancient statuary that
Degas admired and studied
in the Louvre.

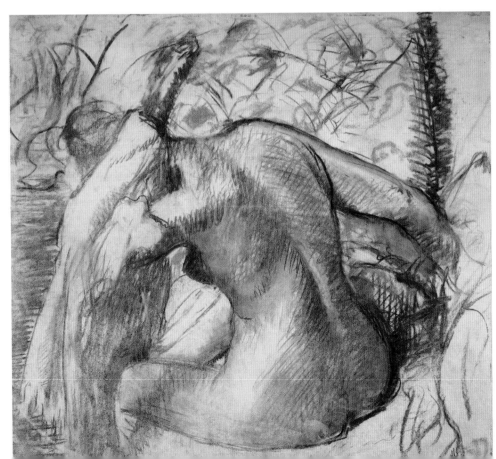

After the Bath, 1903, pastel on paper, Museu de Arte, Sao Paulo, Brazil

At times erotic and alluring, alternatively brutish and animalistic, Degas' nudes express widely contrasting attitudes to the representation of the female body. In this case, the primitive drawing of the body and the pose are very far from the feminine and idealized representations of the nude often exhibited at the Salon. The vibrant blue of the bathtub and the cursory red lines in the background enliven the picture, which seems flooded with light.

Group of Four Dancers, c.1902, charcoal on manila-toned paper, Allen Memorial Art Museum, Oberlin College, Ohio, USA, 73.5 x 51cm (29 x 20in)

This work closely corresponds to the drawing of *Two Dancers Adjusting their Shoulder Straps*, though Degas has altered the position from which we see the principal figures. He has also added two other dancers in the background, interlacing the raised arm of the figure on the far right with the diagonal line of the left arm of the left-hand dancer. These novel and intricate compositions serve to bind the figures together as an ensemble.

*Dancers in the Wing, c.*1905, black chalk and pastel on paper, Fitzwilliam Museum, University of Cambridge, UK, 60 x 44cm (23½ x 17½in)

In this vigorously worked picture of dancers waiting in the stage wings, we see how Degas binds his figures through the use of repeated poses with small adjustments. The pose of the dancer with her hands on her hips is carried through all three dancers, who are shown looking in different directions. Degas crops the space using the scenery to frame the dancers.

Woman Drying Herself, c.1905, charcoal and pastel on tracing paper laid on paper, Museum of Fine Arts, Houston, Texas, USA, 79 x 79cm (31 x 31in)

Many of Degas' drawings create a closed-in, often claustrophobic space, with figures extended across the entire picture surface. In *Woman Drying Herself,* Degas has altered the dimensions of the tracing paper to allow more space. The towel hanging on the back wall visually echoes the woman's cascading red hair. Successive revisions along the contour of the back and arms show Degas altering the foreshortening of the pose and refining his drawing.

After the Bath, 1905–07, gouache on paper, private collection, 77 x 72cm (30 x 28in)

The solitude and avoidance of narrative or anecdote of Degas' bathers is evident in this sparse study of a figure drying her neck, set against a pale pinkish-cream ground. The diversity of these figures is reflected in the altered position of the seated figure, seen here from a slanted, sideward position. This is one of several pictures where the head is obscured and the back, shown in deep shadow, is the focus of the composition.

Woman Combing her Hair, 1896–99, charcoal and pastel on paper, 108 x 75cm (42½ x 29½in)

Degas' bathers are naked figures rather than nudes, breaking with standard conventions of the nude in the grand tradition, despite their frequent references to classical sources. The carefully composed figure, seems awkward and gauche and very much a contemporary Parisian woman. Degas, as in other pictures, has added a suggestive colour note in her red slippers.

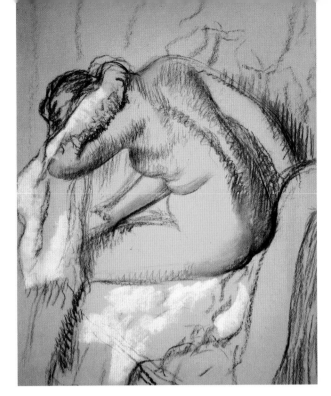

Woman Drying Herself, 1895–1905, charcoal and chalk, private collection, 121 x 101cm (47½ x 40in)

Degas once wrote, "It is essential to do the same subject over again, ten times, a hundred times". This is one of his most repeated motifs, the pose serving not only for the series of seated women drying their necks but also for standing figures such as *Woman Drying Herself* (c.1905). Degas' method was to trace and retrace his motifs, which allowed for reversals and other minor and major variations.

Woman Having her Hair Styled, c.1895–1900, charcoal on paper, Musée Marmottan, Paris, France, 34 x 26cm (13½ x 10in)

The pictures of women à la toilette also include a series of women having their hair combed by their maids. In this seated figure, seen from the rear and turned obliquely away from the viewer, we can just see the hands of another figure tending her hair. While posthumously titled *Woman Having her Hair Styled*, the picture also lends itself to be read as the artist arranging his model.

Nude Combing her Hair, c.1895–1900, charcoal and pastel on paper laid down on board, private collection

Despite its lack of idealism, the pose of this nude, back-combing her red hair upwards, contains an echo of generic classical figures with raised arms. The figure's back is divided into passages of light and dark, suggesting light from a window on her left. Degas shades and models the body through a variety of smudgings, diagonal strokes and hachures.

SCULPTURES

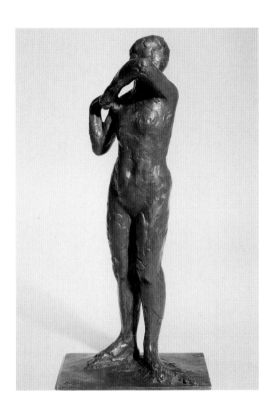

Though primarily known as a painter, Degas was also an innovative and experimental sculptor. Though he never had any of his sculptures cast and only exhibited one work in his lifetime, his work *La Petite Danseuse de Quatorze Ans* was held in high regard by those who knew it. Subsequently, Degas has come to be seen as one of the greatest painter-sculptors of his age. Though he drew on the work of Auguste Rodin and Medardo Rosso, he developed a unique body of sculpture that served as aide-mémoires for his painting, and also had a rich and productive dialogue with it.

Above: Dancer Adjusting the Shoulder Strap of Her Bodice, (bronze).
Left: Dressed Dancer, Study (bronze) c.1879–81.

Jockey on a Horse (bronze),
c. late 1860s to early 1870s,
private collection,
31.5 x 24cm (12½ x 9½in)

Degas did not date his
sculpture and therefore it is
not clear when particular
pieces were made.
According to the artist, his
first sculptures dated from
the late 1860s and were
equestrian maquettes
designed to be aide-
mémoires for his paintings of
horse-racing scenes. If so,
this may be an early work, as
the pose is closer to some
of his horse-racing scenes of
the 1870s that show
horses galloping.

Standing Horse (bronze),
c. late 1860s to early 1870s,
private collection,
25.5 x 35.5cm (10 x 14in)

Equestrian sculptor Joseph
Cuvelier was a close friend
of Degas who shared his
interest in racing motifs. He
was an important influence
in encouraging Degas to
experiment with sculpture
and to take up the racing
motifs that we see in
statuettes such as these.
Cuvelier died prematurely
during the Franco-Prussian
War. *Standing Horse* may
possibly be a tribute to the
work of Degas' friend, as
it closely resembles the
pose of Cuvelier's own
Standing Horse.

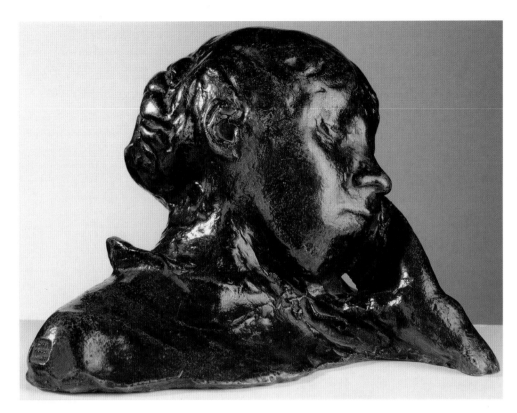

Portrait of a Woman, her Head Supported by her Left Hand (bronze), *c.*1879–81, private collection, 9.5 x 18cm (4 x 7in)

This naturalistic portrait of a woman asleep is an unusual subject for Degas and shows the influence of the Italian sculptor Medardo Rosso. The wax sculptures of Rosso often showed transitional states from waking to sleeping. Degas was impressed with his work, helping him to exhibit in Paris. The model was probably Marie Van Goethen, who modelled for *La Petite Danseuse.*

Grand Arabesque, Second Time (bronze), *c.*1880s, Sterling & Francine Clark Art Institute, Williamstown, USA, 27 x 40.5cm (11 x 16in)

Degas often chose specific positions from ballet-dance manuals for the poses of his sculpture. In doing so, he often pushed sculpture to the limits of the medium's ability, the clay collapsing because it was unable to support the complicated poses Degas sought to represent. Many of his clay maquettes thus perished. Here we see a dancer adopt the classical dance position of the grand arabesque.

Horse with Lowered Head (bronze), *c.*1885–90, Fitzwilliam Museum, University of Cambridge, UK, 18.5 x 27cm (7 x 11in)

This motif of a horse lowering its head occurs in several of Degas' horse-racing scenes, particularly those set before the race commences. The surface of the horse's skin is roughly and vigorously worked to suggest the musculature, and the base has been modelled to suggest a grass ground. Though no jockey is present, the horse's gaping mouth implies it is being restrained, as it strains at the stirrups.

Fourth Position Front, on the Left Leg (bronze), *c.*1880s, Sterling & Francine Clark Art Institute, Williamstown, USA, 57.5 x 30.5cm (23 x 12in)

This bronze shows a ballerina in the fourth ballet position. The majority of Degas' ballerina sculptures are nude, which is consistent with the fact that Degas used such sculpture as models for reference in making his ballerina pictures. Artists often concentrated on anatomy in their preparatory studies before depicting the figure dressed.

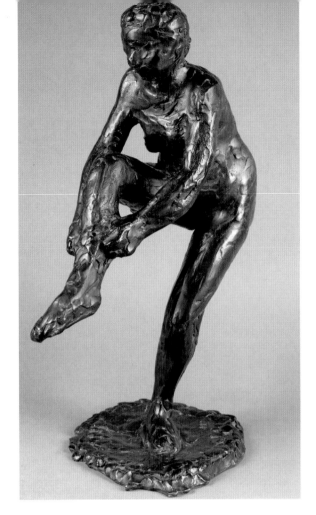

Dancer Putting on her Stockings (bronze), *c.*1880s, private collection, 46 x 20cm (18 x 8in)

The motif of a ballerina pulling on her stockings is present in several of Degas' pictures. However, as this figure is nude, it also takes on a more overtly erotic quality. The sculpture is loosely and roughly modelled with little attention to the head. As in his paintings, emphasis is placed on the movement of the body.

Spanish Dance (bronze), *c.*1880s, private collection, 43 x 17cm (17 x 7in)

Though most of Degas' work on the theme of the dance were of ballerinas, he was interested in other forms of this performance art, from the bizarre dances of the entertainers at the café-concerts, to the exotic foreign folk-dancing troupes that visited and performed in Paris. Degas made paintings after Spanish flamenco dancers and here he shows a dancer in a classic flamenco position.

Trotting Horse (bronze)
*c.*1880s, private collection,
25.5 x 21.5cm (10 x 8½in)

The portrayal of a horse trotting suggests that this sculpture was made after Degas had become familiar with the work of photographer Eadweard Muybridge. Pioneering time-sequence photography, Muybridge took multiple shots of animals that revealed how they moved their limbs, as they trotted and galloped, in a way that had not been understood before. The sculpture is an elegant and economical study in the anatomy and movement of a horse.

Horse at Trough (bronze),
*c.*1880s, private collection,
17 x 10.5cm (7 x 4in)

X-rays of the original wax version of this sculpture show that Degas used a tightly wrapped and intricately twisted framework of wires to create an interior skeletal structure. There is speculation that *Horse at Trough* may have been made as a study for *Mademoiselle Fiocre in the Ballet 'La Source'* (1868) (see page 27), which would date the work to *c.*1866–68, but it might also be an independent work made at another time. The original wax version was presented on a wooden sloped platform.

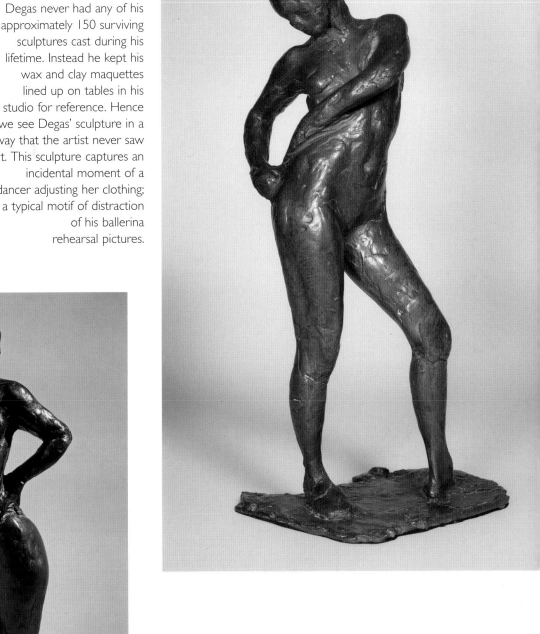

Dancer Fastening the Strings of her Tights (bronze), c.1885–90, San Diego Museum of Art, USA, 42 x 28cm (16½ x 11in)

Degas never had any of his approximately 150 surviving sculptures cast during his lifetime. Instead he kept his wax and clay maquettes lined up on tables in his studio for reference. Hence we see Degas' sculpture in a way that the artist never saw it. This sculpture captures an incidental moment of a dancer adjusting her clothing; a typical motif of distraction of his ballerina rehearsal pictures.

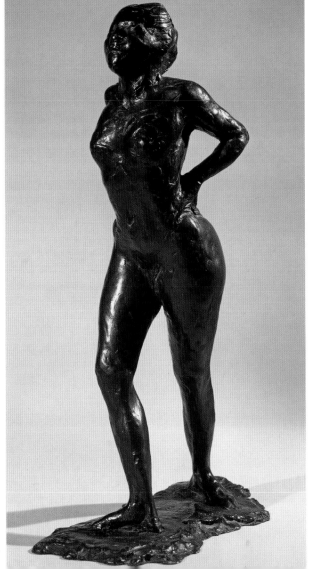

Dancer Resting (bronze), 1882–95, private collection, 43.5 x 25cm (17 x 10in)

Degas often produced several versions of his motifs in sculpture. He produced a nude and a clothed version of this pose. The arched back, tilted head and position of the figure's legs suggests a stretching motion, bringing to mind the many images of ballerinas stretching and relaxing their weary bodies after strenuous rehearsal sessions.

Dancer Looking at the Sole of her Right Foot (bronze), c. mid-1890s, private collection, 45.5 x 26cm (18 x 10in)

Once Degas was interested in a pose he would explore its possibilities in various media. The examples he developed did not simply serve as preparatory studies, but as a developing group of motifs. The pose of *Dancer Looking at the Sole of her Right Foot* appears in various drawings and pastels, as well as in sculpture. In the latter, the lack of contextual setting brings a greater classical tone to the work.

Large Arabesque, Third State (bronze), c. mid-1890s, private collection, 43.5 x 61cm (17 x 24in)

Visitors to Degas' studio in his later years mention how often he could be found working on sculpture. Degas enjoyed and excelled in working in this most tactile medium, especially in a period when his eyesight had become impaired. Sculpture not only informed his painting, but improved his understanding of the body and, in particular, his understanding of dance positions. Here we see a grand arabesque, a complex movement both for dancers to execute and for artists to realize in sculpture.

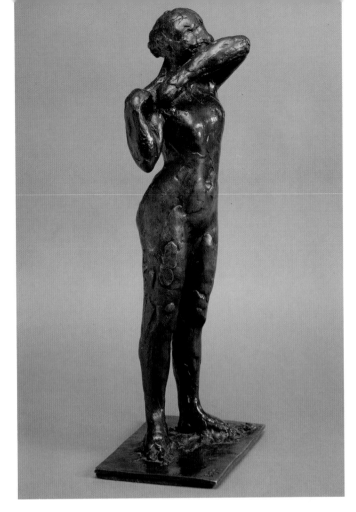

Dancer (bronze), *c.* mid-1890s, private collection, 35 x 21cm (14 x 8¼in)

Degas' sculptures of nude figures acted as aide-mémoires for his bathers as well as his ballerina pictures. However, this is not to suggest they were restricted to this role. Many sculptures more immediately explore classical poses and motifs associated with the tradition of heroic sculpture which enjoyed a revival at the end of the century. In this way Degas' sculpture gains a certain independence from performing the role of preliminary studies for his pictures and gives expression to sculptural ideals independent from his painting.

Preparation for the Dance, Right Foot in Front (bronze), *c.* mid-1890s, private collection, 55.5 x 32cm (22 x 12½in)

Of the 74 surviving sculptures, 38 are dancers, which suggests the importance of these maquettes for Degas, not only as models but as independent works. This sculpture is among the most impressive. Its posthumous casting in bronze accentuates the rippled lighting effect of the careful modelling. Degas has shown care in the detailing of the musculature and head, with subtle tooling to the hair.

The Curtsey (bronze), c.1896
private collection,
33.5 x 18cm (13 x 7in)

The Curtsey is related to a series of Degas' pictures of star ballerinas taking their applause. Degas has modelled the figure nude, which makes the pose appear ungainly. The head is more carefully crafted than many of the maquettes. There is some damage to the figure's left arm. The damaged and fragile state of much of Degas' sculpture meant that only 23 bronze copies could be cast of the sculptures that survived.

Dancer (bronze with brownish-black patina), cast *c.* mid-1890s, private collection, 43.5 x 23cm (17 x 9in)

Though many of Degas' ballerina sculptures are nudes, some, as this example, are clothed. The pose is a familiar and favoured motif from the ballerina pictures of the 1890s, appearing in *Dancers Wearing Green Skirts* and *Three Dancers,* among many others. Degas has tooled the skirt to imitate the folds and movement of the bell tutus worn by the dancers.

Woman Seated Drying her Left Side (bronze), mid-1890s, private collection, 33.5 x 20.5cm (13 x 8in)

This bronze of a woman drying herself is a familiar motif in Degas' paintings from the 1880s and 1890s. Degas always maintained the mutual dialogue between his painting and his sculpture. Sculpture allowed him to model motifs in the round, which could then be used for painting motifs from different angles of vision.

The Tub (bronze), 1889–1919, 24 x 44cm (9½ x 17in)

As Degas was not a trained sculptor and considered himself to be an amateur in this medium, he was less constrained by tradition and convention than most sculptors of his age. This motif is an unusual subject for 19th-century sculpture. Though the motif was common in his oeuvre, the pose is different to those found in his paintings, demonstrating that Degas did not simply transfer motifs to sculpture, but rethought their possibilities within the sculptural medium.

Dancer Holding her Right Foot in her Right Hand (bronze with dark green patina), c.1900s, private collection, 53 x 34.5cm (21 x 13½in)

Dancer Holding her Right Foot in her Right Hand presents another motif found in Degas' ballerinas of the 1890s, though the proportions of this figure bring it closer to the larger, more monumental proportions of some of his late bathers. The head is barely modelled and is posed tilted back in foreshortening.

Dancer Looking at the Sole of her Foot (plaster), c.1900s, private collection, 48 x 26cm (19 x 10in)

Degas worked mainly with wax and clay, sometimes with plastiline (oil-based modelling clay) and plaster, and would have been interested in the different impression a sculpture makes when presented in alternative media. This plaster version of *Dancer Looking at the Sole of her Foot*, appears different to its clay counterpart, later reproduced in bronze. Unlike the rippled lighting effect of the bronze, the plaster version absorbs light and casts deep shadows, creating a more tranquil and well modelled expression of the motif.

Woman Drying her Left Leg II (bronze), 1896–1911, Hirshhorn Museum, Washington, DC, USA, gift of Joseph H. Hirshhorn, 1966, 20 x 15cm (8 x 6in)

The motif of a woman drying her left leg was a common theme of Degas' bathers in the 1880s and 1890s. Transferred to sculpture it makes an astonishing and unusual subject. Degas includes the chair, tub and fabrics that feature in many of the painted variations of this motif.

INDEX